100 Hikes in

SOUTHERN
OREGON

THIRD EDITION

D0048544

William L. Sullivan

Navillus Press

Crater Lake and Phantom Ship from Kerr Notch in April.

©2014, 2012, 2010 by William L. Sullivan. Maps and photography by the author.
All rights reserved. No part of this book may be reproduced in any form without writ-
ten permission from the publisher.

Published by the Navillus Press   *www.oregonhiking.com*
1958 Onyx Street   ISBN 0981570135
Eugene, Oregon 97403   Printed in USA

Cover: Rogue River (Hike #86), Inset: Farewell to Spring *(Clarkia amoena)*.
Spine: Mount Thielsen. Back: Wizard Island from the Devils Backbone (Hike #24).
Frontispiece: Crater Lake from the Sinnott Memorial (Hike #25). This page: East Boul-
der Lake (Hike #93).

UPDATES to this book are available at *www.oregonhiking.com*. Corrections and updates
are welcomed and often rewarded. They may be entered on the website or sent to *sulli-
van@efn.org*. The author has hiked all 100 of the featured trails, and the trails' administrative agencies have reviewed the maps and text. Nonetheless, construction, logging,
and storm damage may cause changes. This book is updated every other year.
SAFETY CONSIDERATIONS: Many of the trails in this book pass through Wilderness and remote country where hikers are exposed to unavoidable risks. On any hike,
the weather may change suddenly. The fact that a hike is included in this book, or that
it may be rated as easy, does not necessarily mean it will be safe or easy for you. Pre-
pare yourself with proper equipment and outdoor skills, and you will be able to enjoy
these hikes with confidence.

Contents

🐎 - Horses OK   🚲 - Bicycles OK   🐕 - Dogs on leash   🚫 - No pets
❁ - Wildflowers (count petals for peak month)   *Parking fee   (pct) - Pacific Crest Trail
C - Crowded or restricted backpacking area   🚙 - Rough access road

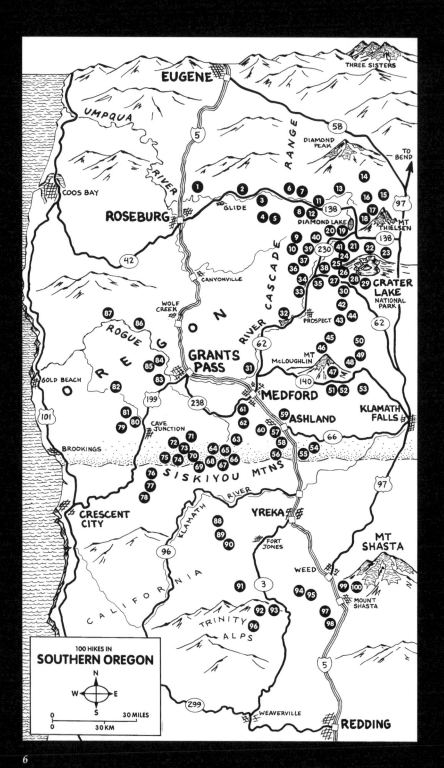

🐴 - Horses OK   🚲 - Bicycles OK   🐕 - Dogs on leash   🚫 - No pets
�֍ - Wildflowers (count petals for peak month)   *Parking fee   (PCT) - Pacific Crest Trail
C - Crowded or restricted backpacking area   ⟿ - Rough access road

Easy	Moderate	Difficult			Great for kids	Open all year	Backpackable	
		●	77. Raspberry Lake	185		C		
●		●	78. Devils Punchbowl	186	●	C		
●	●		79. Babyfoot Lake	188	●		●	🐎
		●	80. Eight Dollar Mountain	190	●	●		
		●	81. Illinois River Beaches	192	●	●		
●		●	82. Illinois River Trail	194	●	●	🐎 🚗
		●	83. Grants Pass Nature Trails	196	●	●		
●		●	84. Taylor Creek	198	●	●	🚲 🐎
●		●	85. Briggs Creek	199	●	●	●	🚲 🐎
		●	86. Rogue River Trail East	201	●	●	C
		●	87. Rogue River Trail West	203	●		C	🚗
			NORTHERN CALIFORNIA	214				
🅟		●	88. Paradise Lake	216		C	🐎
🅟		●	89. Sky High Lakes	217		C	🐎 ❋
	●	●	90. Campbell Lake	219		C	🐎
🅟	●	●	91. Paynes Lake	220		C	🐎
	●	●	92. Trail Gulch Lake	222	●	C	🐎
🅟	●	●	93. East Boulder Lake	224	●	C	🐎 🚗
🅟	●	●	94. Kangaroo Lake	226	●	C	🐎 ❋
🅟	●	●	95. Deadfall Lakes	228	●	C	🐎 ❋
		●	96. Caribou Lake	230		C	🐎
	●	●	97. Castle Lake	231	●		
🅟	●	●	98. Castle Crags*	233		●	🐾
		●	99. Black Butte	235			
	●	●	100. Mount Shasta Meadows	236	●	C	🐾 ❋

Barrier-Free Trails in S Oregon | 238
100 More Hikes in S Oregon | 240
Index | 254
About the Author | 260

🐎 - Horses OK   🚲 - Bicycles OK   🐕 - Dogs on leash   🐾 - No pets
❋ - Wildflowers (count petals for peak month)   *Parking fee   🅟 - Pacific Crest Trail
C - Crowded or restricted backpacking area   🚗 - Rough access road

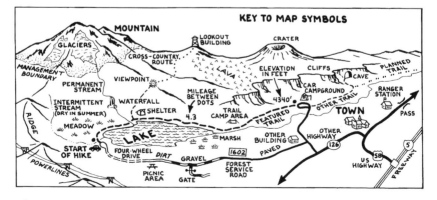

KEY TO MAP SYMBOLS

MOUNTAIN   LOOKOUT BUILDING   CRATER
GLACIERS   CROSS-COUNTRY ROUTE   ELEVATION IN FEET   CLIFFS   CAVE   PLANNED TRAIL
MANAGEMENT BOUNDARY   VIEWPOINT   LAVA   CAR CAMPGROUND   RANGER STATION
PERMANENT STREAM   MILEAGE BETWEEN DOTS   4340'   OTHER TRAIL   TOWN   PASS
INTERMITTENT STREAM (DRY IN SUMMER)   WATERFALL   SHELTER   TRAIL CAMP AREA   4.3   FEATURED TRAIL
RIDGE   MEADOW   LAKE   MARSH   OTHER BUILDING   OTHER HIGHWAY   126
START OF HIKE   FOUR-WHEEL DRIVE   DIRT   GRAVEL   1602   PAVED   5   58
POWERLINES   PICNIC AREA   GATE   FOREST SERVICE ROAD   US HIGHWAY   FREEWAY

Introduction

Welcome to the spectacular trails of Southern Oregon and adjacent Northern California! This comprehensive guide proves there's more to this scenic region than just Crater Lake, the Rogue River, and Mt. Shasta. Come discover a hot springs in the hills behind Roseburg, a wildflower mecca near Ashland, and a rarely visited lake in the Trinity Alps. All of the trips are well suited for day hikers, but you'll also find 50 routes recommended for backpackers, 23 trails for mountain bikers, and 56 paths for equestrians. And don't hang up your hiking boots in winter. Special symbols identify 26 trails that are open all year.

The book features a variety of difficulty levels. If you're hiking with children, look for the symbols identifying 56 carefully chosen kids' hikes—trips that are easy enough for the whole family. Advanced hikers, on the other hand, can choose from 45 unabashedly difficult treks. Hikers with dogs have 85 options. And if you really want to get away from it all, a list at the back of the book describes 100 *more* hikes in Southern Oregon—little-known but intriguing treks for adventurous spirits.

HOW TO USE THIS BOOK

It's Easy to Choose a Trip

The featured hikes are divided into seven regions, from the Umpqua River to Northern California. To choose a trip, simply turn to the area that interests you and look for the following symbols in the upper right-hand corner of each hike's heading. Whether you're hiking with children, backpacking, or looking for a snow-free winter trail, you'll quickly find an outing to match your tastes.

 Children's favorites—walks popular with the 4- to 12-year-old crowd, but fun for hikers of all ages.

 All-year trails, hikable most or all of winter.

 Hikes suitable for backpackers as well as day hikers. No permits required. Crowds unlikely.

 Restricted or crowded backpacking areas. Avoid summer weekends. Advance permits for overnight stays are required in Crater Lake's back-country and in most of Northern California.

The Information Blocks

Each hike is rated by difficulty. **Easy** hikes are between 1 and 7 miles round-trip and gain less than 1000 feet in elevation. Never very steep nor particularly remote, they make good warm-up trips for experienced hikers or first-time trips for novices.

Trips rated as **Moderate** range from 4 to 10 miles round-trip. These routes may gain up to 2000 feet of elevation or may require some pathfinding skills. Hikers must be in good condition and will need to take several rest stops. **Difficult** trails demand top physical condition, with a strong heart and strong knees. These challenging hikes are 6 to 20 miles round-trip and may gain 3000 feet or more. Backpacking can break difficult hikes into manageable segments.

Distances are given in round-trip mileage, except for those trails where a car or bicycle shuttle is so convenient that the suggested hike is one-way only, and is listed as such.

Elevation gains tell much about the difficulty of a hike. Those who puff climbing a few flights of stairs may consider even 500 feet of elevation a strenuous climb, and should watch this listing carefully. Note that the figures are for each hike's *cumulative* elevation gain, adding all the uphill portions, even those on the return trip.

The **hiking season** of any trail varies with the weather. In a cold year, a trail described as "Open May through October" may not yet be clear of snow by May 1, and may be socked in by a blizzard before October 31. Similarly, a trail that is "Open all year" may close due to storms.

The **allowed use** of some featured trails specifically includes horses and bicycle riders. Note that many of the hikes do not have a *use* listing at all. These are open to *hikers only*. For a quick overview of paths recommended for equestrians and mountain bikers, refer to the table of contents. The additional trails listed at the back of the book also include symbols identifying their allowed use.

Dogs are allowed on 97 of the 100 featured hikes, and leashes are required on 8 trails. Restrictions are noted both in the text and in the table of contents.

TOPOGRAPHIC MAPS

All hikers in wilderness and other remote areas should carry a **topographic map,** with contour lines to show elevation. Topographic maps can be downloaded for free at *www.digital-topo-maps.com* and many other Internet sites. Maps of Wilderness Areas can be purchased at outdoor stores, from Nature of the Northwest at *www.naturenw.org,* or at the Northwest Nature Shop at 154 Oak Street in downtown Ashland. It also pays to pick up a Land of Umpqua map (for Hikes #1-20), a Rogue River National Forest map (for Hikes #21-71), or a Coos Bay - Siskiyou National Forest map (for Hikes #72-87) at a ranger station.

TRAILHEAD PARKING FEES

You'll need a **Northwest Forest Pass** to park within ¼ mile of the trailheads for Umpqua Hot Springs, Thielsen Creek, Mt. Thielsen, Mt. McLoughlin, and Mt. Ashland. This permit costs $5 per car per day, or $30 per year, and can be purchased at ranger stations or outdoor stores, or you can pay at the trailhead itself. The permit system may change, but hikes in this book currently requiring a pass are marked with an asterisk in the table of contents.

For trails inside Crater Lake National Park (Hikes #21-30), expect to pay a park entrance fee of $10 a car per week.

WILDERNESS RESTRICTIONS

Thirty-nine of the featured hikes enter designated Wilderness Areas—beautiful, isolated places protected by special restrictions. Day hikers can use all the trails described in this book without having to pick up permits at ranger stations. Advance permits are required only for overnight use in the Trinity Alps Wilderness and Crater Lake National Park's backcountry, or for people planning to use fires or stoves in Northern California outside of car campgrounds. Other important restrictions to expect in Wilderness Areas:

- Groups must be no larger than 12.
- Campfires are discouraged, and are banned within 100 feet of any water source or maintained trail.
- Bicycles and other vehicles (except wheelchairs) are banned.
- Horses and pack stock cannot be tethered within 200 feet of any water source or shelter.
- Motorized equipment, hang gliders, and fireworks are banned.
- Live trees and shrubs must not be cut or damaged.

In addition, some rules apply to all federal lands:

- Collecting arrowheads or other cultural artifacts is a federal crime.
- Permits are required to dig up plants.

SAFETY ON THE TRAIL

Wild Animals
Part of the fun of hiking is watching for wildlife. Lovers of wildness rue the demise of our most impressive species. Grizzly bears were driven to extinction in Southern Oregon and California long ago. The little black bears that remain are so profoundly shy you probably won't see one in years of hiking. To keep them shy, it's important for backpackers to hang food at least 10 feet high and 5 feet from a tree trunk at night. Only where cooler chest goodies are easily accessible have black bears become campground nuisances, particularly at Crater Lake, in Castle Crags State Park, and at river-rafting campsites on the Rogue River.

Rattlesnakes, too, have become relatively rare. The State Health Division reports that only one Oregonian died from a rattlesnake in the most recent decade. Statistically, this makes rattlesnakes less of a threat than horses, bees, dogs, or even cows. Nonetheless, if you hear a rattle or recognize the snake's diamondback pattern, it's your cue to give this reclusive animal some space.

Ticks have received some publicity as carriers of Lyme disease, which begins with flu-like symptoms and an often circular rash. While this is a problem in the Eastern states, only a couple of cases have been reported in Oregon. Nonetheless, brush off your clothes and check your ankles after walking through dry grass or brush.

Mosquitoes can be a nuisance on hikes in the Cascades, particularly in the Sky Lakes and Mt. Thielsen Wilderness Areas. To avoid them, remember that these insects hatch about ten days after the snow melts from the trails and that they remain in force about three weeks. Thus, if a given trail in the Cascades is listed as "Open mid-June," expect mosquitoes there most of July.

Drinking Water
Day hikers should bring all the water they will need—roughly a quart per person. A microscopic parasite, *Giardia*, has forever changed the old custom of dipping a drink from every brook. The symptoms of "beaver fever," debilitating nausea and diarrhea, commence a week or two after ingesting *Giardia*.

If you love fresh water and are willing to gamble, consider that the parasite is spread only by mammals, enters the water by defecation, and moves only downstream. As a result, gushing springs and runoff immediately below snow-fields are less dangerous. If you're backpacking, bring an approved water filter or purification tablet, or boil your water 5 minutes.

Proper Equipment
Even on the tamest hike a surprise storm or a wrong turn can suddenly make the gear you carry very important. Always bring a pack with the 10 essentials: a warm, waterproof coat, drinking water, extra food, knife, matches in a water-proof container, fire starter (butane lighter or candle), first aid kit, flashlight, map (topographic, if possible), and compass. Before leaving on a hike, tell someone where you are going so they can alert the county sheriff to begin a search if you do not return on time. If you're lost, stay put and keep warm. The number one killer in the woods is *hypothermia*—being cold and wet too long.

Global Positioning System (GPS) Devices
Some of the hikes in this book include GPS notations, such as *N43°45.554' W122°37.147'*. This optional information may be used to pinpoint your loca-tion using a handheld, battery-operated GPS device that tracks satellite signals. Though handy, GPS devices are no substitute for a map and compass, because the devices do not always work in dense forest and because their batteries can fail.

THE PACIFIC CREST TRAIL

The 2650-mile Pacific Crest Trail (PCT) from Mexico to Canada is one of the world's great athletic challenges. To follow it through the Central Oregon Cascades, look for PCT symbols beside hikes in the table of contents. Then flip to the specific hike descriptions, where you'll find PCT symbols in the margin highlighting each section of the trail. Although the maps do not always overlap, arrows at the edge of one map indicate the distance to PCT destinations on the next. For an overview of the entire route (without mileages), pick up a *PCT Southern Oregon* map at an outdoor store or online at *www.nationalforeststore.com*.

COURTESY ON THE TRAIL

As our trails become more heavily used, rules of trail etiquette become stricter:

- Pick no flowers.
- Leave no litter. Eggshells and orange peels can last for decades.
- Do not bring pets into wilderness areas. Dogs can frighten wildlife.
- Step off the trail on the downhill side to let horses pass. Speak to them quietly to help keep them from spooking.
- Do not shortcut switchbacks.

For backpackers, low-impact camping is essential, both to protect the land-scape and to preserve a sense of solitude for others. The most important rules:

- Camp out of sight of lakes and trails.
- Build no campfire. Cook on a backpacking stove.
- Wash 100 feet from any lake or stream.
- Camp on duff, rock, or sand—never on meadow vegetation.
- Pack out garbage—don't burn or bury it.

Kangaroo Lake (Hike #94).

FOR MORE INFORMATION

To check on permit requirements, trail maintenance, snow levels, or other questions, call directly to the trail's administrative agency. These offices are listed below, along with the hikes for which they manage trails.

Hike	Managing Agency
57, 58	Ashland Parks — (541) 488-5340
51, 52, 56, 60	Ashland office, Siskiyou Mountains Ranger District — (541) 552-2900
31, 54-5, 59, 62, 80, 86-7	Bureau of Land Mgmt, Medford — (541) 618-2200
1, 2, 4	Bureau of Land Mgmt, Roseburg — (541) 440-4930
43, 45, 46	Butte Falls office, High Cascades Ranger District — (541) 865-2700
98	Castle Crags State Park — (530) 235-2684
73-76, 79-81	Cave Junction office, Wild Rivers Ranger District — (541) 592-4000
15	Chemult Ranger District — (541) 365-7001
21-30	Crater Lake National Park — (541) 594-3000
7, 11-20, 40	Diamond Lake Ranger District — (541) 498-2531
82-85	Grants Pass office, Wild Rivers Ranger District — (541) 471-6500
87	Gold Beach Ranger District — (541) 247-3600
77, 78	Happy Camp/Oak Knoll Ranger District— (530) 493-2243
61	Jacksonville Woodlands Assoc. — (541) 899-7402
44, 47-50, 53	Klamath Ranger District — (541) 883-6714
95, 97, 99, 100	Mount Shasta Ranger District — (530) 926-4511
2-6, 8	North Umpqua Ranger District — (541) 496-3532
72	Oregon Caves Natl Monument — (541) 592-2100
33-35, 37-39, 41, 42	Prospect office, High Cascades Ranger District — (541) 560-3400
88-94, 96	Salmon/Scott Ranger District — (530) 468-5351
63-71	Star Ranger Station, Siskiyou Mountains Ranger District — (541) 899-3800
31	The Nature Conservancy — (541) 770-7933
9, 10, 36	Tiller Ranger District — (541) 825-3201
32	US Army Corps of Engineers — (541) 878-2255

Upper Umpqua River

Cabins, Lookouts & Inns

		Rental units	Private bath	Breakfast	Open (mos.)	Rate range
1	**BUTLER BUTTE CABIN.** On a 5513-foot peak, this cabin sleeps 4-8 and has propane lights, stove, fridge, and heat. Expect to ski or snowshoe in 5 miles in winter. Reservations: 877-444-6777 *(www.recreation.gov)*.	1			●	$40
2	**HOKANSON'S GUEST HOUSE.** Decorated with antiques, this 1882 Victorian home at 848 SE Jackson St. in Roseburg is an elegant bed & breakfast. Reservations: 541-672-2632 or *www.hokansonsguesthouse.com*.	3	●	●	●	$85-125
3	**PICKETT BUTTE LOOKOUT.** Historic 40-foot tower has propane lights, stove, and heat. Sleeps 4, max. You may have to ski in a mile in winter. Reservations: 877-444-6777 *(www.recreation.gov)*.	1			●	$40
4	**STEAMBOAT INN.** Famed for its riverside restaurant (see Hike #3), this inn has 8 rustic cabins ($185 for 1-2 people), 5 cottages ($225 for 1-4), 5 houses ($255 for 1-6), and a row of river suites ($300 for 1-2). Closed Jan-Feb. Reservations: 800-840-8825 or *www.thesteamboatinn.com*.	18	●		III-XII	$185-300
5	**WHISKY CAMP GUARD STATION.** With bunkbeds and propane light/heat, this woodsy 1940s cabin sleeps 8. Bring cookware. Often snow-free in winter. Reservations: 877-444-6777 *(www.recreation.gov)*.	1			●	$40

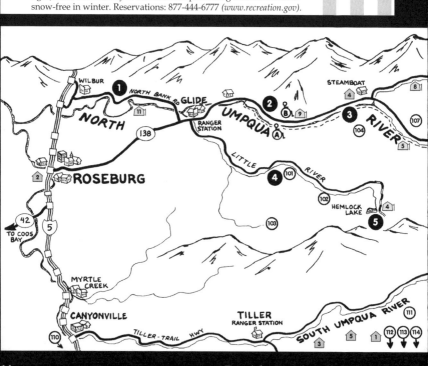

Top right: Lemolo Falls (Hike #13).

Campgrounds

		Campsites	Water	Flush toilet	Open (mos.)	Rate range
1	**BOULDER FLAT.** Between Hwy 138 and the North Umpqua River, this convenient campground includes a launch site for whitewater rafts.	10			V-X	$10
2	**CLEARWATER FALLS.** Off Hwy 138 west of Diamond Lake, this camp has sites both above and below a cascading stream's waterfall.	12			VI-X	$10
3	**EAGLE ROCK.** A rock pillar towers above this riverside camp, with access to the North Umpqua Trail nearby (between Hikes #3 and #7).	26			V-IX	$10
4	**HEMLOCK LAKE.** This small mountain reservoir has a boat ramp, a loop trail (see Hike #5), and lakeshore campsites. No services Nov-May.	13			●	$10
5	**HORSESHOE BEND.** The North Umpqua River loops around this dramatic camp 6 miles east of Steamboat (see Hike #3).	26	●	●	V-IX	$15
6	**KELSAY VALLEY.** This trailhead horse camp accesses both the North Umpqua Trail and the Mt. Thielsen Wilderness.	15			VI-IX	$10
7	**POOLE CREEK.** In the pines beside Lemolo Lake (a reservoir with powerboats), this camp is near the rustic Lemolo Lake Resort.	60	●		VI-X	$15-20
8	**STEAMBOAT FALLS.** Watch steelhead, but don't catch them, at this camp by a waterfall. Open all year, but there are no services Nov-May.	10			●	$10
9	**SUSAN CREEK.** On the North Umpqua River, this convenient camp beside Hwy 138 has hot showers and a trail to Susan Cr Falls (Hike #2).	29	●	●	IV-XI	$14
10	**TOKETEE.** The closest camp to Umpqua Hot Springs (Hike #11), this camp on a small reservoir accesses the North Umpqua Trail.	32			●	$10
11	**WHISTLER'S BEND.** Near Roseburg and Hike #1, this lowland camp fills a broad, grassy bend of the North Umpqua River, offering hot showers and two yurts that sleep 5 ($35). Reservations: 541-957-7001.	23	●	●	IV-X	$15

KEY

100 FEATURED HIKE

All-Accessible Trail – See pages 220-221

200 Other Path – See pages 222-233

0 10 MILES
0 10 KM

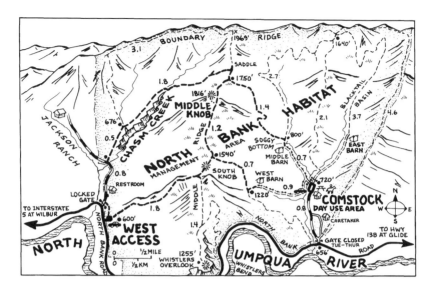

1   North Bank Habitat

Moderate (from Comstock Day Use Area)
4.9-mile loop
1080 feet elevation gain
Open all year, but **gated** Tuesday-Thursday
Use: hikers, horses, bicycles

Moderate (from West Access)
6.1-mile loop
1200 feet elevation gain
Open all year

    Columbia white-tailed deer once roamed most of Western Oregon. But as pioneers began farming the deer's favored valley habitat the whitetails gradually lost ground to their larger, black-tailed cousins from the uplands. By 1970 fewer than 700 of the endangered breed survived. Today Columbia white-tailed deer have staged a comeback, thanks in part to the North Bank Habitat, a 10-square-mile preserve overlooking the North Umpqua River near Roseburg.

    Open all year and just 6 miles from Interstate 5, this quiet hideaway of rolling oak savannahs and forested valleys was once a vast cattle ranch. Now its ancient roads have grown into pleasant, grassy tracks with views that sweep from Whistlers Bend on the North Umpqua River to the Umpqua Community College campus at Winchester. Look for the rare deer, with gray eye rings and flashy white tails. Hawks, eagles, foxes, and blacktail deer are common.

    The Comstock picnic area is the area's best developed trailhead, although you can't drive here Tuesday through Thursday when the access road is gated closed. If you're coming from Roseburg, take Interstate 5 north for 4 miles to Winchester exit 129, turn left toward Wilbur for 2 miles, and turn right on North

Bank Road for 12.1 miles. Just beyond milepost 12, turn left at a white-fenced gate and keep left for 0.7 mile to the parking loop with its picnic shelter, restrooms, and horse staging area.

If you're driving here from Eugene, take Wilbur exit 135, cross the freeway overpass, turn right for 4 miles to the middle of Wilbur, turn left on North Bank Road for 12.1 miles to the entry gate, and keep left for 0.7 mile to the parking loop.

From the picnic area, walk past the left-hand green gate at the end of the loop and then go straight on Soggy Bottom Road amid lichen-draped white oaks. In spring look for the fuzzy blue blooms of minty-smelling pennyroyal, the tall white plumes of camas, the small flowers of blue-eyed grass, and two closely related three-petaled lilies: fuzzy white cats ears and magenta mariposa lilies. In all seasons, poison oak is profuse along the trail, so wear long pants. Long pants also reduce the risk of picking up chiggers — tiny insects that cause weeks of itching. Dogs must be under voice or physical control at all times.

After 0.7 mile you'll see a metal barn on your left. Continue on the main road across a creekbed and then fork left on North Gate Trail. This steeper path passes an incense cedar grove and climbs 1.4 miles to a junction atop a high, grassy ridge (*GPS location N43°20.68' W123°13.39'*).

For the loop, turn left along this view-packed ridgecrest for 1.2 miles. Just beyond an old fenceline, turn left on Thistle Ridge Road down a spur ridge with giant old madrone trees. After 0.7 mile, in a grassy saddle where the main trail heads uphill (*GPS location N43°19.585' W123°13.064'*), turn left at a brown post marked "26-4-8.2." This smaller path descends 400 yards toward a metal-roofed barn. Continue down the valley on a rough old road 0.9 mile to your car.

If the Comstock Day Use Area is closed, start your trip at the West Access parking area instead. To find it from Wilbur, drive North Bank Road 5.4 miles to a large gravel parking lot on the left (*GPS location N43°19.173' W123°15.235'*). Walk uphill past a green gate on Blacktail Ridge Road for 1.6 miles and keep left at a fork to reach a viewpoint in a grassy saddle beside South Knob—a possible turnaround point. For a loop, continue left along Middle Ridge's grassy crest 1.4 miles to a saddle in a cedar grove (*GPS location N43°20.746' W123°13.362'*). Turn left and keep left for 2.3 miles, descending along the gully of Chasm Creek to the Jackson Ranch's gravel road. Then turn left for 0.8 mile to your car.

Oak savannah in the North Bank Habitat Management Area.   Opposite: Madrone trees.

2   Fall Creek Falls

Moderate (to all three waterfalls)
7.2 miles in all
800 feet elevation gain
Open all year
Use: hikers, horses, bicycles

Easy (to Fall Creek Falls)
1.8 miles round-trip
400 feet elevation gain

The shady trail to Fall Creek Falls' plunging double waterfall follows a cascading creek and squeezes through a crack in a house-sized boulder. Because the path is short, it's fun to warm up with two easy hikes to other waterfalls nearby: Fern Falls and Susan Creek Falls.

If you plan to hike to all three waterfalls, start with the smallest, Fern Falls. To find its trailhead from Interstate 5 in Roseburg, take exit 124 and follow "Diamond Lake" signs east on Highway 138 for 22 miles. A mile past the Idleyld Park store, turn right at a "Swiftwater Park" sign, cross the river bridge, and park at the Tioga Trailhead on the left.

The North Umpqua Trail that begins here follows the river 79 miles up to its headwaters in the High Cascades. Although you can tackle longer portions of this well-built route (see Hike #3), here we'll focus on the first 1.7 miles.

From the Tioga Trailhead, the path sets off through a mossy old-growth forest of hemlock, cedar, bigleaf maple, Douglas fir 4 feet in diameter, and an occasional sugarpine—the source of foot-long pine cones along the trail. Big white 3-petaled trilliums bloom in March, while dainty pink calypso orchids bloom in May. The rush of the river masks highway noise from the far shore.

After 0.2 mile, a viewpoint on the left overlooks Deadline Falls, an 8-foot drop in the North Umpqua where salmon and steelhead trout leap. Beware of lush 3-leaved poison oak all around the viewpoint. The second side trail on the left leads to the bedrock shore—a prime sunbathing spot and the only good riverbank access of the hike. At the 0.4-mile mark, ignore side trails on the right

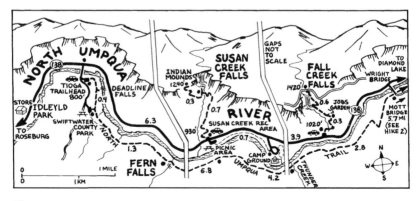

Susan Creek Falls.   Opposite: Footbridges on the trail to Fall Creek Falls.

leading to Swiftwater County Park's picnic shelter. Continue 1.2 miles, with glimpses down to the big green river, before reaching a satisfying turnaround point: the 70-foot bridge across Fern Falls, a mossy fan-shaped cascade where a small side creek pours into the North Umpqua River.

To try the Susan Creek Falls hike, return to your car, drive back to Highway 138, and head 6.3 miles east to the Susan Creek Falls parking area on the left. It's just beyond milepost 28, on the opposite side of the highway from the Susan Creek Picnic Area. The packed gravel path climbs very gradually through old-growth woods, ducks under a powerline, and crosses a footbridge at the base of Susan Creek Falls, a 70-foot punchbowl plume emerging from a slot. A rougher path continues 0.3 mile, switchbacking up a dry, rocky slope (with blue iris, fuzzy white cats ears, and reddish poison oak) to the Indian Mounds, a cyclone-fenced ridgetop of rockpiles and pits. Used as vision quest sites in Native American coming-of-age rituals centuries ago, the rockpiles have grown over with moss and gnarled madrone trees, concealing most of their original panorama.

To visit Fall Creek Falls—the grand finale if you're hiking all three short trails—drive another 3.9 miles east of Susan Creek on Highway 138 and park at the trailhead sign on the left, between mileposts 32 and 33. After hiking 0.3 mile, ignore a fork for the Jobs Garden Trail on the right; this leads 200 yards to a small columnar basalt outcrop and rockpile. The main trail visits the misty plunge pool at the base of Fall Creek Falls' lower, 50-foot cascade, and then switchbacks up to a gravel road crossing the top of a smaller upper falls.

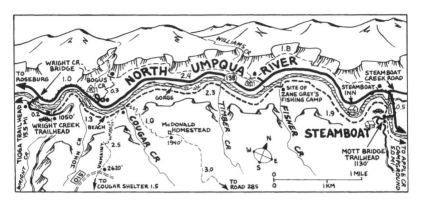

3   North Umpqua River

Moderate (with shuttle)
5.5 miles one way
200 feet elevation gain
Open all year
Use: hikers, horses, bicycles

Difficult
11.7-mile loop
350 feet elevation gain

In all, the North Umpqua Trail follows this whitewater river 79 miles to its headwaters in the High Cascades. If that seems too long a hike, try the 5.5-mile segment featured here—from Wright Creek to the settlement of Steamboat. This portion shows off the river at its best, with access to hidden beaches and rock riverbanks. There's even an optional return loop that's popular with bicyclists. Along the way you'll pass the wooded campsite where Western writer Zane Grey fished. Because his earlier articles had crowded the Rogue River with anglers, Grey never named the North Umpqua in print.

To start the hike, take exit 124 of Interstate 5 in Roseburg and follow "Diamond Lake" signs east on Highway 138 for 33.5 miles. Beyond Fall Creek Falls 1.4 miles, turn right on Wright Creek Road across a bridge. Don't park at the hiker-symbol sign just beyond the bridge, but rather drive 0.2 mile farther to the signed Wright Creek Trailhead on the left. Park here and walk up the road another 100 yards to the actual start of the trail.

An old-growth forest lines the path, with droopy-limbed red cedars, vine maples, and 6-foot-thick Douglas firs. A shag carpet of moss covers the forest floor. Frequent side paths scramble left to the riverbank. Expect some traffic noise from the highway across the river.

After a mile the path dips to a glassy, green-pooled stretch of river where ducks paddle and osprey soar. A small sandy beach nestled among rock banks and wildflowers makes a good turnaround spot for hikers with small children.

The North Umpqua River.   Opposite: Wild iris, also known as Oregon flag.

Poison oak is all but absent up to here, but beyond this point hikers should watch for its telltale triple leaflets along the trail.

After passing the small beach, the path visits two river gorges—rocky narrows where whitewater rafters flail and squeal. At the 3.6-mile mark the path bridges Fisher Creek, where a sign marks Zane Grey's former fishing camp. If you haven't arranged a car shuttle, this might be a good turnaround point. Otherwise continue 1.9 miles, skirting a few houses at the Forest Service settlement of Steamboat, to the Mott Trailhead parking area. (To shuttle a car here, drive east on Highway 138 from Wright Creek Road for 5.1 miles and turn right across Mott Bridge to the trailhead on the right.)

If you're continuing on the 11.7-mile loop, walk across Mott Bridge and turn left along the shoulder of busy Highway 138 for almost half a mile. Then angle uphill to the right on the Riverview Trail. This path follows a historic, early twentieth-century roadbed along the canyon's cliffs, with glimpses of the river through the trees. After 4.2 miles, take a left-hand spur down 0.3 mile to Bogus Creek Campground. Then follow the noisy highway another mile downstream and cross the Wright Creek Bridge to your car.

Other Options

Like to see more of the North Umpqua Trail? Downstream, the path starts 15.7 miles west of Wright Creek at Swiftwater Park (see Hike #2). Upstream from Steamboat, the path mostly traverses forested slopes well above the river for 12.3 miles before briefly joining Highway 138 to cross the river on Marsters Bridge. From there the trail skirts the Boulder Creek Wilderness (see Hike #7), leaves the river for 10 miles to Toketee Lake Campground, passes Umpqua Hot Springs (Hike #11) and Lemolo Falls (Hike #13), detours around the Lemolo Lake reservoir, and then climbs through the Mt. Thielsen Wilderness to the Pacific Crest Trail near Maidu Lake (Hike #15).

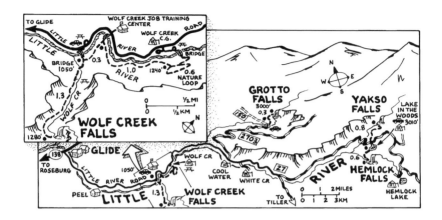

4   Little River Waterfalls

Easy (to Wolf Creek Falls)
2.6 miles round-trip
230 feet elevation gain
Open all year

Moderate (to all four waterfalls)
6 miles in all
Open April through December
870 feet elevation gain

A charming, little-known tributary of the North Umpqua, the Little River tumbles out of a long canyon full of hidden waterfalls. If you only have time to discover one, head for Wolf Creek Falls. The 1.3-mile creekside trail there is ideal for hikers with children. Waterfall connoisseurs will want to round out the day by driving upriver to visit three more cascades at the ends of short trails.

From Interstate 5, take Roseburg exit 124 and follow "Diamond Lake" signs east on Highway 138. At milepost 16, just before the town of Glide, turn right on Little River Road for 10.4 paved miles. Then park at a "Wolf Creek Falls Trail" sign on the right.

The trail starts by crossing the Little River on an arched, 150-foot bridge. In summer, the broad river's bedrock and warm, shallow pools invite wading. Beware of poison oak on the banks. Beyond the bridge go straight on the trail into a cool, shady forest of bigleaf maple and old-growth Douglas fir. In spring, trilliums bloom white in these woods. In summer look for tiny starflower and inside-out flower. In fall, expect a display of scarlet vine maple leaves. After 1.3 miles, the path skirts a 20-foot lower falls and ends at the base of a dramatic, 70-foot cascade. Listen here for the *zeet! zeet!* of robin-sized water ouzels flying along the creek.

To find the three other waterfalls, drive up Little River Road 5.4 miles past the Wolf Creek Trailhead. Opposite Cool Water Campground turn left on gravel

Road 2703 and keep left for 6.3 miles, following "Grotto Falls" signs to a trailhead just after a bridge. This 0.3-mile path climbs steeply across a 1970s clearcut and ends behind Grotto Falls' 45-foot curtain of water.

Now drive back to the junction by Cool Water Campground and continue up Little River Road (known here as Road 27). After 3 miles on pavement and an additional 6.3 miles on gravel, turn right into the Lake in the Woods Campground entrance. Park in the day use area and walk 100 yards along the lakeshore campground road. Then turn at a "Hemlock Falls" sign and follow a switchbacking path 0.6 mile down a densely forested canyon to a 40-foot corkscrew-shaped cataract spilling from a moss-cushioned cliff.

To find the final waterfall, walk back past your car to Road 27. Immediately opposite the Lake in the Woods Campground entrance, take a relatively level 0.8-mile path through the woods to a pebbly beach at the misty base of 50-foot Yakso Falls. This cascade fans out like silver hair—and in fact Yakso means "hair" in Chinook jargon, the old trade language of Northwest Indians.

Other Hiking Options

A 3-mile trail climbs from the far end of the Lake in the Woods Campground loop road to Hemlock Lake (Hike #5), passing several small falls along the way.

Hemlock Falls.   *Opposite: Footbridge over Little River at the Wolf Creek Trail.*

5

Hemlock Lake

Moderate (Yellowjacket Loop)
5.6-mile loop
910 feet elevation gain
Open June through November
Use: hikers, horses, bikes

Moderate (with Flat Rock detour)
7.2-mile loop
1380 feet elevation gain

The spectacular wildflower meadows on this loop trail have the subalpine feel of the High Cascades. But this patch of mountain scenery is less than an hour from Roseburg in an often-overlooked corner of the Old Cascades, the eroded remnants of a much older volcanic range. Thousands of trilliums and shooting stars line the misnamed Yellowjacket Loop in June. For a broader view, climb a side path to a lookout site atop Flat Rock.

To find the trail from Interstate 5, take Roseburg exit 124 and follow "Diamond Lake" signs east on Highway 138 to milepost 16, just before Glide. Then turn right on Little River Road (which becomes Road 27) for 18.8 paved miles and an additional 11.5 miles on gravel, following signs for Hemlock Lake. Finally cross the lake's earthen dam to a T-junction at the campground entrance.

The trail begins at a large mapboard straight ahead. After 100 feet, turn right at a trail junction to start the loop. Then keep left at all junctions for the rest of the hike. The path starts in a forest of Douglas fir and Shasta red fir, but soon crosses the first of many meadow openings. Yellow fawn lilies bloom here within days of the early June snowmelt, followed by white marsh marigolds, purple shooting stars, blue violets, and the huge green leaves of hellebore. Listen for the *ribbet* of frogs and the monotone call of the varied thrush, crying like a slow squeaky wheel in the treetops.

At the 1.1-mile mark, take time to detour right along the 0.8-mile Flat Rock Trail to a clifftop lookout site. Somewhat overgrown, the view stretches from

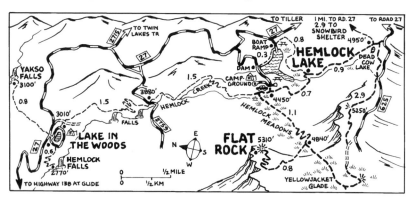

Hellebore (corn lily) in Hemlock Meadows.   *Opposite: Chanterelle mushrooms.*

Roseburg's valley to Crater Lake's rim. Diamond Peak rises to the left of Hemlock Lake, while Mt. Bailey is on the right, with Mt. Thielsen's spire peeking over its shoulder.

Back on the loop trail, you'll cross 2.5 miles of meadows, woods, and a regrown 1970s clearcut before reaching gravel Road 625 in a saddle. The trail is faint here, but just go up the little ridge straight ahead. In another half mile (still keeping left at junctions), you'll pass Dead Cow Lake, an innocent pond in the woods. Then descend 0.9 mile to Hemlock Lake and follow the shoreline path left to your car.

Other Hiking Options

A side trail from Dead Cow Lake continues 3.5 miles along the ridgetop east, passing Snowbird Shelter before ending at Road 2781-100. A proposed 4-mile extension would join the Twin Lakes Trail (Hike #8).

6   Illahee Rock

Easy (to Illahee Rock)
1.4 miles round trip
500 feet elevation gain
Open June to late November
Use: hikers, horses, bicycles

Easy (to Wild Rose Point)
2.8 miles round trip
520 feet elevation gain

Two historic fire lookouts and a panoramic view across the Boulder Creek Wilderness await visitors to this cliff-edged peak. A natural rock garden of wildflowers lines the route to the top. And if the hike seems too short, add a jaunt to nearby Wild Rose Point—a lesser but wilder viewpoint that requires a little bushwhacking to reach.

To find the Illahee Rock trailhead from Interstate 5, take exit 124 in Roseburg and follow "Diamond Lake" signs east on Highway 138 for 47 miles. Just 0.3 mile beyond the Dry Creek Store, turn left on gravel Illahee Road 4760. Follow this one-lane road (ignoring a spur for the "Illahee Flat Trail") for 8 miles, go straight on Road 100 for 1.3 miles, and then turn left at a "Trail" pointer onto steep, rocky Road 104 for 0.2 mile to its end. If you have a low-clearance car you may want to walk this final stretch to the Illahee Rock trailhead.

Just 0.7 mile long, the trail up Illahee Rock is a joy, switchbacking from high forests with woodland flowers (rhododendrons, yellow violets, and more) to shaley rockslides with clumps of bright pink penstemons and fleshy-leaved stonecrop. Cliffs and crags flank the route. In June, whole slopes bloom with fawn lilies—graceful white flowers with six white curving petals and spotted green leaves.

At the top are a 1925-vintage cupola-style lookout and its replacement, a 40-foot lookout tower from 1958. The newer lookout is staffed each summer during

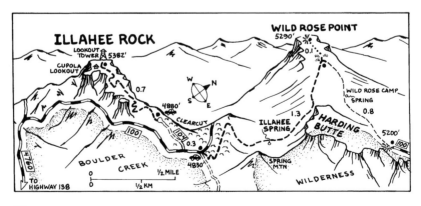

fire season. The older 12-by-12-foot building, painstakingly restored, is one of only eight remaining Oregon lookouts with a hipped cupola roof. Neither of the lookout buildings at Illahee Rock is available for rental.

Agile climbers can scale a rock outcrop near the old lookout for the area's best viewpoint. On the horizon, Mt. Thielsen's spire rises above the uncut forests of Boulder Creek's valley. To the right are broad Mt. Bailey, the tip of Mt. Scott, Crater Lake's rim, and the tip of Mt. McLoughlin. Far to the north, look for the tip of Mt. Jefferson above Wild Rose Point's rock bluff.

If you'd like a longer hike after returning from Illahee Rock, drive back 0.2 mile to Road 100, turn left for 200 yards, and park at a fork in the road. Between the forks is a small "Wild Rose Trail" sign. A forest fire has left this path rough and rocky, with some fallen logs. The route climbs 0.3 mile through a regrowing clearcut and then contours a mile along a slope before reaching a small flat meadow atop a broad ridgecrest.

The main trail curves to the right into the woods (to deadend in 0.8 mile at a different Road 100), but to find Wild Rose Point, walk left through the meadow and then bushwhack 200 yards through the woods—*always keeping uphill on the ridgetop*. You'll reach a rocky bluff atop a 300-foot cliff with a view south to Illahee Rock. Many wildflowers spangle this bluff—red paintbrush, pink heather, yellow lomatiums, purple larkspur, and fuzzy white cats ears—but no wild roses.

The view from the Illahee Rock tower includes Mt. Bailey.   *Opposite: Illahee Rock.*

7 Boulder Creek

Moderate (to Pine Bench viewpoint)
5.5-mile loop
800 feet elevation gain
Open all year
Use: hikers, horses

Moderate (to Boulder Creek)
8.9-mile loop
1100 feet elevation gain

One of Oregon's few official wilderness areas that's hikable in winter, the Boulder Creek valley features a plateau forested with stately ponderosa pines — a rarity west of the Cascades. The trailhead is scheduled to be closed until November 2012 for construction of a fish ladder at the adjacent powerhouse.

To drive here from Interstate 5, take Roseburg exit 124 and follow "Diamond Lake" signs east 55.2 miles on Highway 138. Between mileposts 55 and 56, turn left at a sign for Medicine Creek Road, and *immediately* turn left again onto gravel Soda Springs Road for 1.4 miles to the Soda Springs trailhead parking area on the left. The trail itself begins on the right — and promptly ducks under a huge 12-foot steel pipe that's carrying most of the North Umpqua River to a power station. Because horses can't duck, equestrians have to ride another 200 yards down the road to find a detour path around the pipe.

Beyond the pipe, follow the trail 0.4 miles up to a junction and turn left. This path climbs steadily amid 4-foot-thick Douglas firs and incense cedars. Rhododendrons bloom here in June. Look for the massive trunks and foot-long cones of sugarpines, the world's largest variety of pine. At the 1.3-mile mark the trail finally levels out atop Pine Bench in a grassy forest of Douglas firs and ponderosa pines — easily identified by their 6-inch-long cones, foot-long needles, and orange bark. In June, expect white iris, fuzzy cats ears, starflower, and some mosquitoes. Also keep an eye out for poison oak.

Pine Bench's square-mile plateau is a remnant of a vast lava flow that once filled the North Umpqua's canyon from wall to wall at this elevation. Ponderosa

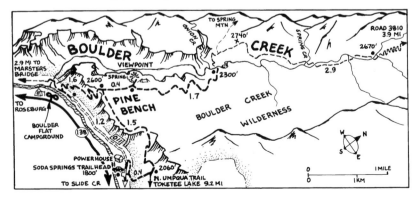

Viewpoint of Boulder Creek's valley.   Opposite: Boulder Creek.

pines are well adapted to such relatively dry spots for several reasons. First, they are among the few conifers with long taproots that enable them to extract water from deep ground layers. Second, they survive wildfire well because their needle clumps are located high in isolated clusters. The ponderosas' unusual bark helps them outlast fires, too, by flaking off in jigsaw-puzzle-piece shapes to dissipate the heat of flames.

Near the far end of Pine Bench, turn right at a T-shaped trail junction and continue 0.4 mile to an unsigned fork. Keep left for 100 yards and follow the sound of water to discover a delicious natural spring, pouring out of a cliff from four mossy spouts. Several campsites are just beyond. For the area's best viewpoint, scramble 50 yards out a rock promontory — using both hands and caution. The vista atop this 200-foot cliff shows how Boulder Creek's valley is recovering from a 1996 fire that swept through nearly half of this Wilderness, burning underbrush and leaving a healthier patchwork of old-growth forest.

If you'd like to continue to Boulder Creek itself, walk back to the fork and take the main trail another 1.7 miles. The path crosses 20-foot-wide, pebbly creek on a fallen log. Flat campsites are scarce here, but lunch sites abound. In summer, it's fun to wade upstream 100 yards to a small waterfall and cold, swimmable pool. Backpackers can follow the Boulder Creek Trail another 6.8 miles beyond this first creek crossing. but the path climbs steeply away from the shore for 1.9 miles, then fords the creek three times before launching uphill on a switchbacking climb to Road 3810.

To return on a loop, hike back to Pine Bench and go straight at all trail junctions. You'll switchback down the Boulder Creek Trail across grassy slopes; watch out for poison oak. At the bottom of the hill the trail joins an ancient roadbed, which soon forks. For a short side trip, take the right-hand fork down 300 yards to a lovely footbridge across Boulder Creek. The pebbly beach here is not only a good place to cool off, it's also a place to see osprey, kingfishers, and ouzels. To complete the loop, however, take the ancient road's left fork 0.2 mile to the small Boulder Creek Trailhead, and continue 1.2 miles along the narrow dirt Soda Springs Road to your car. Although a car shuttle would eliminate this final 1.2-mile roadside walk, the road is rough enough and the river views are pleasant enough to make the walk a good option.

8   Twin Lakes

Easy (around both lakes)
3.2-mile loop
400 feet elevation gain
Open mid-June through November
Use: hikers, horses, bicycles

Moderate (to Twin Lakes Mountain)
5.4-mile loop
850 feet elevation gain

It's hard to imagine a better family backpacking destination than this pair of gorgeous turquoise lakes. The nearly level, 0.9-mile trail to the lakes ambles through old-growth woods and wildflower meadows. At the lakes themselves you'll find two large shelters and a hiker campground with picnic tables—but probably very few other people. If you'd like a bit more exercise, a well-graded 1.1-mile side path climbs to a breathtaking viewpoint atop a mountain cliff.

To start, take Interstate 5 exit 124 in Roseburg and follow "Diamond Lake" signs east on Highway 138 for 49 miles. Immediately after crossing the North Umpqua River on Marsters Bridge (and 0.7 mile before Eagle Rock Campground), turn right on Wilson Creek Road 4770. Follow this one-lane gravel road 9 miles to its end at the trailhead parking area.

The wide path sets off amid Douglas fir with an understory of vine maple, vanilla leaf, and Oregon grape. After 0.3 mile, pass a clifftop viewpoint of three distant, snowy Cascade peaks: Diamond Peak, Mt. Thielsen, and Mt. Bailey. At the 0.6-mile mark, turn right at a T-junction for 150 yards; then turn left through a wildflower meadow for 0.3 mile to a large plank-sided shelter by the lake. The meadow here brims with orange paintbrush, pink owl clover, mint, hellebore, and coneflower.

Turn right at the shelter to find four campsites with log picnic tables, lake views, and June-blooming rhododendrons. Continue around the large lake to the far shore, where a short connecting trail leads to the smaller lake. Turn left around

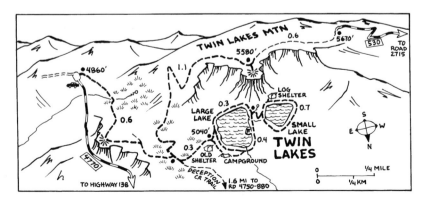

this lake 100 yards and look behind a house-sized boulder to find the 12-by-16-foot Little Twin Shelter, built of logs in 1995 by the Wolf Creek Job Corps and the Forest Service. Both shelters are open on a first-come-first-served basis.

For an optional climb after hiking around the Twin Lakes, head back toward the car but keep right at all junctions to find the trail up Twin Lakes Mountain. This path crests after a mile. Just a few hundred yards after the trail starts downhill, take a right-hand spur through rhododendron bushes to an amazing viewpoint atop a 300-foot cliff. The square-topped peak on the horizon above the small lake is Bohemia Mountain. Above the larger lake is the roadless Boulder Creek Wilderness (see Hike #7), with all Three Sisters peeking over that wild valley's rim.

Twin Lakes Mountain from Large Twin Lake.   Opposite: Twin Lakes from viewpoint.

9   Fish Lake

Easy (to Fish Lake)
3 miles round-trip
630 feet elevation **loss**
Open May to mid-December
Use: hikers, horses

Difficult (to Rocky Ridge)
12.6-mile loop
2800 feet elevation gain
Open July through October

This Fish Lake (not to be confused with the larger, better-known reservoir near Mt. McLoughlin) won its name in 1889 when a group of explorers caught 70 trout in an hour using venison for bait. Fish still jump in this forest-rimmed, half-mile-long natural lake near the South Umpqua River's headwaters, but you'll find other wildlife too: ducks, eagles, and a cute family of river otters. If the stroll down to the lake seems too easy, you can continue on a moderate loop past two smaller lakes, or take a longer loop along Rocky Ridge past dramatic cliffs with views across the Rogue-Umpqua Divide Wilderness.

To start, drive Interstate 5 south of Roseburg 25 miles (or north of Grants Pass 40 miles) to Canyonville exit 98. Following signs for Crater Lake, drive into Canyonville and turn east on 3rd Street—which becomes the Tiller-Trail Highway—for 23.3 miles to Tiller. On the far side of this hamlet, turn left on Road 46 toward South Umpqua Falls. After another 24.2 miles, veer to the right on one-lane, paved Road 2823.

Following "Fish Lake Trailhead" pointers, drive 2.4 miles on Road 2823, fork

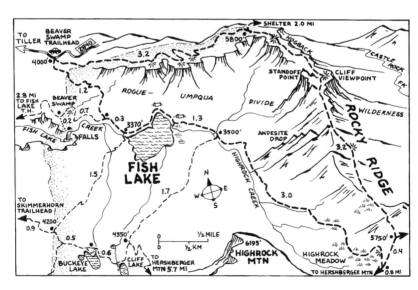

Highrock Mountain from Highrock Meadow.   Opposite: Fish Lake.

to the right on Road 2830 for 3.9 gravel miles, and then fork to the left on Road 2840 for 0.5 mile. Here you'll see the Fish Lake Trailhead – but don't park yet. Although this route to Fish Lake is pleasant enough (and well suited for equestrians), it's 2.3 miles longer than the trail from the Beaver Swamp Trailhead. To find the shorter path, drive onward on Road 2840 for another 4.6 miles to a trail sign on the right.

At this trailhead, take the right-hand path (the "Beaver Swamp Trail") down through a forest of Douglas fir, Incense cedar, and ponderosa pine. In 1907, and again in 2002, fires swept through this area's woods, burning underbrush and downed logs, but leaving most of the large trees intact.

After 1.2 miles, turn left for 0.3 mile to the outlet of Fish Lake. To find the best shore access and lunch spot, hike 0.3 mile along the lakeshore trail to a peninsula. Because camping is banned within 200 feet of the shore, backpackers will want to continue 0.2 mile past the peninsula to an old-growth grove on the left with lots of permissible tent sites.

If you're not yet ready to turn back to your car, continue to a trail junction half a mile beyond Fish Lake. Here you have a choice of two loops.

For a moderate 8.6-mile loop hike, turn right and keep right for 4.4 miles. Climb through the woods to Cliff Lake and Buckeye Lake (see also Hike #10) and descend to the outlet of Fish Lake to join the trail to your car.

For the Rocky Ridge loop, a longer trip with the more dramatic views, turn left and keep left at all trail junctions. You'll climb steeply for 2.5 miles before skirting the left edge of Highrock Meadows, a subalpine slope full of wildflowers and huge-leaved hellebore. The sweet smell is mint. The musty smell is a white flower known as dirty socks. Beyond Highrock Meadows, still keeping left at junctions, you'll contour along Rocky Ridge, with clifftop views east to Fish Mountain and Castle Rock's lava plug. Then the path skirts Standoff Point's weird rock formations of flutes and spires, balances across a narrow hogback ridgecrest, and finally descends to your car through partially burned woods.

10 Buckeye and Cliff Lakes

Cliff Lake from Grasshopper Mtn.

Easy (to lakes)
3.4 miles round-trip
700 feet elevation gain
Open mid-May through November
Use: hikers, horses

Moderate (to Grasshopper Mountain)
8.8-mile loop
1980 feet elevation gain
Open late June to early November

A monumental landslide crumbled half of Grasshopper Mountain about 1000 years ago, damming the Fish Lake Valley with 4 square miles of jumbled debris. Surprisingly, the scene of this ancient disaster has become one of the loveliest subalpine landscapes anywhere. An easy 1.4-mile trail, perfect for hikers with children, crosses the now thoroughly forested landslide to a pair of mountain lakes at the foot of a dramatic mile-long cliff—the origin of the slide. An extra 2-mile climb takes you through wildflower meadows to a viewpoint atop the cliff itself.

To find the trailhead, drive Interstate 5 south of Roseburg 25 miles (or north of Grants Pass 40 miles) to Canyonville exit 98. Following signs for Crater Lake, drive into Canyonville and turn east on 3rd Street—which becomes the Tiller-Trail Highway—for 23.3 miles to Tiller. On the far side of this hamlet, turn left on Road 46 toward South Umpqua Falls. After another 24.2 miles, veer to the right on one-lane, paved Road 2823 and begin following "Skimmerhorn Trailhead" pointers. After 2.4 miles these signs will direct you to fork to the right on Road 2830 for 3.9 gravel miles and then turn left on Road 600 for 1.8 miles to road's end.

The trail starts amid ponderosa pines, sugarpines, and June-blooming rhododendrons. After 0.2 mile, turn left at a T-junction and enter an area burned to black snags by a 2002 fire. In another half mile the path sets off across the hummocky surface of the ancient landslide, strewn with enormous boulders.

Keep straight at two junctions to reenter unburned woods of Douglas fir, mountain hemlock, and Oregon grape. When you reach Buckeye Lake, a small

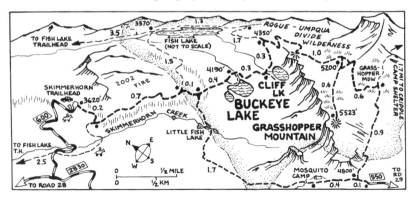

loop trail to the right tours a scenic peninsula where camping is banned. (Tents must be 200 feet from the shore.) Try the echo off Grasshopper Mountain's cliffs.

The main trail continues, crossing Buckeye Lake's outlet below a beaver dam. In 0.3 mile a spur trail to the right leads to Cliff Lake—a smaller pool with a closer view of the landslide cliff. The stripes in the cliff are a cross section of the black basalt lava flows, greenish ash layers, and reddish soil layers that built this portion of the Old Cascades range 16 to 25 million years ago.

If you're not yet ready to turn back, continue on the main trail 0.3 mile, turn right for an uphill mile to a meadow, and fork right for 0.6 mile to the summit of Grasshopper Mountain. From the crumbling cliff edge of this former lookout, Buckeye and Cliff Lakes look like blue-green eggs in a huge forest-furred nest. To the east, note Highrock Mountain's cliffs and the tips of Rabbit Ears' rock spires.

It is quickest to return as you came, but if you keep right at all junctions on the way down you can return on a loop. Longer by 1.6 miles, this route visits Grasshopper Meadow, Mosquito Camp, and shallow Little Fish Lake.

Grasshopper Mountain from Buckeye Lake.

11　Umpqua Hot Springs

Easy (to hot springs)
0.6 miles round-trip
120 feet elevation gain
Open except in winter storms
Use: hikers, horses, bicycles

Easy (to Columnar Falls)
0.6 miles round-trip
100 feet elevation gain

Left: Umpqua Hot Springs Shelter.

A new footbridge has reopened the shortest hiking route to Umpqua Hot Springs, where you'll find a rustic shelter and a series of spa-sized pools as hot as 110° F overlooking the North Umpqua River. After a soak in the hot springs, return to your car and stroll another section of the North Umpqua Trail upstream to a pair of astonishing *cold* springs — a roaring gusher and a mysterious waterfall with no apparent source or outlet.

To start, drivie 59 miles east of Roseburg (or 20 miles west of Diamond Lake) on Highway 138. At milepost 59, turn north onto Toketee-Rigdon Road 34. After 0.2 mile keep left alongside Toketee Lake's dam. Continue 2 miles, fork right onto (possibly unmarked) gravel Thorn Prairie Road 3401, and follow this gravel road 2 miles to a large parking lot on the left.

If you don't have a Northwest Forest Pass, you can pay $5 at a fee box for the required parking permit. Note that nude bathing is common at Umpqua Hot Springs, but visitors are asked to remain conventionally clothed at the trailhead and on the trail.

Hike straight toward the river 100 feet to the footbridge. Then follow the North Umpqua Trail to the right 200 feet. When the path makes a switchback uphill to the left, turn right on a big trail that climbs 0.2 mile to the hot springs.

All the springs in this area resulted when geologically recent High Cascade lava flows buried thousands of stream channels, leaving snowmelt to percolate underground to find an outlet. Here the water has seeped through a hot, active

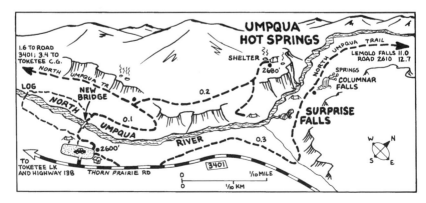

MT. THIELSEN dominates the view from a paved 11.5-mile trail around Diamond Lake (Hike #19).

ABOVE: Lemolo Falls (Hike #13).   INSET: Umpqua Hot Springs (Hike #11).

NORTH UMPQUA RIVER

Driving Highway 138 along the North Umpqua River is pretty, but you'll see the river's many waterfalls only if you stop to take short hikes. Portions of the 79-mile North Umpqua Trail come in handy.

BELOW: Toketee Falls (see Hike #11).   RIGHT: Fall Creek Falls (Hike #2).   BELOW RIGHT: The river from the North Umpqua Trail near Steamboat (Hike #3).

BOUNDARY SPRINGS (Hike #21), the source of the
Rogue River, gushes from a bank of monkeyflowers.

WIZARD ISLAND (Hike #22), in Crater Lake, was
named for its resemblance to a sorcerer's hat.

MT. THIELSEN (Hike #18), has a spire on its summit
that turns back all but the most daring hikers.

WHITEBARK PINES

The bent, struggling trees you see at
timberline on Cascade peaks are often
whitebark pines. These five-needle pines
grow only above 6000 feet. Their amazingly
supple limbs allow them to bend, rather
than break, in winter gales. The pine's seeds
are a favorite food of the Clark's nutcracker.
By flying from peak to peak with the seeds,
this bird helps the whitebark pines spread.

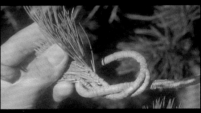

LOWLAND WILDFLOWERS

OOKOW *(Dichelostemma congestum)* blooms in dry, grassy meadows from April to June.

INDIAN WARRIOR *(Pedicularis densiflora).* This snapdragon relative blooms in April and May.

FIREWEED *(Epilobium angustifolium).* After a fire, this plant crowds slopes with tall pink spires.

WILD IRIS *(Iris tenax).* Also called an Oregon flag, this June bloom varies from blue to yellowish white.

PRAIRIE STAR *(Lithophragma parviflora)* blooms in May in dry, rocky fields and slopes.

FOXGLOVE *(Digitalis purpurea).* Showy 5-foot foxglove stalks spangle sunny summer hillsides.

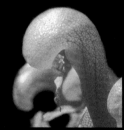

ELEGANT BRODIAEA *(Brodiaea elegans)* blooms in dry grasslands in early summer.

PITCHER PLANT *(Darlingtonia californica),* a bog-dweller, traps and dissolves insects for fertilizer.

SALSIFY *(Tragopogon dubius).* This dry June roadside flower turns to a giant dandelion-like seed puffball.

BACHELOR BUTTON *(Centaurea cyanus).* One of many showy blue composite flowers with this name.

DEATH CAMAS *(Zigadenus spp.).* Dangerously similar to edible camas, this bloom's root is poison.

FAREWELL TO SPRING *(Clarkia amoena).* This Clarkia blooms in dry grasslands as summer arrives.

MEADOW WILDFLOWERS

WILD ONION *(Allium spp.)*. This pungent bloom hugs the ground in dry, rocky areas.

LARKSPUR *(Delphinium menziesii)*. Stalks of larkspur stand up to two feet tall in high meadows.

SCARLET GILIA or SKYROCKET *(Gilia aggregata)* blooms on dry, open slopes all summer.

HELLEBORE or CORN LILY *(Veratrum insolitum)* has poisonous roots and l f i talks of green flowers.

BIGELOW SNEEZEWEED *(Helenium bigelovii)*. These bulbous blooms grow near timberline.

JACOB'S LADDER *(Polemonium occidentale)*, often pale blue, likes damp spots in mid-elevation woods.

INDIAN CARTWHEEL *(Silene hookeri)*. Also called stringflower, this bloom likes dry rocky ground.

FRITILLARY *(Fritillaria spp.)*. This odd, nodding brown "chocolate lily" likes subalpine meadows.

SHOOTING STAR *(Dodecatheon jeffreyi)*. Early in summer, shooting stars carpet wet fields and slopes.

MOUNTAIN BLUEBELL *(Mertensia spp.)*. A favorite browse for elk, these plants fill subalpine meadows.

STONECROP *(Sedum oreganum)*. This plant survives in bare, rocky ground by storing water in fat leaves.

CONEFLOWER (Rudbeckia occidentalis). Like an odd, petalless daisy, coneflower grows waist-high.

FOREST WILDFLOWERS

COLUMBINE *(Aquilegia formosa).* In wet woodlands, this bloom has nectar lobes for hummingbirds.

FAIRY BELLS *(Disporum hookeri).* This lily of moist woodlands later develops pairs of orange berries.

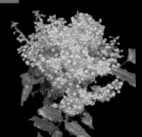

OREGON GRAPE *(Berberis aquifolium).* Oregon's state flower has holly-like leaves and blue berries.

SOURGRASSS *(Oxalis oregana).* The shamrock-shaped leaves carpet forests and taste tart when chewed.

FAIRY SLIPPER *(Calypso bulbosa).* This lovely 6-inch orchid haunts the mossy floor of old-growth forests.

PRINCE'S PINE *(Chimaphila umbellata).* Also known as pipsissewa, this blooms in shade.

BLEEDING HEART *(Dicentra formosa).* Look near woodland creeks for these pink hearts.

TWINFLOWER *(Linnaea borealis).* This double bloom grows in the far North around the globe.

CANDYFLOWER *(Claytonia sibirica).* Common by woodland creeks and trails, candyflower is edible.

STAR-FLOWERED SOLOMONSEAL *(Maianthemum stellata).* These delicate stars decorate deep forests.

WESTERN AZALEA *(Rhododendron occidentale)* blooms in May near the Southern Oregon Coast.

TRILLIUM *(Trillium ovatum).* This spectacular woodland lily blooms in April, a herald of spring.

ALPINE WILDFLOWERS

PHLOX *(Phlox diffusa)*. Like a colorful cushion, phlox hugs arid rock outcrops with a mat of blooms.

PAINTBRUSH *(Castilleja spp.)* has showy red-orange sepals, but the actual flowers are green tubes.

PENSTEMON *(Penstemon spp.)*. Look for these red, purple, or blue trumpets in high, rocky areas.

ELEPHANTS HEAD *(Pedicularis groenlandica)*. You'll see pink elephants like this in alpine bogs.

ASTER *(Aster spp.)*. This purple daisy-like flower blooms late in summer, from July to September.

FAWN LILY *(Erythronium spp.)*. These 6-petaled lilies erupt a week after the snow melts.

BEARGRASS *(Xerophyllum tenax)* resembles a giant bunchgrass until it blooms with a tall, lilied plume.

LUPINE *(Lupinus spp.)* has fragrant blooms in early summer and pea-pod-shaped fruit in fall.

MONKEYFLOWER *(Mimulus spp.)*. Clumps of these showy pink or yellow flowers line alpine brooks.

GENTIAN *(Gentiana calycosa)*. These thumb-sized blooms near alpine lakes open only in full sun.

WESTERN PASQUE FLOWER *(Anemone occidentalis)*. This high alpine flower *(left)* blooms so early it sometimes melts holes in the snow. By August it develops foot-tall, dishmop-shaped seedheads *(right)*

SUN NOTCH'S view of Crater Lake requires a short walk
in summer (Hike #29), but a long ski trek in winter.

Columnar Falls has no apparent inlet or outlet.

fault. Hot water dissolves minerals well. Umpqua Hot Springs doesn't smell of sulfur, but it has carried enough alkali over the centuries to build a 100-foot dome-shaped rock knoll above the river's bank.

On summer weekends, expect to wait for a turn in the hot springs. A pool in the shelter holds four or five people. A string of half a dozen similar pools beside the shelter ranges from very hot to warm. Another warm spring down on the riverbank below the shelter is covered by the river during high water.

After soaking a while and hiking back to your car, be sure to take a look at the interesting cold springs nearby. Take the trail that starts beside the parking lot's outhouse. This path climbs to the road, follows it 100 feet, and then descends into the woods. Officially known as the Dread and Terror Segment of the North Umpqua Trail, this remote but otherwise unthreatening path was named for a nearby ridge that frightened early fire fighters because of its impenetrable thickets.

After a quarter mile you'll reach Surprise Falls, which roars out of the ground just below the trail. Just beyond is Columnar Falls, where lacy springs spill down the angled columns of a mossy basalt cliff and immediately seep back into the ground, vanishing without a trace. This makes a good turnaround point, although backpackers can continue upriver to Lemolo Falls (see Hike #13).

12   Toketee and Watson Falls

Easy (to Toketee Falls)
0.8 miles round-trip
100 feet elevation **loss**
Open except in winter storms

Easy (to Watson Falls)
0.8-mile loop
300 feet elevation gain
Open mid-March through December

A pair of easy 0.4-mile trails lead to the North Umpqua's most spectacular waterfalls—90-foot Toketee Falls, whose name means "pretty" in the Northwest Indians' Chinook jargon, and 272-foot Watson Falls, tallest in Southern Oregon. Both tumble from the eroded edges of basalt lava flows that coursed down this valley from the High Cascades thousands of years ago.

To find the trailhead for Toketee Falls, start by driving 59 miles east of Roseburg (or 20 miles west of Diamond Lake) on Highway 138. At milepost 59, turn north onto Toketee-Rigdon Road 34. Then keep left at all junctions for 0.4 mile to the well-marked gravel Toketee Falls Viewpoint parking lot and a small picnic area.

The trail sets off through a forest of big Douglas fir, red cedar, and bigleaf maple, brightened in April and May with the showy blooms of white trilliums and pink rhododendrons. Staircases help hikers clamber past a churning gorge and descend to the trail's end at a railed deck with a frontal view of the falls.

Below the viewpoint, Toketee Falls pours out of columnar basalt cliffs to smash into a wave-tossed pool. It's hard to imagine how huge this cascade must have been before the North Umpqua hydroelectric projects tapped the river. The enormous 8-foot-thick pipeline alongside this hike's trailhead is shunting most of the river around the falls, from Toketee Lake's reservoir to a power plant at Soda Springs.

To find Watson Falls, drive back to Highway 138 and turn left 2.3 miles. Between mileposts 61 and 62, turn south on Fish Creek Road 37 for 200 yards

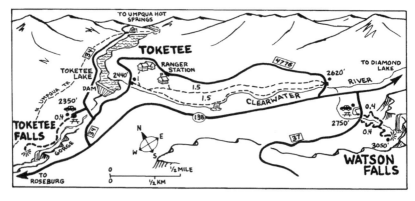

Toketee Falls.   *Opposite: Railed walkway at Watson Falls.*

and park in a paved lot at a picnic area on the right. The trail begins at the end of a turnaround and promptly climbs to a crossing of Road 37 — where parking is not recommended.

After crossing of the road, the path switchbacks up 0.3 mile to a 70-foot, zigzagging footbridge over bouldery Watson Creek. Just beyond is a T-shaped trail junction. To the left is a 100-yard path up to the misty base of Watson Falls' amazingly tall, plunging plume. To the right is the loop's return trail down to the Road 37 crossing and your car.

13   Lemolo Falls

Easy (to Warm Spring Falls)
0.6 mile round-trip
80 feet elevation **loss**
Open May through November
Use: hikers, horses, bicycles

Easy (to Lemolo Falls)
3.4 miles round-trip
400 feet elevation **loss**

Huge waterfalls are the star attractions of these two short hikes below Lemolo Lake, but the North Umpqua Trail is attractive in its own right, passing countless smaller chutes and cascades.

Drive Highway 58 east of Roseburg 70 miles (or west of Diamond Lake 6 miles) and turn north on paved Road 2610 at a sign for the Lemolo Lake Recreation Area. After 5 miles, cross Lemolo Lake's dam. Then keep left on Road 2610 for 0.6 mile.

The North Umpqua Trail crosses the road here, and a bridge across a canal to the left leads to a parking area for the Lemolo Falls hike. But if you'd like to warm up first with a short walk to Warm Spring Falls, continue driving straight on Road 2610 for 2.4 miles, turn left on paved Road 680 (which soon turns to gravel), and follow it 1.6 miles to a partly hidden "Warm Spring Falls Trail" sign on the left.

This path ambles 0.3 mile through a Douglas fir forest full of rhododendrons (with pink blooms in June) and trilliums (with white May blooms). The path ends at an unrailed viewpoint of the massive 70-foot waterfall beside a 100-foot cliff of columnar basalt. This rock is part of a geologically recent lava flow that poured down the North Umpqua River canyon from the Cascades. The river and many side creeks now tumble over the lava flow's eroded lip.

For the second, longer hike to Lemolo Falls, drive back to the North Umpqua River trailhead at the canal bridge. Yellow Oregon grape, white vanilla leaf, and

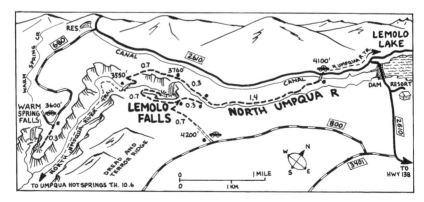

other forest flowers bloom along this riverbank path. Children can splash in pools below small chutes and cascades. At the 1.7-mile mark, a short left spur leads to the top of 100-foot Lemolo Falls—not a safe place for children. For a side view of the falls, continue a few hundred yards on the main trail. If you hike an additional 0.7 mile down the path you'll reach a long footbridge across the river—a pleasant spot for lunch before heading back.

Other Hiking Options

The best view of Lemolo Falls is actually on an older trail on the south side of the river. Although the two trails aren't quite connected, it's not hard to scramble from one to the other. From the top of Lemolo Falls, hike the North Umpqua Trail about a quarter mile upstream, cross the river on a fallen log, and scramble up the far bank less than 300 feet to the old trail. Keep right on this well-built path for a mile to its end at a wave-wracked splash pool below Lemolo Fall's thundering plume.

If you'd rather drive to the old trail, take Road 2610 south of the Lemolo Lake dam 0.5 mile to a curve, turn west onto poorly marked Thorn Prairie Road 3401 for 0.5 mile, turn right on Road 800 for 1.6 miles, and park at a "Lemolo Falls Trail" sign on the right. The path follows an abandoned road 0.6 mile to its end. Keep right through an old picnic area 200 yards to a trail junction and turn left for 0.7 mile to the falls.

Rhododendrons at Warm Springs Falls.   Opposite: Lemolo Falls.

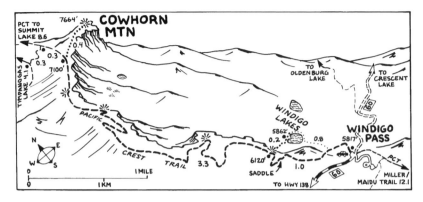

14   Cowhorn Mountain

Difficult
9.4 miles round-trip
1900 feet elevation gain
Open mid-July to late October
Use: hikers, horses

Cowhorn Mountain has been one of the least recognized High Cascade peaks ever since its cowhorn-shaped spire toppled in a 1911 storm. But the summit view is still breathtaking, and few mountain climbs are this convenient. All but the last 0.4 mile of the route follows the well-graded Pacific Crest Trail. On the return trip, hikers can bushwhack a few hundred yards off the trail for a swim at the lovely, rarely visited Windigo Lakes.

To start, drive Highway 138 east of Roseburg 73.5 miles (or north of Diamond Lake 5 miles). Between mileposts 73 and 74, turn north onto Windigo Pass Road 60. Follow this wide, washboard gravel road 4.5 miles to a junction for Lemolo Lake. Curve right, continue on Road 60 another 7.6 miles to Windigo Pass, and park in a large pullout on the left with a trail registration box. Ignore a spur road to the right marked "Windigo Pass Trailhead;" it is for hikers headed south. From the parking pullout, the Pacific Crest Trail climbs gradually northwards through a sparse forest of small mountain hemlock, lodgepole pine, and noble fir. After 0.8 mile the trail dips to a saddle and then switchbacks up 400 yards to the trail's only viewpoint of West Windigo Lake. Make a note of the spot if you'd like to swim on the return trip.

The PCT passes increasingly dramatic cliff-edge viewpoints ahead to Cowhorn Mountain every mile or so as it climbs to alpine elevations with western Pasque flower, purple penstemon, and gnarled whitebark pines. At the 4.3-mile mark, look for pair of rock cairns where the PCT curves left to descend into the woods

The view south from Cowhorn Mountain.   Opposite: Cowhorn Mountain from the trail.

on Cowhorn Mountain's shoulder. Leave the PCT here and follow a faint trail up the ridgecrest, directly toward the summit. At timberline, the route steepens in cinder scree. Crest a false summit of bare black rock, cross a cinder hogback, and scale the actual summit crag on the left—a non-technical scramble requiring the use of hands.

The summit is the eroded remnant of a much larger stratovolcano. The shaley gray andesite is riddled with wall-like dikes, where black lava squeezed into fractures as it rose. But it's the view of Crescent Lake that steals the show at the summit. To the left are the Three Sisters, the sinuous shore of Summit Lake, snowy Diamond Peak, the U-shaped canyon of the Middle Fork Willamette River, and Sawtooth Mountain's bare gray slopes. To the south look for broad Mt. Bailey, Crater Lake's jagged rim, and Mt. Thielsen's spire.

If you decide to visit the Windigo Lakes on the return trip, don't leave the PCT until the lake viewpoint 1 mile from the trailhead. Then bushwhack steeply down 200 yards and continue straight 200 yards to the green lake, an 8-foot-deep pool with a sandy bottom and relatively warm water. Explorers can shortcut back to their cars from the lake's far, southern shore by hiking directly away from the view of Cowhorn Mountain, traversing along a slope 600 yards *without going downhill*, and turning left on the PCT.

15   Miller and Maidu Lakes

Easy (around Miller Lake)
5.1-mile loop
100 feet elevation gain
Open mid-June through October
Use: hikers, horses, bicycles

Moderate (around Maidu Lake)
8.6 miles round-trip
750 feet elevation gain
Open early July through October
Use: hikers, horses

The glaciers that once spanned the crest of the Cascade Range in the Ice Age left behind a broad, forested mountain pass north of Mt. Thielsen. Today hikers can cross this pass on a trail from Miller Lake, on the range's eastern slope, to Maidu Lake, the source of the North Umpqua River. For a shorter hike from the same trailhead, try the 5.1-mile path around Miller Lake, a route popular with anglers. On either trip, be prepared for mosquitoes throughout July.

Access to the trailhead is via the town of Chemult, on Highway 97 halfway between Bend (65 miles to the north) and Klamath Falls (72 miles to the south). Half a mile north of Chemult, between mileposts 202 and 203, turn west onto a side road at a large brown sign for the Chemult Recreation Site. After half a mile of pavement, continue straight for 12 dusty gravel miles to road's end at Digit Point Campground. Keep left to park at the end of the lakeside picnic area loop. (If you're bringing a horse you'll need to park at an equestrian trailhead 2 miles earlier, because the south side of Miller Lake is off limits to stock.)

At Digit Point trailhead, the path begins at the left edge of the picnic area beach. The trail follows Miller Lake's shore through mountain hemlock woods with red huckleberry bushes. The path crosses two small inlet creeks, where lupines bloom and beavers fell trees. After 0.9 mile you'll cross a bridge over Evening Creek and reach a trail junction where you have to make a decision.

For the easy loop around Miller Lake, turn right. This trail follows the shore to the sunny side of the lake, where the forest shifts to pine, the underbrush

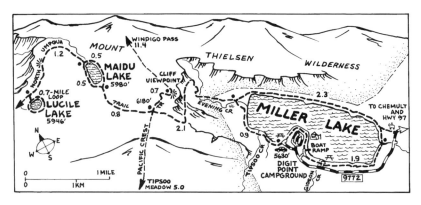

includes huge, creamy Cascade lilies, and the views feature snowy Howlock Mountain. After 2.3 miles, ignore a spur trail to the left that leads to the equestrian trailhead's corral. Keep right, crossing the lake's outlet creek on a footbridge and continuing around the lake another 1.9 miles to your car.

For the longer trip to Maidu Lake, however, keep left at the junction near the start of the hike. Bicycles aren't allowed on this route. The path bridges Evening Creek once more in a meadow of lupine and mountain bluebells (mertensia). Then it climbs steadily through lodgepole pine woods to a junction with the Pacific Crest Trail at the pass. (There are no views at the pass, but if you don't mind a small side trip, you can turn right on the PCT for 0.7 mile to a rock promontory with a fine overlook of Miller Lake's U-shaped glacial valley and Howlock Mountain.)

To go to Maidu Lake, cross the PCT at the pass and descend 0.8 mile to the shallow, forest-rimmed lake. If you're camping, choose a site at least 100 feet from the shore. To help disperse use near this fragile pool, the Forest Service removed an old shelter in 1990 from the open area where the trail meets the lake. Circle the lake on a 1-mile shoreline loop trail before returning the way you came.

Other Hiking Options

For a look west down the huge U-shaped valley left by Maidu Lake's vanished glacier, take the North Umqua Trail 0.7 mile beyond the far end of the Maidu Lake loop to a clifftop viewpoint. On the horizon, look for Sawtooth Mountain, snowy Diamond Peak, and the spire of Cowhorn Mountain. Once you've come this far, you really should continue 0.5 mile and turn left for 100 yards to a 0.7-mile loop path around Lucile Lake, Maidu Lake's little sister.

Maidu Lake.   Opposite: Miller Lake from the Pacific Crest Trail viewpoint.

16 Tipsoo Peak

Moderate
6.2 miles round-trip
1784 feet elevation gain
Open late July to mid-October
Use: hikers, horses

One of the few 8000-foot Cascade peaks with a well-graded trail to its summit, Tipsoo Peak offers a panoramic view from the Three Sisters to Mt. Shasta, with nearby Mt. Thielsen looming above an alpine pumice plain.

To find the trailhead, drive Highway 138 east of Roseburg 75 miles (or north of Diamond Lake 4 miles. Near milepost 75, turn east onto gravel Cinnamon Butte Road 4793. After 1.7 miles, go straight on Wits End Road 100 for 3.2 miles to a wide spot with a small "Tipsoo Trail" sign on the right. The last half mile of the drive is a bit bumpy.

The trail climbs through a mountain hemlock forest with red huckleberry bushes. Grayish green witch's hair lichen grows profusely on tree trunks here, but only above the 8-foot depth of typical winter snow. At the 2.8-mile mark the trail climbs through a corner of Tipsoo Meadow, a vast alpine field of pumice that was blasted here when when Mt. Mazama collapsed to form Crater Lake. The intervening 7700 years have allowed wildflowers to spread—dwarf blue lupine, tiny purple penstemon, white partridge foot, and pink heather. At this elevation the sparse, wind-bent mountain hemlocks and whitebark pines grow no larger than Christmas trees.

Finally the trail turns right at a snowy pass and climbs a ridgecrest of craggy, black and red lava to the summit. The view to the south, across Tipsoo Meadow, includes Howlock Mountain and the Matterhorn-shaped Mt.Thielsen. Completing the panorama to the right are Diamond Lake, Mt. Bailey, Lemolo Lake, snowy

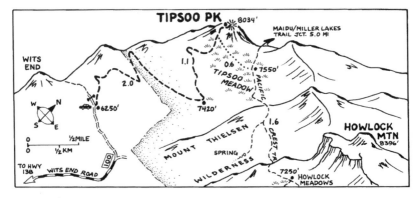

Mt. Thielsen from Tipsoo Peak.   Opposite: Alectoria, *or witch's hair lichen.*

Diamond Peak, Cowhorn Mountain, and the Three Sisters. The green lakes at the north base of Tipsoo Peak are Lucile and Maidu Lakes, while larger Miller Lake lies to the east.

If you'd like to explore Tipsoo Peak's high country, or if you're backpacking, it's easy to walk down 0.6 mile cross-country through Tipsoo Meadow to the Pacific Crest Trail—but note your route carefully for the return trip. Once on the PCT, you could either go 5.8 miles north to Maidu Lake (see Hike #15) or head south 1.6 miles to Howlock Meadows (see Hike #17).

Diamond and Crater Lakes

Campgrounds

	Campsites	Water	Flush toilet	Open (mos.)	Rate range
BROKEN ARROW. Amid lodgepole pines, this is the least crowded camp at Diamond Lake. Res: 877-444-6777 (*www.recreation.gov*).	130	●	●	V-IX	$15-20
🐴 **COLLIER STATE PARK.** An outdoor museum of logging and log cabins adjoins this riverside camp on Highway 97. Four primitive campsites with horse corrals are $14 each.	68	●	●	IV-X	$14-22
DIAMOND LAKE. Strung along 2 miles of shore, this camp is crowded, noisy, smoky, and *very* popular. Res: 877-444-6777 (*www.recreation.gov*).	238	●	●	V-X	$16-27
DIGIT POINT. On a wide, pine-forested peninsula at Miller Lake (see Hike #15), this camp has a boat ramp and swimming area.	64	●	●	VI-IX	$12
FAREWELL BEND. On the upper Rogue River near Union Creek (see Hike #35), this forested camp is close to Crater Lake National Park.	61	●	●	V-X	$18
JACKSON F. KIMBALL STATE PARK. This small, primitive camp near Crater Lake has a path to a bubbling spring, Wood River's origin.	10	●		IV-X	$5-10
LOST CREEK. Only tents are allowed at this uncrowded Crater Lake camp in pines near The Pinnacles. Bears visit at night, so lock up food.	16	●	●	VII-IX	$21
MAZAMA. Crater Lake's largest camp has a store, trails (see Hike #28), evening ranger talks, and crowds. Bears visit at night, so lock up food. Reservations: *www.craterlakelodges.com.*	200	●	●	VI-X	$21-29
THIELSEN VIEW. Diamond Lake's prettiest camp (see Hike #19). Reservations: 877-444-6777 (*www.recreation.gov*).	60	●		VI-X	$15-20
UNION CREEK. In old-growth forest along the Rogue River (Hike #35). Res: 541-560-3900 (*www.roguerec.com*).	78	●		V-X	$14

◁ *Diamond Lake Lodge.*

Cabins, Lookouts & Inns

	Rental units	Private bath	Breakfast	Open (mos.)	Rate range
CRATER LAKE LODGE. This grand old 1915 lodge perches on the lake's rim (see Hike #26). Res: 888-774-2728 (*www.craterlakelodges.com*).	71	●		V-X	$165-292
DIAMOND LAKE RESORT. Rustic but inelegant, this 1922 resort rents 38 motel units, 10 studios, 42 two-bedroom cabins that sleep 6, and a house that sleeps 20. See Hike #20. Res: 888-774-2728 (*www.diamondlake.net*).	91	●		●	$89-999
THE CABINS AT MAZAMA VILLAGE. This board-and-batten motel has no view but is near services. Reservations: 888-774-2728.	40	●		V-IX	$140
ROCKY POINT RESORT. Rustic Klamath Lake lodge with dock, store, and 4 cabins ($140-160). Res: 541-356-2287 (*www.rockypointoregon.com*).	9	●		IV-X	$85
UNION CREEK RESORT. This 1920s waystation on the road to Crater Lake includes a rustic lodge (with 9 rooms at $58-63), store, cafe, and 22 cabins. See Hike #35. Res: 866-560-3565 (*www.unioncreekoregon.com*).	31	●		●	$58-245

Top right: Crater Lake in April.

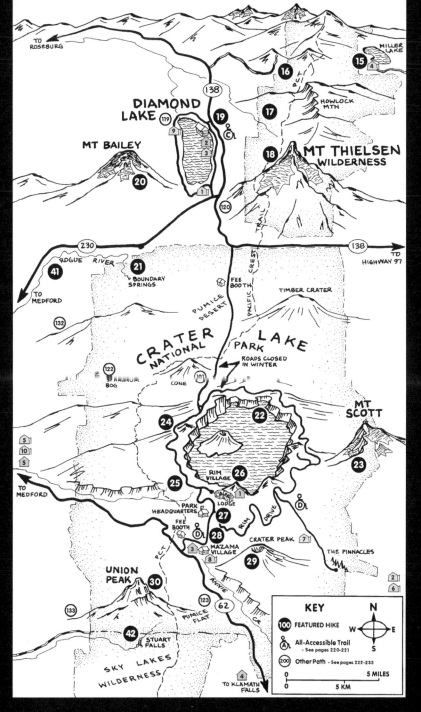

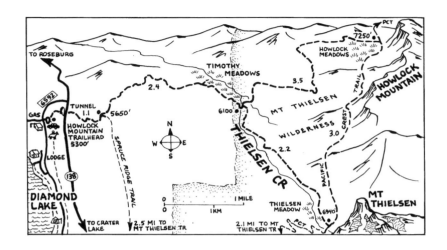

17   Thielsen Creek

Difficult (to Thielsen Meadow)
11.4 miles round-trip
1650 feet elevation gain
Open end of July through October
Use: hikers and horses

Difficult (to Howlock Meadows)
15.7-mile loop
2000 feet elevation gain

Mt. Thielsen looms like the Matterhorn above Thielsen Meadow, an alpine glen with a bubbling mountain stream. If you have extra energy after hiking to Thielsen Meadow you can return on a Pacific Crest Trail loop via Howlock Meadows, a broader field at another mountain's base. In either case, be prepared for mosquitoes from late July until mid-August and expect horse traffic on the first few dusty miles from the trailhead.

To find the trailhead from Medford, follow "Diamond Lake" signs east on Highway 62 for 57 miles and go straight on Highway 230 for another 23.6 miles. Then turn left at a "Diamond Lake Recreation Area" sign and follow Road 6592 for 4.2 miles to the Howlock Mountain Trailhead on the right, opposite a gas station. If you're coming from Roseburg, take Highway 138 east 78.6 miles. Between mileposts 78 and 79, turn right at a "Diamond Lake Recreation Area" sign for 0.3 mile, and park at the Howlock Mountain Trailhead on the left. If you don't have a Northwest Forest parking permit, you can buy one here. Horse rentals and guided rides are also available at this busy trailhead.

Start at the message board at the far end of the parking loop, and set off on the left-hand trail. In 0.2 mile follow the path through a tunnel under Highway 138. Then continue straight, ignoring horse loop trails to the left. The sparse lodgepole pine trees, pinemat manzanita bushes, and white lupines here are struggling to grow in 6 feet of dusty pumice and ash dumped here by the eruption of Crater Lake's Mt. Mazama 7700 years ago.

After 3.5 miles you'll be glad to reach Thielsen Creek, in a cool, grassy oasis at the head of Timothy Meadows. Cross on a log and walk 100 feet to a trail junction. Turn right on a path that parallels the creek upstream 2.2 miles to the Pacific Crest Trail. Just before the PCT, a short spur to the right leads to Thielsen Meadow, where the creek meanders through a heather glen overtowered by Mt. Thielsen's spire 2000 feet above. If you're backpacking, do not camp on the fragile meadow, but rather on forest duff well away from the creek.

If you're interested in the longer loop hike, turn left on the PCT. This route contours 3 miles through mountain hemlock woods to Howlock Meadows, a pumice barrens. At the far side of the field, where a sweeping view opens up of Howlock Mountain's cliffs and Mt. Thielsen's spire, turn left at a pointer for Diamond Lake and descend 3.5 miles to Thielsen Creek and the trail back to your car.

Mt. Thielsen from Thielsen Meadow.   Opposite: Thielsen Creek at Timothy Meadow.

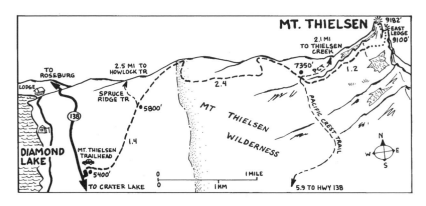

18   Mount Thielsen

Difficult (to Pacific Crest Trail)
7.6 miles round-trip
1950 feet elevation gain
Open end of July through October

Very Difficult (to summit)
10 miles round-trip
3800 feet elevation gain

Towering above Diamond Lake, Mt. Thielsen's stony spire commands views from Mt. Shasta to the Three Sisters. A popular path climbs to the Pacific Crest Trail on Mt. Thielsen's flank. Hardy hikers can continue to a dizzying ledge at the base of the summit spire, and many dare to scale the final pitch as well.

Originally a broad, 11,000-foot volcano, Mt. Thielsen stopped erupting about 100,000 years ago when a lava plug blocked its throat. Since then, erosion by Ice Age glaciers has left this hard lava core exposed as the summit spire. The peak's nickname, "Lightning Rod of the Cascades," reflects both its shape and its weather. Lightning has left the summit boulders spattered with black *fulgurite*—glassy recrystalized rock. The name Thielsen (pronounced *TEEL-sun*) honors a Danish-American pioneer railroad engineer.

To drive here from Medford, take Highway 62 east and follow "Diamond Lake" signs a total of 81 miles. At that point *do not* take the "Diamond Lake Recreation Area" turnoff. Instead continue 300 yards to a "Roseburg" pointer and turn left onto Highway 138. In 1.4 miles you'll find the Mt. Thielsen Trailhead parking area on the right. If you're coming from Roseburg, take Highway 138 east for 81.6 miles. Ignore a "Diamond Lake Recreation Area" turnoff and continue 3 miles to the large trailhead sign on the left. If you don't have the required parking permit, you can buy one here.

The trail climbs a dry, sparsely forested ridge, so bring plenty of water. As you gain elevation, lodgepole pine trees and manzanita bushes give way to mountain hemlock and red huckleberry. Notice how the trail cut exposes tan pumice gravel blasted here by the eruption of Crater Lake's Mt. Mazama 7700 years ago. Since then, only an inch or two of forest duff has managed to form atop the debris.

After 3.8 miles the path officially ends at the Pacific Crest Trail, but a climbers' trail continues straight up the ridgecrest. The best views are up this unofficial path, which climbs through the purple penstemon blooms and gnarled whitebark pines of timberline. To the north, the snowy peaks on the horizon are the Three Sisters and Diamond Peak. To the west, Mt. Bailey rises above Diamond Lake. To the south is Crater Lake's jagged rim.

Above timberline the braided, rocky path gives out amidst slippery scree and broken rock. Only sure-footed hikers should venture upward. The correct route veers slightly to the right, spiraling around to a dizzying ledge at the eastern base of the summit spire. This ledge, practically overhanging Thielsen Creek 2000 feet below, is an excellent place to declare victory and turn back. The final 80 feet are nearly vertical and require the adept use of hands and feet to chimney up cracks in the rock. Hikers attempting this do so at their own risk.

Mt. Thielsen from the trail.   Opposite: Mt. Thielsen's summit register.

19 Diamond Lake

Easy (North Shore)
3.4 miles round-trip
No elevation gain
Open mid-May through November
Use: hikers and bicycles

Easy (Silent Creek)
2.3-mile loop
100 feet elevation gain

Difficult (entire lakeshore)
11.5-mile loop
100 feet elevation gain

Crater Lake may be a dramatic draw for out-of-staters, but Oregonians visit neighboring Diamond Lake five times as often. This popular getaway is surrounded by mountain views, over 400 campsites, five boat ramps, a resort lodge, and a paved 11.5-mile loop trail. It's easiest to tour the lakeshore trail by bicycle, but a quiet section along the lake's north shore makes a lovely stroll, and the beautiful, unpaved spur trail through the wildflower meadows of glassy Silent Creek is open only to foot traffic.

The 3,015-acre lake has an average depth of only 20 feet, so it becomes swimmably warm in August. It's also stocked with rainbow trout. Waterskiing is allowed, but not jet skis. Mosquitoes are a problem in June.

Diamond Lake's basin once cradled a broad Ice Age glacier that descended from the flanks of Mt. Thielsen, Mt. Bailey, and Crater Lake's volcano, Mt. Mazama. A lake had replaced the glacier by the time Mt. Mazama's eruption sent a glowing avalanche of frothy pumice and hot gases racing toward the North Umpqua River canyon. The lake did not vaporize under that hot blast,

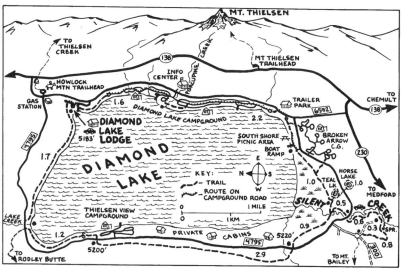

perhaps because earlier eruptions had left a blanket of pumice floating on the lake as an insulating bridge.

The Diamond Lake Lodge makes a good starting point for a lakeshore tour. To find it, turn off either Highway 138 or Highway 230 at "Diamond Lake Recreation Area" signs and follow paved Road 6592 to a "Lodge" pointer. Turn here and drive past the boat ramp before parking on the left at the lodge. The compound includes not only a restaurant and store, but also a marina shop where you can rent boats and bicycles.

If you're hiking, simply walk to the sandy picnic beach in front of the lodge, follow the lakeshore to the right, and climb to the paved bike path. If you're pedaling, bike from the lodge parking lot directly away from the lake (past a "Dead End" sign) for 150 yards to the paved path on the left.

Ducks, shadowy trout, and zillions of dragonflies patrol the lapping shore. Raucous gray jays and scampering golden-mantled ground squirrels watch passersby. Look on the grassy banks for tiny blue forget-me-nots and large mountain bluebells (*mertensia*). At times the trail dips into a forest of Douglas fir, lodgepole pine, and long-needled ponderosa pine. Look here for white trilliums in May and star-flowered solomonseal in June. Views ahead are to broad Mt. Bailey (Hike #20). Spire-tipped Mt. Thielsen (Hike #18) is behind you. After 1.7 miles, the trail briefly joins a road to cross Lake Creek, the lake's outlet. This is a good turnaround spot for hikers with children. If you're continuing, you'll find the trail wedged between the shore and the road for the next 1.2 miles. Beyond this the paved path crosses the road, traverses a viewless forest slope for 2.9 miles to avoid private cabins, recrosses the road, strikes off across brushy marshlands for 1.9 miles to the South Shore boat ramp, and then mostly follows campground roads (where the route is identified by painted bike symbols on

Diamond Lake.   Opposite: Silent Creek.

the pavement) for the final 3.8 miles back to the lodge.

Perhaps the most beautiful short hike at Diamond Lake follows Silent Creek to the largest spring feeding the lake. To find this unpaved trail from the Diamond Lake Lodge, drive 2.7 miles south on Road 6592, turn right at a "South Shore Picnic Area" pointer, follow Road 4795 for 1.5 miles, and park on the left immediately after the Silent Creek bridge.

This path heads upstream through an oasis in the dry lodgepole pine forests. In June, Silent Creek's mossy banks are ablaze with white marsh marigolds, purple shooting stars, and yellow violets. Alas, the mosquitoes here are thickest when the flowers are at their best. After the trail passes the spring it curves to the right through dry woods and meets a faint dirt road at the 1.4-mile mark. The official trail follows this track left 100 yards to a dusty trailhead on Road 300, but for a pleasant loop route back to your car, turn right instead. Follow the faint road 0.3 mile to its end, bushwhack straight ahead 20 feet through the woods, and turn left on the Silent Creek Trail for 0.6 mile to your car.

20   Mount Bailey

Difficult (from upper road)
5.4 miles round-trip
2330 feet elevation gain
Open end of July through October

Difficult (from lower road)
9.8 miles round-trip
3130 feet elevation gain

The two major mountains looming on opposite sides of Diamond Lake are both popular climbing goals for hikers. Mt. Thielsen is taller and has a more dizzying view, but the route to its top ends with a trailless scramble and a hair-raising rock climb (see Hike #18). Mt. Bailey is almost as challenging, but its steep trail leads all the way to the top. What's more, the final mile is full of surprises: a hidden crater, a rock garden of wildflowers, a double summit, and a rock wall with a window overlooking Diamond Lake.

Most hikers start the climb at a lower trailhead on Road 300, which is easily accessible for passenger cars. If you're driving a high-clearance vehicle, however, it's possible to shorten the hike by 2.2 miles (and 800 feet of elevation) by starting at an upper trailhead on a deeply rutted dirt road full of large rocks.

To find the lower trailhead, drive Highway 230 or 138 to Diamond Lake, take the "Diamond Lake Recreation Area" turnoff, drive along Road 6592 to a "South Shore Picnic Area" pointer, and turn onto paved Road 4795 for 1.7 miles. Continue 400 yards past Silent Creek and turn left on dirt Road 300 for 0.4 mile to a dusty parking area in a stand of lodgepole pines.

The trail starts by a sign on the right and soon climbs from the lodgepole pine woods into a forest of Shasta red fir and manzanita. After 1.6 miles you'll

Mt. Bailey's summit.   Opposite: Mt. Bailey from Diamond Lake.

get a first teasing glimpse of Diamond Lake through the trees. Take a 200-foot side trip up a rock knoll to the right for a better viewpoint. Then continue on the main trail, which levels off for 0.6 mile to an upper trailhead at a dirt road.

Along this stretch you might keep an eye out to the left of the trail for the Hemlock Butte Ski Cabin, an unlocked three-story A-frame cabin that's open to the public for free. Built by the Edelweiss ski club of Roseburg in the late 1980s, the cabin sleeps 16 and has a wood stove. Reservations are required only during the ski season from Thanksgiving through April; call the Diamond Lake Ranger District at 541-498-2531.

If you have a rugged vehicle, you can drive to the upper trailhead beside Hemlock Butte by taking Highway 230 west from the Diamond Lake turnoff toward Medford 3 miles. Near milepost 21, turn right on gravel Three Lakes Road 3703 for 2 miles, turn right on rutted dirt Road 300 for 0.2 mile, and fork left on unmarked Road 380 for 1.5 miles.

From this upper trailhead the path launches steeply up through a dense mountain hemlock forest. The trees become smaller and the rocks larger as you climb. Finally the path reaches a ridgecrest with views across Diamond Lake to Mt. Thielsen, and across the Crater Lake rim to Mt. Scott. The forest thins to

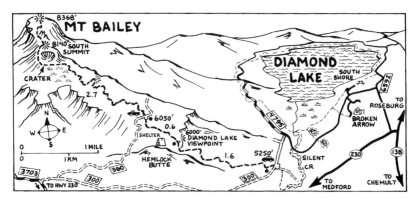

a few gnarled whitebark pines, but flowers brighten the black lava rockfields. Look for purple penstemon, white partridge foot, blue lupine, fuzzy pasque flower seedheads, and three colors of buckwheat blooms.

The trail skirts a snowfield in a 300-foot-wide crater and climbs to Mt. Bailey's south summit. While enjoying the view here, notice the glacier-carved valley to the east, where a massive 1965 winter avalanche mowed down forests halfway to Diamond Lake.

If you're not wearing boots with soles that grip well, consider turning back at the south summit. Ahead, the path dips across a cinder saddle, climbs along the left side of a 30-foot rock wall with a window-like peephole, edges briefly across the slippery top of a talus scree slope, and then climbs steeply to a ridgecrest and the true summit, a broad rockfield with alpine dandelions.

21   Boundary Springs

Easy
5 miles round-trip
400 feet elevation gain
Open June to mid-November

Few rivers begin as dramatically as the Rogue. At Boundary Springs, in the dry forests of Crater Lake National Park, the river pours out of the ground 20 feet wide, rushes through a meadow of yellow monkeyflowers, and tumbles over a 15-foot waterfall. Pets are banned on park trails and camping is forbidden within a quarter mile of the springs.

The headwaters of the Rogue were buried by the eruption of Crater Lake's Mt. Mazama 7700 years ago, when a glowing avalanche of hot pumice roared 40 miles downstream in a few minutes. Below Boundary Springs the river has managed to wriggle loose by carving a 100-foot-deep canyon into the vast debris field. Above the springs, snowmelt from the Crater Lake high country still has to percolate underground. Other than this seepage, the springs are not an outlet for Crater Lake itself, as was once believed.

The hike to Boundary Springs starts at Mount Mazama Viewpoint, a Highway 230 pullout located 5 miles west of the junction with Highway 138 at Diamond Lake. To drive here from Medford, take Highway 62 east 57 miles and continue straight on Highway 230 toward Diamond Lake for 18.6 miles to the viewpoint on the right, between mileposts 18 and 19.

Start out on the Upper Rogue River Trail through open woods of lodgepole pine, Shasta red fir, and mountain hemlock. After half a mile turn left on the Boundary Springs Trail and begin following the Rogue River. Along the river look for robin-sized water ouzels that dip in the river, lush blue lupine (best in July), and green islands of monkeyflowers.

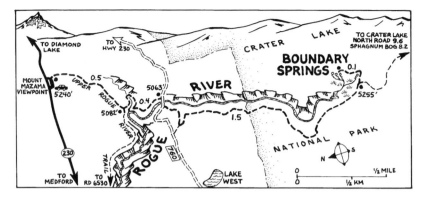

At the 0.9-mile mark you'll meet a dirt road. Turn right on it 100 feet to find the continuation of the trail upstream. After another 1.5 miles the trail forks at the edge of a brushy meadow. Keep left 100 yards to a 3-foot-wide spring. The trail peters out here, but don't turn back. Contour onward around a low ridge toward the sound of water 200 yards to find Boundary Springs' massive vent.

Other Hiking Options

If you'd like to shorten this hike by 1.8 miles, start at dirt Road 760. To find this trailhead from the Mount Mazama Viewpoint, drive east on Highway 230 for 2.2 miles and turn right past a "Lake West" sign for 3.4 miles. If you'd like to lengthen the hike, head downstream. From the junction of the Boundary Springs Trail and Upper Rogue River Trail it's 4.2 miles downriver to Rough Rider Falls (see Hike #41), and 47.4 miles to trail's end at Prospect.

Boundary Springs   Opposite: Waterfall below Boundary Springs.

The Cleetwood Cove boat dock.   Opposite: Wizard Island from the boat tour.

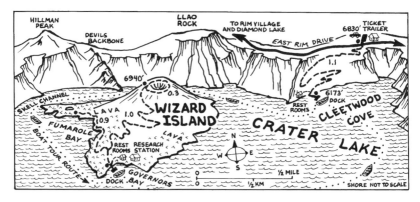

22   Wizard Island

Easy (to Cleetwood Cove)
2.2 miles round-trip
700 feet elevation **loss**
Open late June to mid-October

Moderate (to Wizard Island summit)
4.5 miles round-trip
1460 feet elevation gain
Open early July to early September

The switchbacking trail down to Cleetwood Cove's tour boat dock is the most popular path in Crater Lake National Park — and the only route to the lakeshore. Although the trail is "easy" by the standards of this book, the climb back up from the lakeshore can seem hot, steep, and difficult indeed if you are not used to hiking. Hikers who'd like to explore the inside of Crater Lake's collapsed volcano more fully can take the boat tour and climb to Wizard Island's summit crater. Pets are not allowed on park trails.

To drive here from Crater Lake's Rim Village, take the Rim Drive clockwise 10.6 miles to the trailhead. If you're coming from the park's north entrance off Highway 138, turn left along the Rim Drive for 4.6 miles. If you plan to take the boat tour, be sure to stop by the ticket trailer in the large parking lot across the road from the trailhead. Some reservations are now accepted for boat trips at 000-774-2728, but you still have to pick up tickets at the kiosk before hiking down.

Weather permitting, boat tours leave every 60 minutes between 9:30am and 3:30pm from mid-July to early September. The ticket trailer opens at 8am, and if you want to visit Wizard Island on a busy summer weekend, it's not a bad idea to arrive by 9am. Only the boats that leave at 9:30am and 12:30pm will stop at Wizard Island, and the only pickup times for the return trip are 2:30pm and 5:45pm. Overnight stays on Wizard Island are not allowed.

A private concession company sets boat tour prices; expect to pay about $27 for kids age 3-11 and $45 for adults ($5-$10 less if you don't get off at Wizard Island). To make sure hikers don't miss their boat, sales for each tour stop 40 minutes before it leaves.

The trail down to the boat dock is wide enough that the concessioner's tractors can carry supplies on it. The route passes lodgepole pines, Shasta red firs, mountain hemlocks, manzanita bushes, and lots of glimpses down to the glowing blue lake. The amazing color results from the lake's purity (it has no inlet other than precipitation) and its 1943-foot depth (it is the deepest lake in the U.S.). In recorded history the lake has only frozen twice and its surface level has fluctuated only 16 feet.

Gutsy swimmers sometimes brave the 50° F water at the dock's rocky shore. Fishing has been permitted without a license ever since rangers realized that introduced trout and kokanee salmon are hurting the lake's biological balance. Still, angling in this vast transparent pool is all but hopeless.

The roofless tour boats carry up to 40 passengers and an interpretive ranger.

It's a 45-minute ride to Wizard Island. The island is actually one of two cinder cones that erupted from the ruins of Mt. Mazama shortly after its cataclysmic collapse 7700 years ago. The other, Merriam Cone, was left under 486 feet of water after rain and melting snow gradually filled the lake. Wizard Island was named by Crater Lake's early promoter William Steel, who thought the cone resembled a sorcerer's hat. Although Steel helped win national park status, it's lucky some of his development schemes were ignored. He not only pushed for a rim road and a lodge, but also an aerial tramway from the rim to the island's top.

The trail on Wizard Island sets off through blocky black basalt lava colonized by golden-mantled ground squirrels, the red blooms of bleeding hearts, and gnarled Shasta red firs. Take the trail's right fork to switchback up the cinder cone. At the top, a path circles the 90-foot-deep crater's rim amid storm-blasted pines, red paintbrush, and constant panoramas. On the way back down, don't miss the rocky 0.4-mile side trail to the house-sized lava boulders and emerald lakeshore at Fumarole Bay. A rougher path continues around the bay 0.5 mile.

The return boat trip passes the place where an unauthorized private helicopter crashed in 1995. It promptly sank with its passengers in 1500 feet of water and has never been recovered. The boat tour also circles Phantom Ship, a small craggy island that is actually a remnant of a 400,000-year-old volcanic plug—the oldest rock exposed on the lake. On the return trip, sharp-eyed passengers sometimes spot the Old Man of the Lake, a floating vertical log that's been roaming the lake for a century. Bring warm clothes for the sometimes chilly boat ride, and be sure to save energy for 1.1-mile climb back to your car.

23   Mount Scott

Moderate
5 miles round-trip
1250 feet elevation gain
Open mid-July through October

Mt. Scott's lookout tower is the only place where hikers can fit the whole breathtaking sweep of Crater Lake into an average camera viewfinder. And although this is a major mountain—tenth tallest in Oregon's Cascades—the trail is so well-graded that even families with children sometimes tackle it.

Heavy winter snows make the Rim Drive near Mt. Scott the last road in Crater Lake National Park to open each summer. If you're driving here from Medford or Klamath Falls on Highway 62, turn north past the park entrance booth 4 miles and turn right on East Rim Drive for 11 miles to a parking pullout and trail sign on the right. If you're coming from Diamond Lake, turn left on East Rim Drive for 13 miles to the trailhead. Remember that pets are banned on park trails.

Crater Lake from Mt. Scott.   Opposite: Mt. Scott's lookout.

The trail begins as an ancient road track amid 5-needle whitebark pines and sparse meadows. Expect to cross a few snow patches until August. Also expect the company of Clark's nutcrackers, the gray-and-black cawing birds that tempt visitors to defy the park's ban on feeding wildlife. In fact, these "camp robbers" don't need handouts. Their sharp, strong beaks are adapted to break open whitebark pine cones for seeds, which they eat or cache for later. In return, the rugged whitebark pines, which only grow above 7000 feet, rely on the nutcrackers to spread their seeds from peak to peak.

The trail's second mile switchbacks up a slope of pumice pebbles, strewn like ochre hailstones from Mt. Mazama's fiery storm 7700 years ago. Views open up to the south across Klamath Lake's flats to the blue silhouette of the Mountain Lakes highland and the white tip of Mt. Shasta. To the right, Mt. McLoughlin's snowy cone rises above the summits of the Sky Lakes Wilderness. Wildflowers along the way include red paintbrush, purple penstemon, and the fuzzy seed stalks of western pasque flower.

At the summit you'll find a two-story stone-and-frame lookout. Built in 1953, the lookout replaced a similar stone cabin from the 1920s. To the north, look for Mt. Thielsen's spire and the distant Three Sisters. As for Mt. Scott, it honors Levi Scott, an 1844 Oregon Trail pioneer who founded Douglas County's Scottsburg and helped scout the Applegate Trail to Southern Oregon.

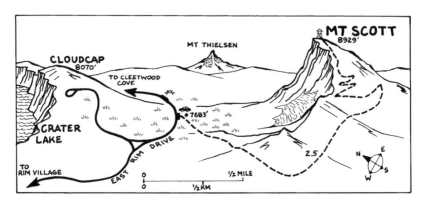

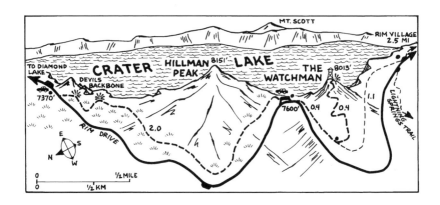

24   The Watchman

Easy (to Watchman Lookout)
1.6 miles round-trip
420 feet elevation gain
Open mid-July through October

Easy (past Hillman Peak)
4 miles round-trip
250 feet elevation gain

High on Crater Lake's western rim, The Watchman's lookout tower commands an eagle's-eye view across the amazingly blue lake to Wizard Island. The steep little climb up The Watchman is one of the most popular paths in the national park. It's also short enough that you might want to extend the hike by taking an adjacent 2-mile path around Hillman Peak to a viewpoint above the Devils Backbone. Pets are banned on all park trails.

The Watchman won its name in 1886, when the U.S. Geological Survey set up a watch point here while surveyors in a boat sounded the lake with a reel of piano wire. Other names that stuck from that 1886 expedition are Cleetwood Cove (for the boat) and Dutton Cliff (for its captain). The survey recorded a maximum lake depth of 1996 feet—a figure that has since been corrected by sonar to 1943 feet.

The Watchman Trail begins at a large, rail-fenced parking area and viewpoint on Crater Lake's Rim Drive. The parking area is not well marked, but you'll find it by driving 4 miles north of Rim Village or 2.2 miles south of the junction with the north entrance road. From the parking area, follow a paved sidewalk along the highway 100 yards to the actual trailhead. Look here for the fuzzy seedheads of western pasque flower and the blue trumpets of penstemon.

The wide path—a portion of the long-abandoned 1917 rim road—traverses a rockslide of giant cream-colored boulders. These rocks are dacite, originally part of a 50,000-year-old lava flow on Mt. Mazama's shoulder. After Mazama's cataclysmic decapitation 7700 years ago, the old lava flow was left as The Watchman, a crest on the gaping caldera's rim.

At the 0.3-mile mark, a snowfield lingers across the trail until August. Turn left at a junction just beyond the snow and climb 0.4 mile amid struggling mountain hemlock, white lupine, and patches of pinkish 5-petaled phlox. The summit tower, built in 1932, is staffed each summer with friendly rangers who help spot fires and answer hikers' questions. Soak in the view from the lookout's stone patio before heading back to your car.

If you'd like more exercise and different views, hike right on past your car and up a sandy ridge to find a trail that opened in 1995. This route skirts Hillman Peak for 2 miles, passing wildflower meadows, snow patches, rockfields with cat-sized marmots, and views across the Pumice Desert to the Three Sisters.

If you can't arrange to shuttle a car to the far end of the section—a lakeview pullout 2.2 miles from The Watchman's parking lot—turn back when the trail reaches a dramatic Crater Lake viewpoint beside the Devils Backbone. This craggy wall protruding from the lake's rim is a volcanic dike, formed when magma squeezed into a vertical crack inside ancient Mt. Mazama.

Wizard Island from The Watchman.   *Opposite: The lookout tower's patio.*

25   Discovery Point

Easy (to Discovery Point)
2.2 miles round-trip
100 feet elevation gain
Open July through October

Difficult (to Lightning Spring)
12.9-mile loop
1900 feet elevation gain

Explore the shattered flank of Crater Lake's ancient Mt. Mazama on these two very different hikes from Rim Village. The first is an easy view-packed stroll to Discovery Point. The second hike continues on a much longer loop that descends past Lightning Spring and returns through forests. If you plan to backpack on this longer loop you'll need to pick up an overnight permit at a national park office. Pets are banned on all national park trails.

Start in Rim Village at the huge paved parking area between the gift shop and visitor center. Take the sidewalk back along Crater Lake's rim, heading clockwise around the lake. The pavement and the tourist crowds end just beyond the parking lot. After another 200 yards you'll briefly follow the Rim Road's shoulder. Then the path swerves back to the caldera rim for 0.7 mile of glorious views.

The picture-postcard setting features cone-shaped Wizard Island below the massive dacite cliffs of Llao Rock, with a frame of gnarled whitebark pines and mountain hemlocks. Look for lavender cushions of 5-petaled phlox along the path and raucous gray-and-black Clark's nutcrackers in the trees.

At the 1-mile mark the trail switchbacks down to cross a highway parking pullout. Then it climbs 200 yards to Discovery Point, where a bronze plaque commemorates the viewpoint from which John Wesley Hillman's prospecting

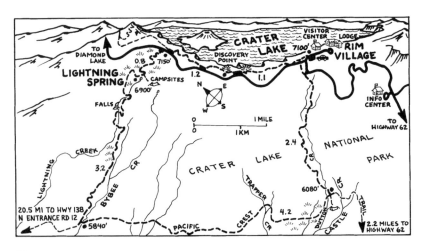

Crater Lake from Discovery Point.   Opposite: Golden-mantled ground squirrel.

party may have first spotted the lake in 1853.

For the easy hike, turn back here. If you're ready to tackle the longer loop, however, continue 1.2 miles along the rim-edge trail. When you reach the third highway parking pullout, cross the road and walk 100 yards along it to the gravel Lightning Springs trailhead on the left. This path—actually a long-abandoned roadbed—descends a dry, sandy slope in sweeping curves. Mt. Mazama's pumice and ash fell so deep here 7700 years ago that only a few lupine, phlox, and dogbane plants have yet taken hold. After 0.8 miles you'll pass Lightning Spring, where a deliciously cold, 3-foot-wide creek emerges from the dry slope.

Beyond the spring the trail/road descends a wooded dale for 3.2 miles, passing a 15-foot falls along the way. Then you'll meet the Pacific Crest Trail—one of the few trails in the national park where horses are allowed. Turn left on this level but relatively dull route through lodgepole pine woods for 4.2 miles. Finally, at an X-shaped trail junction by scenic little Dutton Creek, turn left for the 2.4-mile climb back to Rim Village. This last trail segment starts amid lovely meadowed openings of blue lupine, scarlet gilia, green hellebore, and chattering songbirds before crossing 6-foot-wide Castle Creek and climbing more seriously through mountain hemlock woods to your car.

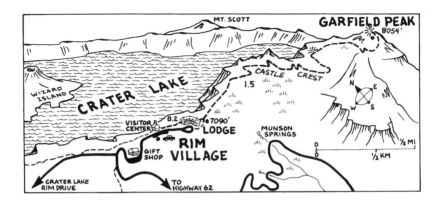

26   Garfield Peak

Moderate
3.4 miles round-trip
1010 feet elevation gain
Open mid-July through October

Perhaps the prettiest trail in Crater Lake National Park follows the lake's craggy rim from the historic lodge to the wildflowers and views of Garfield Peak. As on all park trails, pets and flower-picking are banned.

The path starts from the back porch of the grand old Crater Lake Lodge. To find it, follow signs to Crater Lake's Rim Village and continue straight through this beehive of tourists 0.3 mile to a turnaround at road's end.

Truth be told, the lodge here wasn't always grand. Built from 1909-1915 at a cost of just $50,000, the building originally opened with tarpaper on its outside walls and flimsy beaverboard between rooms. Years of makeshift maintenance and harsh winters left the building slated for demolition in the 1980s. But a public outcry pushed the Park Service to renovate it instead. After a $35 million makeover, the lodge reopened in 1995 with elegant woodwork in the Great Hall, a modern bath in each guestroom, and its rustic ambiance remarkably intact.

Walk behind the lodge and turn right on the paved pathway along Crater Lake's rim. Pavement soon yields to a broad trail through meadows of pale blue lupine, bright orange paintbrush, yellow groundsel, purple daisy-shaped flea-bane, and white pearly everlasting. Views improve with each switchback. The trail climbs past cliffs of *breccia*—welded volcanic rubble from Mt. Mazama's early mountain-building eruptions. The breccia here was long buried with lava flows, but these were stripped away by glaciers. The glaciers, in turn, vanished after Mt. Mazama lost its summit in a cataclysmic blast 7700 years ago.

Garfield Peak rises behind Crater Lake Lodge.   Opposite: Chairs on the lodge porch.

Snow patches linger across the trail until August near the top. At this elevation, only gnarled, 5-needle whitebark pines survive. These trees' limber limbs, so flexible they can be tied in knots, help the pines bend rather than break in winter gales.

Garfield Peak was named for the Interior Secretary of Teddy Roosevelt, who created the national park in 1902. When you reach the peak's summit, the glowing blue of Crater Lake gapes below like a 4-cubic-mile pool from a high-dive tower. If you're quiet you might see foot-long marmots and guinea-pig-sized pikas watching from cliff-edge rocks 100 feet north of the summit. To the east, Mt. Scott looms above Phantom Ship's small craggy island. To the south stretch the distant flats of Klamath Lake, with the tip of Mt. Shasta and the cone of Mt. McLoughlin to the right.

Crater Lake from the trail to Garfield Peak.

The Steel Visitor Information Center.   Below: The Castle Crest wildflower trail.

27   Park Headquarters

Easy (Lady of the Woods Loop)
0.5-mile loop
120 feet elevation gain

Easy (Castle Crest wildflowers)
1.2-mile loop
70 feet elevation gain
Open mid-June through November

When you stop at Crater Lake National Park's main visitor center, stretch your legs with a 0.5-mile loop trail through the park headquarters' forest to see a dozen historic stone buildings on the Lady of the Woods Loop. If you like, you can add a second tour from the same trailhead—a loop to the wildflowers and mossy springs of Castle Crest. Pets are not allowed.

Drive north from Highway 62 for 3.8 miles (or south from Rim Village 2.6 miles). Turn into the park headquarters parking lot and pull up in front of the Steel Visitor Information Center. Built of massive stones and timbers in the rustic national park style, this building opened in 1932 as a ranger dormitory. Now it's a visitor center with displays, books, brochures, and helpful rangers. A booklet describing the Lady of the Woods Loop may be available here for $2.

To find the trailhead, walk around the left-hand end of the visitor information building. Then cross a footbridge over a branch of Munson Creek and fork uphill to the right on a dirt path into the woods. After 200 yards you'll reach a post marked #3. A doctor visiting the park in 1917 spent two weeks chiseling a reclining nude into a boulder here. Early park guides touted the unfinished sculpture as a tourist attraction under the name "The Lady of the Woods."

Next the loop switchbacks up alongside a woodsy creek and crosses the driveway of the 1933 superintendent's residence, now renovated as a educational center. At this point the path enters a creekside meadow with pink monkeyflower, purple aster, green hellebore, yellow groundsel, and views of

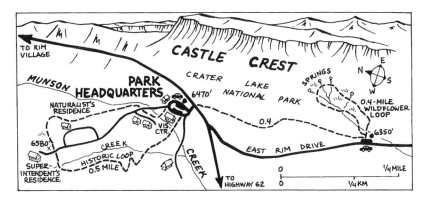

Castle Crest's cliff. The historic tour route passes below the 1932 naturalist's residence and crosses a road beside a row of mid-1920s employee residences before returning to the visitor center parking lot.

The second short hike at park headquarters tours the wildflower meadow at Castle Crest. If you're short on time you can drive to the start of the loop by turning right 200 yards on the highway and forking left on Rim Drive 0.4 mile to a pullout on the left, just beyond a "Congested Area" sign.

But why not leave your car where it is and take a connector trail instead? From the entrance to the visitor center parking lot, simply walk across the highway on a crosswalk and follow a path through the trees 0.4 mile to the Castle Crest parking pullout, where the loop itself begins.

Walk the loop counter-clockwise. Start by crossing a 10-foot-wide branch of Munson Creek and climbing to a mossy slope of springs and flowers.

The pink blooms here are trumpet-shaped monkeyflowers and dart-shaped shooting stars. The blue flowers are pea-like lupines, tiny forget-me-nots, and elephant heads—stalks clustered with scores of tiny blooms that really look like elephant heads. The white ball-shaped flowers are American bistort.

The loop crosses the creek twice more before returning to the parking pullout—and the 0.4-mile connector back to the visitor center.

The historic walking tour crosses a creek below the 1933 superintendent's residence.

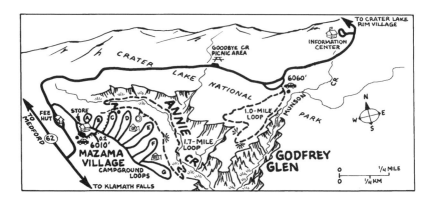

Godfrey Glen.   Opposite: Annie Creek.

28 Annie Creek & Godfrey Glen

Easy (Annie Creek Canyon)
1.7-mile loop
200 feet elevation gain
Open mid-June through November

Easy (Godfrey Glen)
1-mile loop
50 feet elevation gain

Wildflowers, tumbling brooks, and strange ash pinnacles highlight these short loop trails near popular Mazama Campground in Crater Lake National Park. Although not connected, the two paths are just 2 miles apart, so it's easy to hike them both in a day. Note that pets are banned on park trails.

The 1.7-mile loop through Annie Creek Canyon starts conveniently in the national park's only campground. From the national park entrance on Highway 62, drive 0.3 mile toward the Rim Village and turn right at a sign for Mazama Campground. If you're not camping here, keep right and park in front of the store. Then walk through the campground to the end of camping loop C, where you'll find the trailhead behind site C-11.

The loop starts to the right, following the wooded rim of Annie Creek's canyon along the edge of the campground. Black bears do visit these woods daily, looking for campsites with obvious cooler chests, but you're unlikely to see these unaggressive bears. On the other hand, you're almost certain to spot three species of squirrels and chipmunks. The lively, orange-bellied Douglas squirrels have no stripes and often chatter in trees. Golden-mantled ground squirrels have striped sides and scamper into burrows. Genuine chipmunks are smaller and have side stripes that extend all the way past their eyes.

After 0.5 mile the Annie Creek trail switchbacks down into a canyon with several weird-looking ash pinnacles. The story behind the pinnacles begins in the Ice Age, when glaciers scoured U-shaped valleys through Annie Creek's canyon and adjacent Godfrey Glen. After the ice retreated, the eruption of Crater Lake's Mt. Mazama filled both valleys to the brim with glowing avalanches of hot pumice and ash. When the loose debris stopped moving, superheated gas rose through it, welding ash into solid rock along the vents. Since then streams have cut narrow V-shaped canyons into the softer ash, exposing the old vents as spires.

Beyond the ash pinnacles the path follows the lovely cascading stream up through wildflower meadows a mile before climbing back to the loop's start at campground site C-11.

To take the all-accessible 1-mile loop hike to Godfrey Glen, drive back to the park's main entrance road, turn right toward Rim Village for 2.1 miles, and turn right at a "Godfrey Glen Nature Loop" sign for 200 yards to the trailhead. The trail here promptly forks for the loop; keep left for the quickest route to the astonishing overlook of Godfrey Glen, a green oasis 300 feet below in a box canyon flanked by fluted spires of beige ash. Watch children near this dangerously unrailed viewpoint. Then continue on the loop through the woods to your car.

29 Crater Peak

Easy (to Sun Notch)
0.5-mile loop
115 feet elevation gain
Open July to early November

Moderate (to Crater Peak)
6.8 miles round-trip
1010 feet elevation gain

These two uncrowded hikes on the south side of Crater Lake reveal the difference between a crater and a caldera. The 0.2-mile Sun Notch Trail climbs to a spectacular Crater Lake viewpoint above Phantom Ship's craggy little island. But the astonishingly blue, 6-mile-wide lake you see here is not in a crater at all—it fills a *caldera*, a giant pit created by a mountain's collapse. To see a true volcanic crater, take the nearby 3.2-mile path to Crater Peak, a cinder cone with a wildflower meadow in a cute little summit bowl. Pets are not allowed on either trail.

Start at the national park headquarters and visitor information building located halfway between Crater Lake's Rim Village and Highway 62. Drive 200 yards down the road toward Highway 62, turn left at a "Rim Drive (East)" sign, and follow this road 4.3 miles to the Sun Notch Trailhead on the left. Then hike the short path up through mountain hemlock woods to the cliff-edge viewpoint.

Much of Crater Lake's geologic story is exposed at Sun Notch's viewpoint. When eruptions started building Mt. Mazama 400,000 years ago, they began near here. Phantom Ship is a fragment of the volcanic plug from those early eruptions. As Mt. Mazama grew to an estimated height of 12,000 feet, the volcanic

Cloudcap from Sun Notch.   Above: Phantom Ship from Sun Notch.

Lupine in Crater Peak's summit meadow.

vents moved farther north, finally pouring out a thick dacite flow to create Llao Rock, the largest cliff visible across the lake. By then, glaciers were scouring deep U-shaped valleys into the mountain's flanks. Sun Notch is a remnant of one of the largest of these glacial troughs, amputated when the mountain exploded 7700 years ago.

If you'd like to see a genuine crater after visiting Sun Notch, drive 1.4 miles back on Rim Drive and turn left down to the Vidae Falls Picnic Area. Park here and hike the Crater Peak Trail, which traverses a slope below Rim Drive for 0.6 mile. Then the path strikes off along a broad ridge through mountain hemlock woods with patches of blue lupine, scarlet gilia, and golden currant bushes. After 2.1 mostly level miles the path climbs 0.5 mile to the mouth of the summit crater. Pumice and ash that rained down from Mt. Mazama's eruption filled this little crater halfway to the top. Since then lupine, dogbane, and grass have colonized the bowl, making it a popular grazing spot for elk; look for their hoofprints and sign. A patch of snow lingers in the crater until August.

For a view-packed 0.4-mile loop, walk clockwise around Crater Peak's rim. To the north, note Mt. Thielsen's distant spire above Sun Notch. To the east is Mt. Scott; to the west is Union Peak's spire; and to the south are Klamath Lake, distant Mt. Shasta, and snowy Mt. McLoughlin.

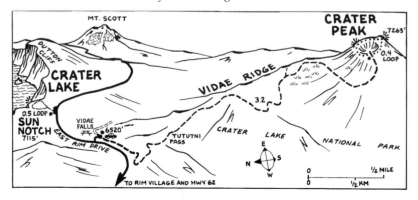

30　Union Peak

Difficult 11 miles round-trip
1600 feet elevation gain
Open mid-July through October

The oldest mountain in Crater Lake National Park, Union Peak's rocky volcanic plug affords a view across ancient Mt. Mazama's forested flanks to Cascade peaks from Mt. Thielsen to Mt. Shasta. The panorama comes with a price, however—the hike's first 4.7 miles are a trudge through viewless woods, while the final 0.8 mile is an invigorating climb up three dozen switchbacks. A few other cautions: backpackers must pick up an overnight permit at a national park office, pets are not permitted, and there is no water.

 Start by driving 72 miles east of Medford (or 1 mile west of Crater Lake National Park's Mazama Village) to the summit of Highway 62. At a "Pacific Crest Trail Parking" sign, turn south to a dirt turnaround. The nearly level trail sets off through a sparse forest that alternates between stands of almost pure lodgepole pine and groves of almost pure mountain hemlock. The pumice that fell here 10 feet deep during the eruption of Crater Lake's Mt. Mazama 7700 years ago is responsible for the utter lack of underbrush.

In an open pumice plain at the 2.9-mile mark, turn right at a sign for the Union Peak Trail and gain a first glimpse of Union Peak ahead. The path now climbs gradually through meadow openings with blue lupine and lots of elk sign. Once hunted nearly to extinction, elk were restocked here from Yellowstone National Park in the 1960s and are thriving.

Suddenly the trail emerges from the woods at the base of Union Peak—a gigantic rockpile surmounted with a fortress of black crags. As you switchback up, look for the dishmop-shaped seedheads of western pasque flower and the

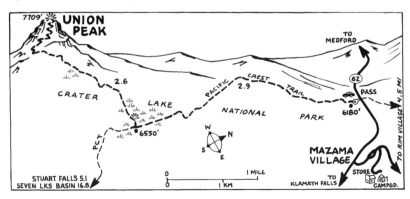

Crater Lake's rim from Union Peak.   Opposite: Union Peak from Crater Lake's rim.

purple trumpets of penstemon. The final short switchbacks are so rugged you may need to use your hands as you climb.

The summit's black boulders have shiny spots of melted rock where lightning has struck, proving this is no place to be in a storm. On a clear day, however, distant Mt. Shasta floats ghost-like on the southern horizon above Devils Peak, with the cone of Mt. McLoughlin to the right. To the west is the Rogue Valley's haze. To the north, it's easy to imagine Mt. Mazama's former shape, although the mountain's forested flanks now rise to a broken hole. Crater Lake itself is hidden inside but Llao Rock's cliff, on the lake's far shore, peeks out above Rim Village.

Upper Rogue River

Cabins, Lookouts & Inns

		Rental units	Private bath	Breakfast	Open (mos.)	Rate range
1	**PROSPECT HISTORICAL HOTEL.** Teddy Roosevelt stayed in this 1889 stagecoach inn en route to Crater Lake. Restaurant open May-Oct. 14 motel units run $70-120. Res: 800-944-6490 *(www.prospecthotel.com).*	10	●	●	●	$120 -205
2	**THE WHITE HOUSE.** This Medford bed & breakfast has just one large suite with rocking chairs on the porch, at 212 Valley View Drive. Reservations: 541-301-2086 *(www.thewhitehouse-bedandbreakfast.com).*	1	●	●	●	$135
3	**UNION CREEK RESORT.** This rustic wayside lodge has 9 rooms, 22 cabins, and a tiny general store. Open all year despite heavy winter snow. Res: 866-560-3565 *(www.unioncreekoregon.com).*	32	●		●	$55- 245
4	**VALLEY OF THE ROGUE.** This handy state park campground beside I-5 rents 6 yurts. Res: 800-452-5687.	6			●	$36

◁ *Upper Rogue River (Hike #34)*

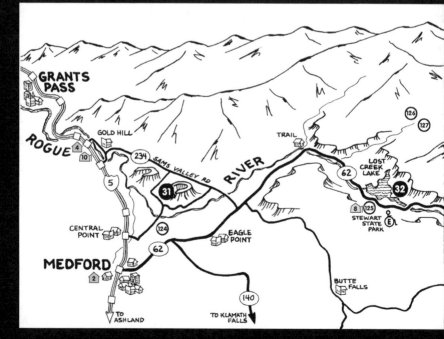

Top right: Hershberger Mountain (Hike #37).

Campgrounds

		Campsites	Water	Flush toilet	Open (mos.)	Rate range
1	**ABBOTT CREEK.** This overlooked camp at the confluence of two creeks is just a mile from the Rogue River's Takelma Gorge trailhead (see Hike #33).	25	●		V-X	$12
2	**FAREWELL BEND.** Very popular, this camp along the Rogue River at Union Creek is a good stop on the way to Crater Lake. See Hike #35.	61	●	●	V-X	$18
3	**HAMAKER.** Because this campground along the upper Rogue River is a mile off Highway 230, it's often overlooked. In a forest, with meadows nearby and trails in both directions. See Hike #41.	10	●		V-X	$14
4	**HUCKLEBERRY MOUNTAIN.** All-terrain vehicle trails pass this 1930s CCC camp, hidden on a rough back road above Union Creek.	25			V-X	free
5	**MILL CREEK.** Just 3 miles north of Prospect, but hidden a mile off Highway 62, this creekside camp has quiet, primitive sites.	10			V-X	$8
6	**NATURAL BRIDGE.** The Upper Rogue Trail traces the riverfront through this forested campground (see Hike #34).	17			V-X	$10
7	**RIVER BRIDGE.** A rustic campground with spacious sites along the river, on the Upper Rogue Trail (see Hike #33 map).	11			V-X	$8
8	**JOSEPH H. STEWART STATE PARK.** On Lost Creek Reservoir (swimming, waterskiing, 19-mile hiker/biker loop trail), this park has campsites in meadows and woods. See Hike #32. Res: 800-452-5687.	201	●	●	III-X	$13-20
9	**UNION CREEK.** In an old-growth forest where Union Creek meets the Rogue River, this lovely, spacious camp was built by the CCC in the 1930s. See Hikes #34-35. Reservations: 541-560-3900 (*www.roguerec.com*).	78	●		V-X	$14
10	**VALLEY OF THE ROGUE.** Between Interstate 5 and the Rogue River, this state park is noisy and crowded, but convenient. Res: 800-452-5687.	168	●	●	●	$15-24

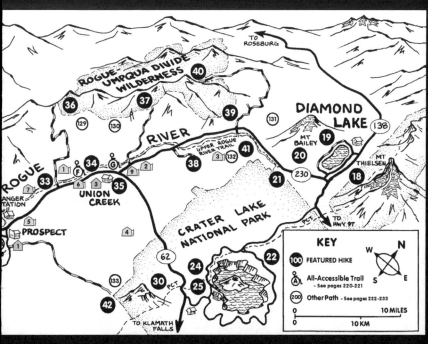

31 Upper and Lower Table Rocks

Easy (Upper Table Rock)
2.8 miles round-trip
720 feet elevation gain
Open all year

Moderate (Lower Table Rock)
5.2 miles round-trip
780 feet elevation gain

Once a sanctuary for Takelma Indians, today these cliff-edged mesas near Medford are a haven for hikers and endangered wildflowers. Views from the cliffs extend across the Rogue River to the Siskiyous and the Cascades. Visit in spring to catch the best flower displays and to avoid summer's merciless heat. Dogs, horses, fires, and flower picking are banned on both Table Rocks trails. Stay on designated paths.

The 125-foot-thick andesite rims capping these U-shaped mesas are remnants of a lava flow that poured down the Rogue River Valley 7 million years ago from a vent near Lost Creek Lake. Since then, erosion has worn away the softer surrounding rock, leaving the hard andesite perched 800 feet above the plain.

An 1850 gold strike at Jacksonville attracted so many miners and settlers to

Lower Table Rock.   Above: Lower Table Rock from the trailhead.

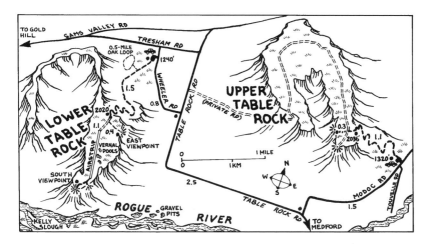

the Rogue Valley that the local Takelma Indians launched attacks to reclaim their homeland. When the U.S. Army retaliated in 1853, the tribe retreated to Upper Table Rock, a natural fortress that long defied capture. To this day, the mesas remain sacred to the Takelmas.

When real estate speculators proposed a subdivision inside Lower Table Rock's bowl in 1979, The Nature Conservancy raised $500,000 to save it. The Bureau of Land Management has since formed a partnership with this public-spirited non-profit group, building trails and designating additional land. In 2009 The Nature Conservancy bought the last private land on the two mesas for $3.9 million.

Today each mesa has its own trail. For information about the free, guided hikes led here on April and May weekends, call the Medford BLM office at 541-618-2200 or check *www.blm.gov/or/resources/recreation/tablerock*.

Of the two trails, the path up Upper Table Rock is shorter and slightly easier. To find it from Interstate 5, take Central Point exit 33 just north of Medford, drive east on Biddle Road 1 mile, turn left on Table Rock Road for 5.2 miles to a curve, and turn right on Modoc Road for 1.5 miles to a parking lot on the left.

The Upper Table Rock Trail climbs through a scrub oak grassland ablaze with spring wildflowers. In April expect blue camas and pink fawn lilies. In May look for pink, four-petaled clarkias (alias "farewell to spring"), California blue-eyed grass (with six small petals), and elegant brodiaea (with six long purple petals). By June, orange paintbrush and tall purple ookow are blooming too. In all seasons, beware of triple-leafleted poison oak.

At the 1.1-mile mark, after a final steep pitch, the trail suddenly emerges onto the table's amazingly flat, grassy summit. Continue straight across the mesa 0.3 mile to trail's end at a 200-foot cliff with a view west.

Although the trail to Lower Table Rock is longer and rockier, it climbs through shadier woods and leads to a taller cliff. To find this trailhead get back in your car, continue driving on Table Rock Road north of Medford to milepost 10 and turn left on Wheeler Road 0.8 mile. The trail sets off through grasslands with the same profusion of flowers as at the other mesa. The path climbs, steeply at times, through a dry forest of madrone and black oak. After 1.5 miles the path suddenly crests at the plateau and becomes an old road.

The quickest route to a viewpoint is to walk the road 200 yards and fork left on a trail 0.3 mile to a cliff. From here you can see your car far below. The snowy rim of Crater Lake rises above Upper Table Rock. The Rogue River, like a great green snake, curves across a quilt of orchards, ranches, and gravel pit ponds toward the distant white cone of Mt. McLoughlin. Turkey vultures soar on updrafts.

For the best view of all, however, hike back to the road and follow it a mile across the mesa. The road becomes an old grassy airstrip bordered by vernal pools — ponds that dry up by May, leaving a haze of flowers. Look here for dwarf meadowfoam, a subspecies that exists only on the Table Rocks. At the airstrip's end, continue right on a path to a viewpoint overtowering the Rogue River.

32   Lost Creek Lake

Easy (to The Grotto)
5 miles round-trip
100 feet elevation gain
Open all year

Moderate (north shore, with shuttle)
9.6 miles one way
200 feet elevation gain

Difficult (entire lakeshore)
18.7-mile loop
400 feet elevation gain

Waterskiers and fishermen are familiar with this reservoir on the upper Rogue River, but surprisingly few hikers have discovered its shoreline trail. The path is nicest in spring when the reservoir is full, the wildflowers are blooming, the birdlife is at its most active, and the powerboats aren't yet too noisy.

Most visitors to Lost Creek Lake cluster around the dam's outlet (with picnic areas and the nation's third-largest steelhead hatchery) or Joseph Stewart State Park (with a campgound, swimming beach, boat ramp, marina, cafe, and store). But trails in those areas are mostly paved. For a wilder walk on the quieter side of the lake, head for The Grotto, a box canyon of colored ash formations.

To find the trailhead, drive Crater Lake Highway 62 east of Medford 35.5 miles. Just after crossing the bridge at the far end of Lost Creek Lake, turn left on Lewis Road for 1 mile to the Lewis Road Trailhead on the left. The path starts in an open forest of Douglas fir, ponderosa pine, and black oak. Watch out for poison oak here. Also notice orange paintbrush, pink 5-petaled geraniums, blue lupine, and yellow salsify. Lizards run through the dust. Fish-hunting osprey soar above the lake. Look back to the east to see Needle Rock, a lava-capped mesa with a window arch.

After 0.9 mile the trail passes a gravel boat ramp and crosses a footbridge to Fire Glen Camp, a cluster of walk-in sites commemorating a 50-acre blaze in 1979. The best swimming spot of the hike is 0.3 mile farther, at a small beach.

At the 2.4-mile mark, just before a footbridge over an inlet, turn right at a "Grotto" sign and climb to a viewpoint of a secluded gulch where a tiny creek drips 40 feet. The soft greenish rock here is ash from Crater Lake's volcano, and the hard basalt layer atop it is lava from the same source. In June, The Grotto is

Lost Creek Lake.   Opposite: Salsify.

abloom with *pretty face*, a delicate, 6-petaled yellow amaryllis.

If you're not yet ready to turn back—and if you can arrange a car shuttle—continue onward around the lake's roadless north shore 7.2 miles to Takelma Park's boat ramp.

If you can't arrange a shuttle and you're up to an athletic challenge, trek 18.7 miles around the entire lake. Along the way you'll cross the reservoir's dam, follow 2 miles of paved paths in busy Stewart State Park, and finally hoof 1.3 miles along the Highway 62 bridge and Lewis Road to your car.

Other Hiking Options

Long-distance hikers are supposed to be able to follow the Upper Rogue River Trail from Lost Creek Lake to the river's source near Crater Lake. But if you hike from Peyton Bridge along the reservoir's upper arm, you'll find the trail peters out after 4.7 miles, where government property ends. Rather than bushwhack the next 4 miles, skip to the Forest Service trailhead near Prospect. To find it from the ranger station in Prospect, drive 0.4 mile south on Highway 62 and turn right on a gravel road beside a canal for half a mile.

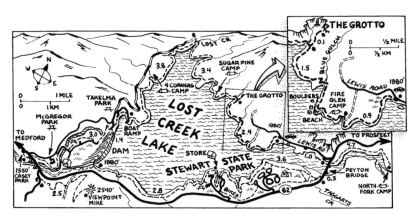

33 Takelma Gorge

Easy (to Takelma Gorge)
3.2 miles round-trip
No elevation gain
Open March to mid-December

Easy (to River Bridge, with shuttle)
4.6 miles one way
160 feet elevation **loss**

Tormented by an ancient lava flow, the Rogue River twists around a hairpin curve, rages down a chute, and foams for nearly a mile through Takelma Gorge's 150-foot-deep rock slot. Several thousand years ago, Crater Lake's volcano filled the Rogue's valley with 650 feet of lava and ash. Through Takelma Gorge the river follows a crack in the lava—a weak spot where water eroded a canyon.

The gorge is named for the Upland Takelma (or Latgawa), a tribe native to this area. A warlike band, they often raided the Lowland Takelma in what is now the Grants Pass area for food and slaves. In their Penutian language—unrelated to the languages of other Southern Oregon tribes—Takelma means "those who live by the river." Early French trappers called them *coquins* ("rogues"), and later white settlers dubbed them Rogue River Indians. Today the Upper Rogue River Trail wends through an old-growth forest along the gorge's rim.

To hike here, start by driving east from Medford on Crater Lake Highway 62. Between mileposts 51 and 52 (past the Prospect Ranger Station 6 miles) turn left onto paved Woodruff Meadows Road. After 1.7 miles turn left into the Woodruff Bridge picnic area. Park at the far end of the turnaround.

The path curves left to the riverbank among 7-foot-thick Douglas fir. In early summer look here for tiny white starflower, the delicate double bells of twinflower, 5-petaled white anemone, and yellow Oregon grape blooms. In fall, vine maple lines the river with scarlet pinwheel-shaped leaves.

After 1.6 miles the trail reaches the first Takelma Gorge viewpoint, on a cliff-

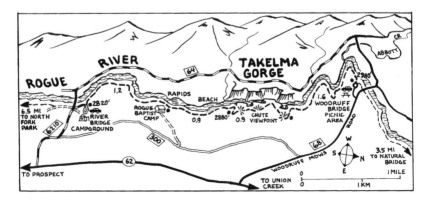

Takelma Gorge.   Opposite: Townsend's chipmunk.

top above the spectacular, churning chasm. Hikers with small children could turn back here, but it would take willpower, because the next 0.9 mile of trail follows the gorge's rim past a succession of stunning viewpoints. Finally the trail switchbacks down to a tamer stretch of river. In another 0.3 mile the path passes a small sandy beach suitable for sunning or wading—another possible turnaround point.

If you'd like to hike the entire 4.6-mile trail section from Woodruff Bridge to River Bridge one way, plan to leave a shuttle car at the far end. To find that trailhead, turn off Highway 62 a ways south of milepost 51. Take gravel Road 6210 west 1 mile, turn right into the River Bridge Campground entrance, and keep left for 0.2 mile to a trail sign at the day-use parking area.

Other Hiking Options

Long-range hikers can continue along the Upper Rogue River Trail for days. If you're walking downstream, it's 6.5 miles to trail's end at North Fork Park. (To find this trailhead, drive 0.4 mile south of the Prospect Ranger Station on Highway 62 and turn right on a gravel road beside a canal for half a mile.) The trail is prettier upstream, however. From Woodruff Bridge it's 3.5 miles to Natural Bridge (see Hike #34) and 36.8 miles to the Mount Mazama Viewpoint trailhead near the Rogue River's source (see Hikes #41 and #21).

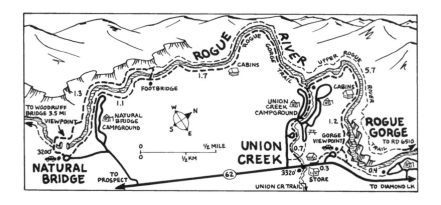

34   Natural Bridge

Easy (to Natural Bridge)
2.4-mile loop
300 feet elevation gain
Open mid-March through November

Easy (Rogue Gorge and Union Creek)
2.2-mile loop
No elevation gain

The upper Rogue River puts on its two most spectacular performances in the popular Union Creek resort area: a disappearing act where the river vanishes underground and a daredevil act where it squeezes through a rock chasm. Easy loop hikes visit each of the attractions. If you'd like to see both, a moderate 8-mile hike combines the two loops in one.

The secret behind both of the river's stunts is its use of lava tubes. Several thousand years ago Crater Lake's volcano filled this canyon with a long basalt lava flow. When the lava's crusted surface stopped moving, the molten rock underneath kept on flowing, leaving long caves. At Natural Bridge the Rogue River funnels through one of these tubes like water through a hose. At Rogue Gorge the river has ripped open the cave's roof, leaving a slot of raging whitewater.

For the Natural Bridge loop, drive Crater Lake Highway 62 east from Medford 55 miles (or west of Union Creek 1.1 mile), and turn off the highway at a "Natural Bridge Campground" sign near milepost 55. Then keep left for 0.7 mile to the Natural Bridge parking area. The trail starts at an information kiosk at the far right-hand end of the lot.

The paved path crosses the river on a long footbridge. Pavement ends in 0.2 mile at a railed viewpoint of the natural bridge. Below, the frothing river appears to be sucked into solid rock. Water pressure in the 200-foot lava tube is so great that spray sputters out from cracks in the cave roof.

Most tourists turn back here. But a lovely, quiet portion of the Upper Rogue River Trail continues upstream. In early summer, large patches of 5-petaled white anemones bloom here beneath old Douglas firs. Also look for vanilla leaf, with three big leaves and a stalk of tiny white flowers.

A mile beyond Natural Bridge take a fork to the right, cross the river on a footbridge over a churning chasm, and come to a T-junction with the Rogue Gorge Trail. Only turn left if you're interested in the 8-mile hike combining both loops. To complete the first short loop, turn right and hike 1.1 mile to your car.

The other easy loop hike, to Rogue Gorge, is a more civilized tour, passing summer cabins, campgrounds, and an ice cream shop in the village of Union Creek. To start, drive Highway 62 to Union Creek at milepost 56. A few hundred yards north of town, follow a "Rogue Gorge" sign to a parking lot. First take a minute to explore a paved 0.2-mile loop trail that visits fenced viewpoints of the 100-foot-deep gorge. This is all most tourists will see. For a more thorough,

Rogue River footbridge on the Natural Bridge loop.   Opposite: Trillium.

2.2-mile tour of the Union Creek area, however, follow the fence downstream and continue on the unpaved Rogue Gorge Trail.

After 1.2 miles along the wooded riverbank, cross a footbridge over Union Creek to a trail junction. To the right the Rogue Gorge Trail continues 1.7 miles along the river to the Natural Bridge loop described above. For the short loop back to your car, however, turn left along Union Creek. This creekside path actually goes through a few campground sites, but the campers know they're beside a trail and don't seem to mind passersby. After stubbornly following the creekbank 0.7 mile upstream, turn left along Highway 62. Just beyond the ice cream shop, angle left beside a propane tank on a short trail back to your car.

35   Union Creek

Easy (to falls from Road 610)
0.6 mile round-trip
120 feet elevation **loss**
Open April through November

Moderate (to falls from Highway 62)
8.2 miles round-trip
330 feet elevation gain

Left: Union Creek.   *Opposite: Cascade lily.*

A nearly level trail from the rustic resort village of Union Creek follows a cool mountain stream through old-growth woods to a small, mossy waterfall. This 4.1-mile path is lovely, but if you're pressed for time, a backdoor route will take you down to the falls in just 0.3 mile.

Begin by driving Crater Lake Highway 62 east from Medford. At milepost 56, park near the store in the hamlet of Union Creek. This is the start of the longer, prettier route to Union Creek Falls.

Walk behind the store to Cabin #21 to find the path heading upstream along Union Creek. The Douglas firs in these woods are as much as 7 feet in diameter.

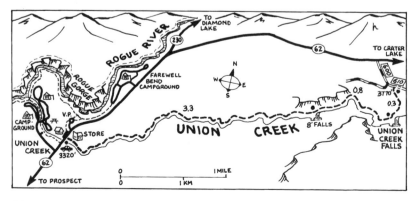

The scraggly, flat-needled trees along the creek are yew; its bark yields the cancer drug taxol, and its resilient wood was once used by Indians for bows. Bracken fern and vanilla leaf add greenery to the forest floor. Star-flowered solomonseal blooms in June with sprays of tiny stars.

The farther you hike, the livelier the creek becomes, bubbling through miniature waterfalls and gorges. Watch for ouzels near an 8-foot cascade at the 3.3-mile mark. These dark gray, robin-sized birds dive underwater and flap their wings, "flying" along the creekbed in search of insect larvae.

Union Creek Falls is only 10 feet tall, but it tops a dramatic series of water slides, chutes, and rock channels—a nice lunch spot. Beyond the falls, the trail leaves the creek and climbs through smaller woods 0.3 mile to Road 610. To start your hike here (or to leave a shuttle car here for a one-way hike), drive Highway 62 north of Union Creek 1.3 miles, veer right on Highway 62 toward Crater Lake for 2 miles, turn right on gravel Road 600 for 0.2 mile, and fork left on dirt Road 610 for 200 yards to the trailhead on the right.

36 Abbott Butte

Moderate (to Abbott Butte)
6.8 miles round-trip
1500 feet elevation gain
Open July through October
Use: hikers, horses

Difficult (to Elephanthead Pond)
9.8 miles round-trip
1950 feet elevation gain

Wildflowers and vistas line this spectacular, often overlooked portion of the Rogue-Umpqua Divide Wilderness's ridgecrest. The chief destination here is Abbott Butte, where an abandoned lookout tower straddles a small cabin. But an equally interesting goal is Elephanthead Pond, in the shadow of an enormous, elephant-shaped cliff.

To drive here from Medford, head east on Crater Lake Highway 62. Between mileposts 51 and 52 (past the ranger station in Prospect 6 miles) turn left onto paved Woodruff Meadows Road 68. Stick to Road 68 through numerous well-marked junctions for 4.9 miles of pavement and another 7.4 miles of 1-lane gravel road. At a pass, park in a gravel pullout on the right by a sign for the Abbott Butte Trailhead.

If you're coming from Roseburg, you'll want to take Interstate 5 south 25 miles to Canyonville exit 98. Following signs for Crater Lake, drive into Canyonville and turn east on 3rd Street—which becomes the Tiller-Trail Highway—for 23.3 miles to Tiller. On the far side of this hamlet, fork left onto Road 46 at a South Umpqua Falls pointer for 5.3 miles; then turn right on Jackson Creek Road 29 for 12.5 miles and finally turn right at a "Huckleberry Gap" sign for 15 gravel miles to the trailhead on the left, just beyond a pass.

The trail sets out through a mountain hemlock forest full of beargrass (with blooms in early July), blue huckleberries (ripe in late August), and a host of woodland wildflowers, including anemones and inside-out flowers. After 1.4 miles, at Windy Gap, the path dips to within 30 feet of the abandoned road to the Abbott Butte lookout, and 0.4 mile later at Sandy Gap the path joins the old road. The views from Sandy Gap's pass stretch from Mt. Scott to Mt. McLoughlin and distant white Mt. Shasta. The sand in this pass is strewn with the sunny wildflowers one might expect in the Siskiyous, including sunflower-like balsamroot and tall blue ookow. Beyond the pass, follow the road because the parallel trail is no longer maintained.

At the 2.5-mile mark the road crosses the path in a lush meadow of white lupine, green hellebore, purple larkspur, and black coneflower. If you're headed for Abbott Butte, simply keep on the roadbed another mile uphill to the summit. The 30-foot lookout tower lacks glass or stairs, but still shelters a 10-foot cabin where the lookout staff once slept. The view is a bit overgrown. Bunches of huge Cascade lilies brighten the slopes nearby.

If you're ready to head back, return as you came. If you'd like to visit Elephant-head Pond, however, walk down the lookout road 0.7 mile from Abbott Butte

Elephanthead from Elephanthead Pond.

The abandoned Abbott Butte lookout and its cabin.

to the third switchback and hike cross-country 100 yards downhill to the trail. Turn right and follow this increasingly faint path as it contours across the meadow. Cairns and poles help mark the mostly level route 0.4 mile to an open pass with views of Mt. Bailey and Mt. Thielsen. From here the trail descends 0.9 mile through profuse wildflower meadows to a boardwalk at the marshy outlet of Elephanthead Pond, a shallow lake with a surprising view of a 300-foot rock cliff sporting a natural bas-relief sculpture of an elephant's head, complete with trunk, ear, and eye.

Other Hiking Options

Backpackers can continue along the Rogue-Umpqua Divide Trail beyond Elephanthead Pond 12 miles to Hershberger Mountain (see Hike #37), 13 miles to Highrock Meadows (Hike #9), or 19 miles to Fish Creek Valley (Hike #40).

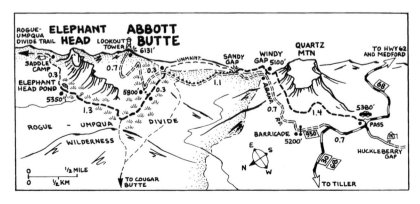

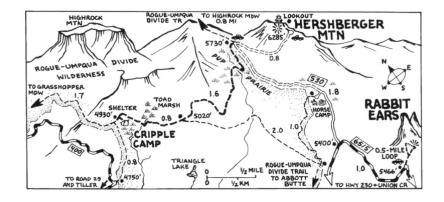

37   Hershberger Mountain

Easy (to Rabbit Ears and lookout tower)
1 mile round-trip
360 feet elevation gain
Open July through October

Moderate (to Cripple Camp shelter)
4.8 miles round-trip
840 feet elevation **loss**
Use: hikers, horses

    Short paths lead to two spectacular landmarks of the Rogue-Umpqua Divide high country: the historic Hershberger Mountain lookout and the 400-foot rock spires of Rabbit Ears. To round out the day with a longer hike, try the nearby trail to Cripple Camp's shelter, in a wildflower meadow surrounded by huge Douglas firs.

    To start, drive east from Medford on Crater Lake Highway 62 for 57 miles, veer left onto Highway 230 toward Diamond Lake for 0.9 mile, and turn left across a Rogue River bridge onto Road 6510 for 1.6 miles. Fork to the right on gravel Road 6520 for 0.5 mile and then turn left on Road 6515 for 5.6 increasingly rough miles to a sharp left bend at a small ridge-end meadow. Park at an unmarked parking area on the right *(GPS location N43°00.461′ W122°26.873′)* and follow a trail to the right along the wooded ridgecrest 300 yards to the base of Rabbit Ears—a pair of huge, overhanging spires. The eroded remnants of a volcanic plug, these pillars were first scaled in 1921. They still attract technical rock climbers and nesting falcons. Even from the base, the view extends south to snowy Mt. McLoughlin and distant Mt. Shasta.

    After inspecting Rabbit Ears, return to your car, continue driving up Road 6515 exactly one more mile. Then turn right on Road 530 for 1.8 steep, rough miles to a switchback with a parking space on the left for the Rogue-Umpqua Divide Trail. This is where you'll start the hike to Cripple Camp, and if you're

Rabbit Ears from Hershberger Mountain.   Opposite: Hershberger Mountain's lookout.

in a low-slung passenger car, this is definitely as far as you should drive. If your vehicle has high clearance, however, drive onward and upward on a steep 0.8-mile track to road's end atop Hershberger Mountain. From this parking area, a 100-foot path scrambles to the white wooden lookout on the summit.

Built in 1925, the 12-foot-square building has an inside ladder to a cupola—a small second story full of windows. Views sweep from Mt. Bailey to Mt. Shasta. The lookout was restored with the intention of making it available for rental, but the access road doesn't meet regulations, so the empty lookout is left unlocked and open to overnight users for free on a first-come-first-served basis. Don't expect furniture, lights, heat, or anything else except a view.

For the more substantial hike to Cripple Camp's shelter, drive 0.8 mile down from the lookout to the road's switchback. Two trails start here, but take the Acker Divide Trail down to the left. It descends through Douglas fir woods 0.5 mile to Pup Prairie, an astonishingly lush wildflower meadow with head-high stalks of purple larkspur. Also look for green hellebore, mountain bluebells, red paintbrush, fuzzy-topped mint flowers, red columbine, and brown coneflower. Mosquitoes peak along with the flowers in late July and early August.

Continue a mile past Pup Prairie to a junction and go straight 0.6 mile to Toad Marsh, a former lake that really does foster toads. Fist-sized and warty, the khaki amphibians stumble across the trail. Hike another 0.2 mile to Cripple Camp, a meadow with large orange tiger lilies and a leaky shake-roofed shelter from 1937. Droopy incense cedars and 8-foot-thick Douglas firs add to the ambience.

Other Hiking Options

Backpackers can continue past Cripple Camp shelter on a grand 13.4-mile loop to Buckeye Lake (see Hike #10), Fish Lake (Hike #9), and Highrock Meadow before returning to the Hershberger Mountain trailhead. The Rogue-Umpqua Divide Trail offers other long-distance choices. If you follow this path south along the crest of the Wilderness you'll reach Abbott Butte in 13 miles (see Hike #36). Follow it north instead and you'll reach Fish Creek Valley beside Rattlesnake Mountain (Hike #40) in 7 miles.

38 National Creek Falls

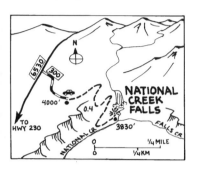

Easy
0.8 mile round-trip
170 feet elevation **loss**
Open mid-April through November

This very short hike to a cool, misty waterfall glen makes a good family outing for a hot summer day. National Creek was a favorite stop for travelers as early as the 1860s, when miners and stockmen blazed a route past here on their way from Southern Oregon to the newly discovered John Day gold fields.

Drive Crater Lake Highway 62 east of Medford 57 miles and fork left onto Highway 230 toward Diamond Lake. After 6 miles, near a sign marking the

National Creek Falls.   *Opposite: Hellebore (corn lily).*

Jackson County line, turn east on paved Road 6530 for 1.3 miles. Then fork left to keep on Road 6530 for another 2.4 miles and finally turn right on gravel Road 300 for a few hundred yards to the trailhead at road's end.

The trail sets off through woods of mixed Douglas fir, hemlock, flat-needled grand fir, and white pine. Look on the trail for spiny golf-ball-sized "porcupine eggs" — the seeds of the broadleaf chinkapin trees that form a scraggly understory here. In May, Oregon grape has clusters of yellow flowers and vanilla leaf puts up fuzzy white flower stalks resembling bottle brushes.

After ambling 0.2 mile the trail passes the top of the falls. Don't venture near the cliffs for a view. Instead continue down the trail another 0.2 mile to its end at the base of the falls, a side-by-side pair of 80-foot fans that spray out over a basalt cliff. The rock is actually the broken edge of a lava flow from Mt. Mazama, Crater Lake's ancient volcano.

39   Muir Creek

Easy (Highway 230 to Muir Falls)
5.4 miles round-trip
250 feet elevation gain
Open May through November
Use: hikers, horses

Moderate (Road 400 to Upper Mdw)
5.6 miles round-trip
500 feet elevation gain
Open June to mid-November

Elk and deer love the brushy meadows along this mountain stream so much that early morning hikers almost always see them. If you're not an early riser, you'll still be able to see Muir Falls, wildflowers, and plenty of elk tracks. The two easy hikes recommended here sample the trail's highlights. More ambitious trekkers can connect these trail segments or continue for a backpack trip into the beautiful, uncrowded Rogue-Umpqua Divide Wilderness. Be aware that cows graze these meadows from July to early October.

The flattest and most accessible trail in this area leads from Highway 230 to Muir Falls. To find it, drive east from Medford on Highway 62 for 57 miles and veer left onto Highway 230 (toward Diamond Lake) for 10.3 miles. Immediately before a bridge labeled "Muir Creek", pull into an unmarked parking area on the left. (If you're coming from Diamond Lake, drive 0.6 mile past milepost 11 and park just after the Muir Creek bridge.)

The trail promptly leaves Muir Creek and sets off through a forest of hemlock and Douglas fir with low huckleberry bushes and princes pine plants. After crossing two bridgeless side creeks (look for logs up or down the stream), the path finally returns to Muir Creek at the 1.4-mile mark. A lovely viewpoint by the creekbank here overlooks the brushy, marshy meadows popular with elk and songbirds. Mosquitoes can be a problem the last half of June. Continue another 1.3 miles — along a trail muddied in places by hooves — until you hear

Buck Canyon's upper meadow.

(and glimpse) Muir Falls to the right. Bushwhack 50 yards through alder brush to the creekbank for a closer look at this cascade, a series of 10-foot falls where Muir Creek forks. Turn back here unless you're ready to connect the two short hikes in a single long trek.

The second short hike along Muir Creek climbs through prettier wildflower meadows to a subalpine bowl dammed by an ancient landslide. To find this trail from the first trailhead, drive Highway 230 north 1.9 miles. Shortly after milepost 12, turn west on gravel Fish Creek Road 6560 for 1.8 miles. Then turn left on Road 400 for 1.3 miles to its end at the Hummingbird Meadows trailhead.

This path sets off through high-elevation woods with incense cedar, 5-foot-thick Douglas fir, and the white blooms of trilliums. In between are meadowed slopes with huge-leaved hellebore (corn lily), purple larkspur, and delicate yellow fawn lilies. There's also lots of cattle and elk sign. After 0.3 mile, hop across Muir Creek on rocks. Shortly afterwards, turn right on the Buck Canyon Trail.

In another 1.6 miles, keep left at a fork and climb through lichen-draped woods to a 10-foot waterfall beside the Devils Slide. This half-mile-long rockslide dammed the canyon several thousand years ago, creating the waterfall and a quarter-mile-long lake. Since then, the lake has filled with silt and become a subalpine meadow traced with the meanders of the clear, swift, deep-pooled creek. In June look for marsh marigolds and fawn lilies in the meadow. Also listen for the *meep!* of pikas, the rabbit-like denizens of the nearby rockslide.

This upper meadow makes a good turnaround point. Beyond, the trail climbs 1000 feet to a broad pass before gradually descending to Alkali Meadows, with a spring, a campsite, and more wildflowers.

Other Hiking Options

Backpackers with map and compass can complete a 15.5-mile loop from the Muir Creek trailhead on Highway 230. Hike up Muir Creek and continue through Alkali Meadows to the Road 700 trailhead. The trail once continued east, but has been supplanted by logging Road 760. Follow it to its end and bushwhack downhill to the Muir Creek Trail.

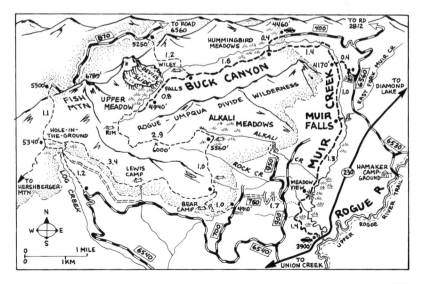

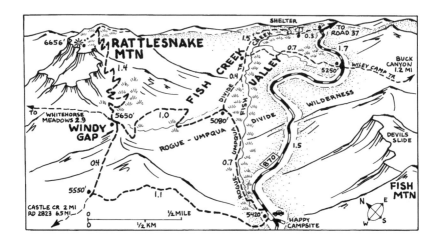

40 Rattlesnake Mountain

Easy (to Windy Gap)
3.2-mile loop
740 feet elevation gain
Open July through October
Use: hikers, horses

Moderate (to Rattlesnake Mountain)
6-mile loop
1750 feet elevation gain

Right next door to the popular Diamond Lake area, but overlooked by tourists, the Rogue-Umpqua Divide Wilderness is a hidden haven of subalpine wildflower meadows, viewpoints, and quiet trails. One of the best hikes starts from a gravel road that sneaks into the heart of the wilderness. For an easy loop, hike to Windy Gap and the flowers along Fish Creek. For a longer trip, climb to the views atop Rattlesnake Mountain—a snakeless summit with a meadow.

From Medford, take Crater Lake Highway 62 east for 57 miles, and then veer left onto Highway 230 for 12.2 miles, following a "Diamond Lake" pointer. At the Hamaker Campground junction shortly after milepost 12, turn left onto Fish Creek Road 6560. Follow this gravel road 4 miles to a pass where it becomes Road 37. Continue another 0.5 mile, fork left onto Incense Cedar Loop Road 800 for 2.8 miles, and then turn left on Fish Creek Valley Road 870 for 4.2 miles. This increasingly rough road passes three other trailheads before you reach the one you want—a small "Rogue-Umpqua Divide Trail" sign on the right, 100 yards before a parking pullout and a spur road to Happy Campsite, a primitive tent spot.

If you're driving to this trailhead from Roseburg, it's quicker to head east on

Highway 138. Between mileposts 60 and 61 turn right on Fish Creek Road 37 for 13 miles. Then turn right on Incense Cedar Loop Road 800 for 3 miles and finally turn right on Fish Creek Valley Road 870 for 4.2 miles.

The trail sets off downhill through a meadow with a rainbow of summer wildflowers. Look for goldenrod, red paintbrush, white yarrow, purple aster, blue lupine, black coneflower, and sweet-smelling mint. From late August to early October you may also find cows grazing here. The path follows Fish Creek, a splashing mountain brook, 0.7 mile to a junction. Turn left and climb 1 mile to Windy Gap, a wooded saddle where four trails meet.

For the easy loop, turn left on a faint path along the wooded ridgecrest, past a sign for Trail 1576 and Hummingbird Camp. In another 0.4 mile, turn left on an abandoned roadbed with views west to Castle Rock's plug-shaped lava knob. After 1.1 mile, the road/trail ends at Road 870 a few yards from your car.

If you like views, however, don't miss the side trip up Rattlesnake Mountain. When you first reach Windy Gap, go straight 50 feet to find the trail. It forks uphill to the right and promptly starts switchbacking up through meadows of lavender owl clover, bracken, aster, white lupine, and scarlet gilia. The path is faint, but maintained and not extremely steep. The only switchback that's easy to overlook is the second one, in a meadowed gully with a view of Fish Mountain.

When you reach a steep meadow near the summit, turn left at a trail junction. After another 100 yards the trail ends at a large rock cairn, but continue straight across the meadow 150 yards to a clifftop viewpoint virtually overhanging Castle Creek's broad wilderness valley. To the left, your view of the horizon's peaks sweeps from forested Fish Mountain, past the tip of Mt. McLoughlin, Union Peak's steep pyramid, Crater Lake's rim, flat-topped Mt. Scott, pointy Mt. Thielsen, and broad Mt. Bailey.

Other Hiking Options

The Rogue-Umpqua Divide Trail extends 23.8 miles in all. Hike it east 1.9 miles to Fish Creek Shelter, or head west to Highrock Meadow, Hershberger Mountain, and Abbott Butte (Hikes #9, #37, and #36).

Rattlesnake Mountain.   Opposite: Mt. Thielsen from Rattlesnake Mountain.

41   Upper Rogue River

Easy (to No Name Falls)
3.4 miles round-trip
200 feet elevation gain
Open mid-May to mid-November

Moderate (to Rough Rider Falls)
7.8 miles round-trip
650 feet elevation gain

Moderate (Highway 230 to Road 6530)
8.6 miles one-way
1200 feet elevation **loss**
Open June to mid-November

Near its headwaters the Rogue River churns through a rarely visited canyon of waterfalls. For an easy hike, take a nearly level stroll through the woods to an unnamed 40-foot S-shaped falls. For a longer hike, continue upstream to roaring, 50-foot Rough Rider Falls. Better yet, arrange a car shuttle and hike this entire 8.3-mile stretch of the Upper Rogue River Trail one way.

If a car shuttle isn't in the cards, start at the lower trailhead. From Medford, take Highway 62 east for 57 miles and continue straight on Highway 230 toward Diamond Lake 12.2 miles. At a "Hamaker Campground" sign shortly after milepost 12, turn right onto gravel Road 6530. In another 0.5 mile, keep left at a fork to stay on Road 6530. Then drive 0.2 mile, *watching closely for a small "Upper Rogue River Trail" sign on the left*. Park on the shoulder here. (If you're driving here from Diamond Lake, take Highway 230 toward Medford 11.4 miles and keep left on Road 6530 for 0.7 mile to the small trail sign on the left.)

The trail sets off through a quiet forest of big Douglas fir (up to 6 feet in diameter), flat-needled grand fir, droopy-limbed incense cedar, white pine, and chinkapin brush. The trail briefly swings beside the Rogue River after 0.4 mile, but then returns to the woods until just before the unnamed waterfall. This long cascade churns through two curves before frothing into a 120-foot-wide pool. White lupine and 4-petaled bunchberry bloom here.

If you decide to continue past the unnamed falls you'll follow the glassy river

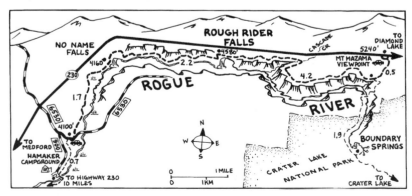

Rough Rider Falls.   Opposite: Blacktail deer.

through the most remote and scenic part of its canyon. At a switchback 2.2 miles farther up the trail, bushwhack straight ahead 100 yards to reach a scenic river islet at the base of Rough Rider Falls. This turnaround spot affords a fine view of the cascade pounding down onto mossy boulders.

If you have access to two cars you can hike the trail one way — all downhill. After leaving one car at the lower trailhead on Road 6530, drive the other back to Highway 230 and turn right for 6.4 miles to the Crater Rim Viewpoint parking pullout, where the Upper Rogue River Trail begins. Follow this path 0.5 mile, keep right at a junction, and head downstream 8.1 miles to the first car.

The upper 4.2 miles of this trail is often within earshot of the highway, but follows the scenic rim of a 200-foot-deep canyon. The Rogue carved this chasm out of the vast ash layer deposited when Crater Lake's Mt. Mazama erupted 7700 years ago.

Other Hiking Options

Backpackers and equestrians can follow the Upper Rogue River Trail downstream even farther. From the lower trailhead at Road 6530, it's 0.7 mile to Hamaker Campground, 10.7 miles to Highway 230, 24.7 miles to Natural Bridge (Hike #34), and 39.3 miles to trail's end near Prospect.

42

Stuart Falls

Moderate
8.6 miles round-trip
1500 feet elevation gain
Open mid-June to mid-November
Use: hikers, horses

Waterfalls and huckleberries draw hikers to this canyon between the Sky Lakes Wilderness and Crater Lake National Park. In addition to Stuart Falls—a 40-foot fan on a columnar basalt cliff—the route passes Red Blanket Falls and several unnamed cascades. Blue huckleberries along the way ripen in profusion by late August. Expect some mosquitoes during the first three weeks of July.

To find the trailhead, take Crater Lake Highway 62 east of Medford 45 miles to a turnoff for Prospect and turn right for 0.7 mile to the center of this village. Just beyond the Prospect Hotel turn left onto Butte Falls Road, and 1 mile later turn left again on Red Blanket Road. In another 0.4 mile fork left on gravel Road 6205 for 11.4 miles to its end at a large parking turnaround.

The path begins in a park-like stand of Douglas fir, hemlock, and grand fir, with an understory of dogwood and hazel. The shiny leaves of holly-like Oregon grape and tiny twinflower serve as ground cover. After 100 yards the trail enters the official Wilderness near one of the corner markers for Crater Lake National Park. These monuments were built in 1902 to warn sheepherders and timber cutters away from the newly created reserve.

After 2 miles of well-graded but viewless climbing, the trail follows a canyon rim with glimpses of roaring waterfalls. The best view is of Red Blanket Falls, which tumbles 40 feet into a bubbling pool. The falls and creek are named for the red blankets that early Prospect-area settlers used to purchase the land here from the Takelma tribe.

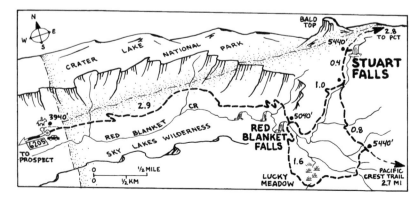

Stuart Falls.   Opposite: Shasta red fir cone opened by a squirrel for its seeds.

At the top of Red Blanket Falls, keep left for 1.4 miles along a lovely mountain brook to a lodgepole pine forest at the base of splashing Stuart Falls. Look for water ouzels here, the robin-sized dippers that can "fly" underwater. Backpackers are directed away from this heavily used area to a camping area downstream and saddle stock are limited to an area away from the creek.

Other Hiking Options

If you're willing to add 1.4 miles to your trip back, you can return on a loop through the area's best huckleberry fields. Walk back from Stuart Falls 0.4 mile and fork left at a "Pacific Crest Trail" pointer. In 0.8 mile, after crossing three creeks, look carefully for a "Lucky Camp Trail" sign to the right. This rockier path, crowded with huckleberry bushes, descends past Lucky Meadow (a grassy bog with hellebore and columbine) and crosses 30-foot-wide Red Blanket Creek (on a log just above the falls) before rejoining the trail to your car.

Southern Cascades

Campgrounds

	Campsites	Water	Flush toilet	Open (mos.)	Rate range
1 **ASPEN POINT.** Swim or waterski at this lakeside campground near the Lake of the Woods Resort. Res: 877-444-6777 (*www.recreation.gov*).	60	●	●	V-IX	$17-34
2 **FISH LAKE & DOE POINT.** These two camps on Fish Lake (near a resort with boat rentals) access the High Lakes Trail (Hike #51).	43	●	●	V-X	$18
3 **FOURMILE LAKE.** At a large alpine lake by Mt. McLoughlin, this camp amid lodgepole pines has a boat ramp and trails (Hike #48).	29	●		VI-X	$17-34
4 **HOWARD PRAIRIE.** This giant county park on a busy reservoir amid pines has showers, boat rentals, a cafe, and a store. Res: hplake.com	300	●	●	IV-X	$18-30
5 **HYATT LAKE.** On a reservoir beside the Pacific Crest Trail, this camp has showers, 2 boat ramps, and 1 horse campsite.	54	●	●	IV-X	$10-15
6 **NORTH FORK.** This small, pretty camp beside Fish Lake's outlet creek (at a trailhead for Hike #51) is usually uncrowded.	9	●		IV-XI	$10
7 **ODESSA CREEK.** Launch a canoe tour of Upper Klamath Lake from this convenient camp amid brushy, open woods.	5			●	free
8 **SOUTH FORK.** In old-growth timber along the South Fork Rogue River (see Hike #45), this camp is just west of the Sky Lakes Wilderness.	6			V-X	$10
9 **SUNSET.** Mt. McLoughlin mirrors in Lake of the Woods at this lakeshore camp with a boat ramp. Res: 877-444-6777 (*www.recreation.gov*).	64	●	●	VI-IX	$17-34
10 **WHISKEY SPRINGS.** A mile-long barrier-free nature trail loops from this wooded camp.	34	●		V-X	$14
11 **WILLOW PRAIRIE.** At this meadow in tall timber, each campsite has 4 horse corrals. Nearby is a rental cabin (see below). Reservations: 877-444-6777 (*www.recreation.gov*).	10	●		V-X	$10

◁ *Lake of the Woods Resort.*

Cabins, Lookouts & Inns

	Rental units	Private bath	Breakfast	Open (mos.)	Rate range
1 **FISH LAKE RESORT.** Modernized 1940s resort (boat rentals, general store) has 60 campsites ($20-30) and 11 cabins. Res: 541-949-8500.	11	●		●	$75-250
2 **IMNAHA GUARD STATION.** 3-room cabin (sleeps 4-6), running water, flush toilet. See Hike #45 map. Res: 877-444-6777 (*www.recreation.gov*).	1	●		V-X	$40
3 **LAKE OF THE WOODS RESORT.** This old-timey mountain lodge rents 26 rustic cabins. Res: 866-201-4194 (*www.lakeofthewoodsresort.com*)	27	●		●	$99-325
4 **WILLOW LAKE RESORT.** This resort has 63 campsites ($20-30), 4 cabins that sleep 6, and 2 yurts ($35). Reservations: 541-865-3474.	6	●		IV-X	$100-125
5 **WILLOW PRAIRIE CABIN.** Historic log cabin (sleeps 2-4), woodstove, horse corrals. Ski in a mile in winter. Res: 877-444-6777 (*www.recreation.gov*).	1			●	$15
6 **WILSON'S COTTAGES.** Near Crater Lake in Fort Klamath, these cabins have kitchenettes. Res: 541-381-2209 (*www.thewilsoncottages.com*).	10	●		●	$75-110

Top right: Devils Peak (Hike #44).

113

43 Seven Lakes West

Moderate (to Alta Lake)
8.4 miles round-trip
1750 feet elevation gain
Open early July through October
Use: hikers, horses

Difficult (to Cliff Lake)
10.4 miles round-trip
2300 feet elevation gain

Difficult (to Devils Peak)
13.7-mile loop
3050 feet elevation gain

From Devils Peak's lofty summit, the pools of the forested Seven Lakes Basin look like pips on a pair of green dice. Up close, each lake has its own character. Half-mile-long Alta Lake, for example, is so narrow you can throw a rock across it. Cliff Lake has a mountain view and a diving rock popular with swimmers.

The Seven Lakes Trail is the shortest route to this popular basin, but it climbs across a high ridge. For a gentler route from the east, see Hike #44. In either case, be warned that mosquitoes are a problem from mid-July to mid-August. Group size is limited to eight people and 12 animals. Backpackers must tent at least 100 feet from lakeshores and are encouraged to use the four signed camp areas. Equestrians are required to use the eight designated horse camps. In addition, horses are not allowed within 200 feet of lakeshores (except on trails or at designated watering spots) and grazing is usually banned.

To find the Seven Lakes Trailhead, take Highway 62 east from Medford 14.5 miles, turn right on the Butte Falls Highway for 15 miles to the town of Butte Falls, continue straight for another 1 mile, turn left at a sign for Prospect for 9 miles,

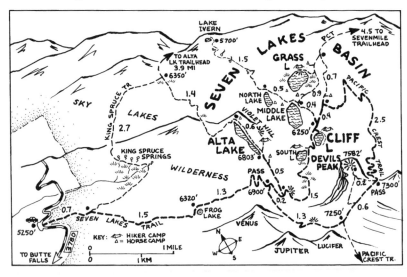

turn right onto Lodgepole Road 34 for 8.5 miles, continue straight on Road 37 for 0.4 mile, and then veer right onto gravel Road 3780 for 4.1 miles.

The trail starts behind a guardrail and climbs steadily up a broad forested ridge. The path is a bit dusty and rocky from heavy use by horses and hikers, especially on summer weekends. Fork to the right at the 0.7-mile mark, and after another 1.5 miles take a break beside Frog Lake, a shallow pool rimmed with heather and lodgepole pine. Then continue 1.3 miles to a pass with a trail junction and a view ahead to Devils Peak. The thumb-shaped outcrop on the peak's left shoulder is the old volcano's original plug, stripped bare by the vanished Ice Age glacier that carved the lake basin below.

Go straight down the far side of the pass 0.2 mile to a second trail junction—this one for Alta Lake. For a moderate hike, turn left half a mile to this amazingly straight, skinny pool, aligned on the crack of a major north-south fault. Before turning back, be sure to follow a "Camping" pointer right 100 yards to the cliffy lip of Violet Hill and a view across the Seven Lakes Basin.

If you're up to a more difficult hike, skip the Alta Lake side trail and continue straight 1.5 miles to Cliff Lake. Along the way you'll descend through subalpine meadows with the tiny blooms of pink heather and white partridge foot. Pause at the rockslide between South Lake and Cliff Lake to watch for pikas, the round-eared "rock rabbits" that *meep!* at passing hikers.

If you're backpacking, or if you can manage an even longer day hike, continue on a spectacular loop to Devils Peak. Go straight past Cliff Lake 0.4 mile, turn right on the Pacific Crest Trail, take this well-graded route 2.5 miles to a pass, and turn right on an unmarked path up a rocky ridge 0.2 mile to Devils Peak's summit. The panorama here spins from Mt. Thielsen and the Crater Lake rim to Klamath Lake and Mt. McLoughlin's snowy cone. On the way down, keep right at trail junctions for 1.9 view-packed miles. Then turn left on the Seven Lakes Trail for 3.5 miles to your car.

Other Hiking Options

Experienced hikers can return from Alta Lake on a different, 9.6-mile loop that passes the coneflower meadows and giant Engelmann spruce trees at King Spruce Springs. From the far, north end of Alta Lake, head left on a faint, rocky path. After half a mile this infrequently maintained route briefly vanishes in a meadow, but follow the field's left edge to keep on track. At the 1.4-mile mark, watch closely for a small trail sign on a tree to the right. Turn left here for 2.7 miles to return to the Seven Lakes Trail, just 0.7 mile from your car.

The Seven Lakes Basin from Devils Peak.   Opposite: Alta Lake.

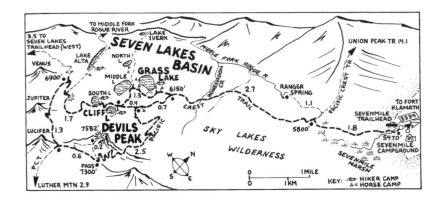

44   Seven Lakes East

Difficult (to Cliff Lake)
11.4-mile loop
900 feet elevation gain
Open early July through October
Use: hikers, horses

Difficult (to Devils Peak)
17.3-mile loop
2150 feet elevation gain

This eastern "back door" route to the popular Seven Lakes Basin may be a trifle longer than the official Seven Lakes Trail from the west (Hike #43), but a delightful lack of elevation gain makes it seem easier.

The popularity of this lake-dotted basin has brought a few rules. Maximum group size is eight people and 12 animals. Backpackers must tent at least 100 feet from lakeshores and are encouraged to use the four signed camp areas. Equestrians are required to use the eight designated horse camps. Horses are not allowed within 200 feet of lakeshores (except on trails or at designated watering spots) and grazing is usually banned. Also remember that mosquitoes are plentiful from mid-July to mid-August.

Start by driving to Fort Klamath, a hamlet near milepost 90 of Highway 62, east of Crater Lake 16 miles and 38 miles north of Klamath Falls. At an abandoned gas station in the middle of town, turn west on Nicholson Road. Follow this paved road absolutely straight 3.9 miles. Heeding "Sevenmile Trailhead" signs, fork left on gravel Road 3300 for 0.4 mile, and then fork to the right on Road 3334 for 5.6 miles to road's end.

From the left side of the parking area, hop across a creek on rocks to find the start of the trail. Heavy horse use has left the path dusty in the dry lodgepole pine woods. After 1.8 miles, turn left on the Pacific Crest Trail in a cooler forest of mountain hemlock and Shasta red fir. The distant river roar audible in the canyon to the right is the Middle Fork Rogue, gushing from Ranger Spring.

At the 4.5-mile mark, fork to the right on the Seven Lakes Trail—the start of a delightful little loop tour. In another 0.3 mile, side trails branch off to the right to designated camp areas by Grass Lake. Take time for a detour here, ambling to the right along Grass Lake's shore to a viewpoint of the peaks rimming this basin. Along the reedy shore expect fuzzy pink spirea blooms, blue dragonflies, and zillions of thumbnail-sized Cascade toads.

Then return to the Seven Lakes Trail and continue the loop tour 1 mile to a junction, passing huckleberry patches, wildflower meadows, and sandy-bottomed Middle Lake along the way. At the junction, turn right 100 yards to find a short spur trail on the left to Cliff Lake. With a dramatic view of Devils Peak, a rockslide full of curious pikas, and a 30-foot diving cliff popular with daredevil swimmers, Cliff Lake is a popular destination. Heavy use has left much of its lakeshore closed for revegetation, but there's an approved camping area on a low ridge close by.

Day hikers will probably have to turn back here, completing the little loop tour by following signs back to the Pacific Crest Trail. Backpackers, however, can continue on a spectacular, larger loop to the top of Devils Peak. From Cliff Lake, continue west on the Seven Lakes Trail 1.7 miles to a forested pass, turn left for 1.3 view-packed miles to a junction in another pass, turn left on the Pacific Crest Trail along a slope for 0.3 mile, and take a steep unmarked side trail to the left 0.3 mile to Devils Peak's summit. The view here encompasses the entire route of your hike—and most of the Sky Lakes Wilderness from Crater Lake to Mt. McLoughlin. The shaley rock of the summit provides a foothold for wind-bent whitebark pines and the dishmop-shaped seed heads of western pasque flowers.

On the way down from Devils Peak, fork left to find a different route to the PCT. Then go left on this well-graded trail to complete the loop.

Devils Peak from Cliff Lake.   *Opposite: Cliff and Middle Lakes from Devils Peak.*

South Fork Rogue River.   Below: Old-growth Douglas firs along the trail.

45   South Fork Rogue River

Moderate (upper portion)
6 miles one way
450 feet elevation gain
Open May through November

Moderate (lower portion)
6.8 miles one way
550 feet elevation **loss**

A well-built trail follows the brawling, bouldery South Fork Rogue River more than 12 miles through old-growth woods. There are three trailheads. If you can arrange a shuttle, it's fun to start at the middle trailhead and hike one-way for 6 miles to one of the trail's ends. If you don't have a shuttle, start in the middle anyway. You'll find good turnaround points for short hikes in either direction.

To drive to the central trailhead on Road 34, take Crater Lake Highway 62 east from Medford 14.5 miles, turn right on the Butte Falls Highway for 15 miles to the town of Butte Falls, continue straight for another 1 mile, turn left at a sign for Prospect for 9 miles, and turn right onto Lodgepole Road 34 for 8.5 miles. Half a mile past South Fork Campground, turn right at a hiker-symbol sign to the parking area.

The upper portion of the trail (on the right half of the map) visits quieter woods with bigger trees. To try it, start at the trail sign at the end of the parking area. The path crosses a forested flat and a cattle-proof fence before joining the 30-foot-wide river. Oregon grape, twinflower, pathfinder plant, and princes pine form a green carpet beneath the Douglas firs. If you're hiking with small children, you might make your destination Big Ben Creek at the 0.7-mile mark. A side trail to the left follows a cascading creek up toward Big Ben Campground, while the main trail crosses the creek on a 70-foot, railed log. Small gravel bars and logs along the river here make for good exploring.

If you decide to follow the main trail upriver, you'll cross three more large side creeks and gravel Road 800 before reaching the upper trailhead on Road 37. Douglas firs 7 feet in diameter line the upper part of the path. These ancient woods also host a remarkably dense understory of yew—a gnarly, shaggy-barked tree with flat needles, poisonous red berries, and a mystique dating to the days when its tough wood was used for bows. To shuttle a car here from the middle trailhead, drive 100 yards east on Road 34 and turn right on Road 37 for 5.3 miles to a parking area on the right, just before a river bridge. If you don't have a second car to shuttle, leave a bicycle at the upper trailhead for a quick ride back on the paved road.

If you'd prefer to try the lower portion of the South Rogue River Trail instead, walk from the middle trailhead back to the parking area's entrance, cross Road 34, and look for an unsigned trail into the woods. This lower path follows a very scenic part of the river's canyon, crossing two side creeks on bridges in the first 1.4 miles. For a short trip, turn right after the second bridge on a side trail that crosses Road 3775 and climbs 0.2 mile to a giant sugarpine tree. If you continue down the lower portion of the South Rogue River Trail, you'll see many more sugarpines, with tall, column-like trunks and foot-long cones dangling from the tips of long upper branches. Douglas firs 4 feet thick are common here, too.

At the 6.7-mile mark the trail passes an overlook of a diversion dam, where most of the river is shunted into a canal for power production. Just beyond is the Road 690 trailhead. To drive (or bike) here from the middle trailhead, go 100 feet up Road 34, turn left on gravel Road 3775 for 5 miles, and turn left on narrow Road 690 for 0.4 mile to its end.

Other Hiking Options

A much rockier, steeper portion of the South Fork Trail begins at Road 720 and traces the river to its headwaters at Blue Lake. This wilderness path fords the river on the way, and is not recommended for horses. An easier route to the Blue Lake Basin is described in Hike #46.

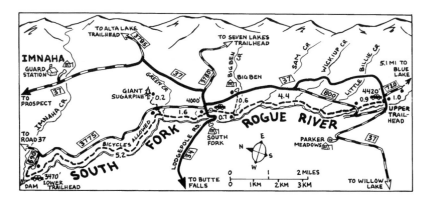

46 Blue Lake Basin

Easy (to Blue Lake)
4.6 miles round-trip
640 feet elevation **loss**
Open early July through October
Use: hikers, horses

Moderate (to Horseshoe Lake)
6.2 miles round-trip
700 feet elevation gain

Difficult (to Island Lake)
11 miles round-trip
1300 feet elevation gain

The high lakes in this corner of the Sky Lakes Wilderness have been popular destinations since at least 1888. That's the year Judge John Waldo of Salem led a party of five horsemen from Willamette Pass to Mt. Shasta, becoming the first to trace the route of the present-day Pacific Crest Trail through Southern Oregon. While camped at Island Lake, Waldo's group carved their names in a large Shasta red fir. Today hikers who trek 5.5 miles along the Blue Canyon Trail can still read the inscription. But it's tempting to turn back at one of the smaller, prettier lakes along the way.

The area's popularity has brought a few rules. Maximum group size is eight people and 12 animals. Backpackers must tent at least 100 feet from lakeshores. Equestrians are required to use designated horse camps. Horses are not allowed within 200 feet of lakeshores or 50 feet of streams (except on trails or at designated watering spots) and grazing is usually banned. Also remember that mosquitoes are a problem from mid-July to mid-August.

To find the Blue Canyon Trail, drive Highway 62 east from Medford 14.5 miles, turn right on the Butte Falls Highway for 15 miles to the town of Butte Falls, continue straight for another 1 mile, turn left at a sign for Prospect for 9 miles, turn right onto Lodgepole Road 34 for 8.5 miles, turn right on Road 37

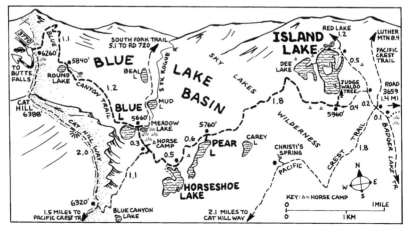

Island Lake.   Opposite: The Waldo Tree.

for 5.3 miles of pavement and an additional 2.1 miles of gravel, and finally turn left on gravel Road 3770 for 5.3 miles to a large parking pullout on the right.

The trail heads downhill into a forest of Shasta red fir with blue lupine blooms in late July and ripe blue huckleberries in late August. After 1.1 mile the path passes Round Lake—a scenic pool, but no match for Blue Lake, another 1.2 miles down the trail. Backed by a rockslide from a dramatic 300-foot cliff, Blue Lake is filled with deep green water suitable for swimming. From the mountain hemlock woods along the shore, you can watch dragonflies zoom or listen to the *meep!* of pikas scampering about the rockslide.

Hikers with children may want to turn back here. To continue, however, turn right at a trail junction near Blue Lake's outlet and then go straight 0.8 mile to Horseshoe Lake. The trail only touches the small end of this lopsided horseshoe. To find the prettier end, backtrack 100 yards on the trail and take a side path out to the lake's peninsula—off-limits to tenters, of course.

If you're headed for more distant lakes, note that neither Pear Lake nor Island Lake is visible from the main trail. Beyond Horseshoe Lake 0.6 mile, look for a short spur on the right that leads to Pear Lake, obviously named before bananas were common. Another 1.8 miles along the main trail, a large unmarked fork leads 140 yards to Judge Waldo's railed tree and the only grassy bank along the shore of large, brush-rimmed Island Lake.

To return on a loop through the area's best huckleberry fields, consider taking the somewhat rockier and steeper trail over forested Cat Hill. Look for the turnoff between Blue and Horseshoe Lakes. Follow this path up 1.1 mile to a crest and turn right on Cat Hill Way for 2 miles to your car, passing the area's only full view of Mt. McLoughlin along the way.

47   Mount McLoughlin

Difficult
10.6 miles round-trip
3915 feet elevation gain
Open July through October

Mt. McLoughlin overlooks half the state—and a good share of California, too. For years there was no official trail to the summit, so climbers spread out on a maze of scramble paths, spray-painting dots on rocks to help them find the route back. In the mid-1990s, however, Forest Service crews laid out a single clear route and chipped away the ugly, misleading markings. The hike is still one of the most demanding—and rewarding—in Southern Oregon. Only set out in good weather, bring sunscreen, and carry plenty of water. Maximum group size is eight.

From a distance, Mt. McLoughlin's relatively smooth cone suggests it is one of the youngest Cascade volcanoes. Climbers, however, can see massive gouges left by Ice Age glaciers on the peak's hidden north face, exposing a thumb-shaped lava plug. The most recent eruption, 12,000 years ago, poured blocky basalt from a vent low on the mountain's south slope.

The tallest peak in Southern Oregon has had many names. Klamath Indians called it *Kesh yainatat*, home of the dwarf old woman who commanded the west wind. The Takelma tribe dubbed it *Alwilamchaildis* after a mythic hero of their legends, and thought it was the home of Acorn Woman, who made oaks bear fruit each year. In 1838, the first map to show the peak labeled it Mt. McLoughlin in honor of the Hudson's Bay Company leader at Fort Vancouver. After Rogue Valley settlers began calling the peak Mt. Pitt (for California's Pit River), the Oregon legislature resolved in 1905 to restore the McLoughlin name.

To find the trailhead from Medford, take Highway 62 east 6 miles and turn right toward Klamath Falls on Highway 140 for 36 miles. Between mileposts 35 and 36, turn left at a "Fourmile Lake" pointer onto gravel Road 3661 for 2.9 miles, and then turn left on Road 3650 for 0.2 mile to a large parking lot. (From Klamath Falls, take Highway 140 west to just beyond milepost 36, turn right on Road 3661 for 2.9 miles, and turn left on Road 3650.)

The trail promptly crosses Cascade Canal, which shunts Fourmile Lake's outlet stream west toward Rogue Valley irrigators. Then the path marches steadily up through a mixed forest of Shasta red fir. After a mile, veer right onto the Pacific Crest Trail. In another 0.2 mile, an unmarked spur to the right leads over a rise to Freye Lake, a shallow pool with a view of the mountain's top half. To continue your climb, return to the PCT, follow it a few hundred yards uphill, and fork left on the Mt. McLoughlin Trail.

The next 1.5 miles are relatively easy, through boulder-strewn mountain hemlock woods. But then the route launches uphill with a vengeance to timberline,

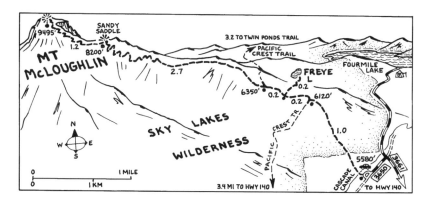

where only pinemat manzanita and gnarled whitebark pines survive. At the 4.1-mile mark the trail clambers to a sandy saddle where the sweeping view includes your first glimpse of Mt. McLoughlin's true summit. The final 1.2 miles gain a staggering 1300 feet along a craggy ridgecrest.

A crumbling rock wall at the top remains from the foundation of a vanished 1929-vintage lookout. On a clear day, the panorama includes every major Cascade peak from South Sister to Mt. Lassen. Even with a bit of haze you'll be able to spot snowy Mt. Shasta to the south and pointy Mt. Thielsen above Crater Lake's rim to the north. To the east, Upper Klamath Lake floods the Cascade foothills. Whale-shaped Fourmile Lake swims through the wilderness forests at the mountain's base, with Squaw Lake a calf at its side. To the southwest, beyond Howard Prairie Reservoir and the Rogue Valley, rise the peaks of the Siskiyous.

When you hike down, stick to the ridgecrest trail you followed on the way up. Don't be tempted to romp down a snowfield (or by August, a scree slope) to the right of the ridge. Nearly every year, search parties are organized for hikers lured far south of the trail by this "shortcut."

The final pitch to the summit.   Opposite: Mt. McLoughlin and Fourmile Lake from the air.

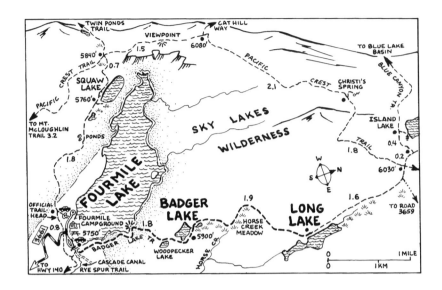

48   Fourmile Lake

Easy (to Badger Lake)
3.6 miles round-trip
200 feet elevation gain
Open early July through October
Use: hikers, horses

Moderate (to Long Lake)
7.4 miles round-trip
360 feet elevation gain

Difficult (around Fourmile Lake)
14-mile loop
680 feet elevation gain

Mt. McLoughlin rises like an Egyptian pyramid above the driftwood-jammed shores of Fourmile Lake. Although the Sky Lakes Wilderness surrounds this mountain, surprisingly few other lakes in the area offer views of it. The next best view is a glimpse from cute, swimmable little Badger Lake. Catch both of these vistas on an easy, nearly level walk from the Fourmile Campground. Or continue past a wildflower meadow to skinny Long Lake. Or tackle a 14-mile loop hike that uses the Pacific Crest Trail to complete a grand circuit around Fourmile Lake. Maximum group size is eight people and 12 animals.

To start, drive east of Medford on Highway 62 for 6 miles and turn right onto Highway 140 toward Klamath Falls for 36 miles. Between mileposts 35 and 36, turn left at a "Fourmile Lake" sign on gravel Road 3661 for 5.7 miles to Fourmile Campground. (If you're coming from Klamath Falls, head west on Highway 140 to just beyond milepost 36, and turn right on Road 3661 for 5.7 miles.)

Once you reach Fourmile Campground, signs point you left to an official trailhead turnaround where parking is free. But you can trim the least interesting 0.8 mile from the hike to Badger Lake by driving to the *right* through the campground instead. For this shortcut, park at a day-use pullout beside the boat ramp's picnic area, where you may have to pay a $5 day-use fee. From here, hike 100 yards to the end of the campground's loop road and walk past a gate with a "Road Closed" sign. Beyond the gate, go straight 100 yards on the largest dirt road to a sign for the Rye Spur Trail by a canal. Continue straight on the road another 100 feet and turn left to join the official Badger Lake Trail.

After this, the trail parallels Fourmile Lake's shore for nearly a mile through lodgepole pine woods with red and blue huckleberry bushes. The best viewpoint and shore access is at the 0.9-mile mark, just before the trail turns inland. From here it's painfully obvious that this mountain lake has been converted to a reservoir. Bleached snags and drift logs line the barren, rocky shore. The lake once drained east toward Klamath Lake, but now a concrete dam and canal near the campground divert its water west to irrigate Medford orchards.

After leaving Fourmile Lake, the trail passes shallow Woodpecker Lake before skirting Badger Lake at the 1.8-mile mark—an excellent goal, especially if you're hiking with children. If you decide to continue on the trail, you'll pass a lilypad pond and a long meadow. Look here for white marsh marigolds in July and bulbous yellow Bigelow's sneezeweed in August. Then the path crosses a low ridge to the densely forested edge of Long Lake.

If you hate to backtrack, consider marching onward on a 14-mile loop. Although the route ahead offers only one good viewpoint (across a forest to Fourmile Lake) and touches the shore of only one lake (Squaw Lake), the nearly level trail is so well built that joggers sometimes do the loop just for exercise. Simply follow the Badger Lake Trail 1.6 miles past Long Lake, turn left on the Pacific Crest Trail for 5.1 miles, and turn left on the Twin Ponds Trail for 2.5 miles to the Fourmile Trailhead. Of course, if you didn't park at the official trailhead, you'll have to continue 0.8 mile, following a "Badger Lake Trail" pointer on a path that skirts around the campground through the woods.

Other Hiking Options

For a different short trip, start at Fourmile Campground's official trailhead and hike clockwise around Fourmile Lake 1.8 miles to Squaw Lake.

Mt. McLoughlin from Fourmile Lake.   *Opposite: Fourmile Lake from the PCT.*

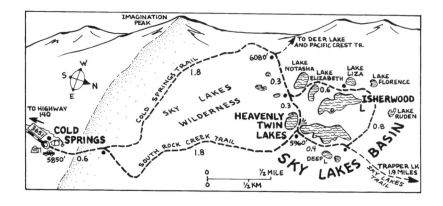

49 Sky Lakes via Cold Springs

Easy
6.9-mile loop
400 feet elevation gain
Open early July through October
Use: hikers, horses

By far the easiest route into the famous lake-dotted high country of the Sky Lakes Wilderness, this loop passes half a dozen pools in a nearly level, forested basin. The drawbacks? The area's easy access draws crowds on summer weekends, mosquitoes are a nuisance from mid-July until late August, and the basin has few mountain views. Maximum group size is eight people and 12 animals.

To find the trailhead, drive east of Medford 6 miles on Highway 62, turn right on Highway 140 toward Klamath Falls to milepost 41, and turn left at a "Cold Springs Trailhead" pointer onto Road 3651. Follow this gravel road 10.1 miles to its end at a turnaround with a primitive campground and a restored, shake-sided shelter beside a cold, piped spring. (If you're coming from Klamath Falls, take Highway 140 west to milepost 41 and turn right on Road 3651.)

The broad, dusty trail sets off amid mountain hemlocks and Shasta red firs up to 4 feet in diameter. White woodland flowers here include large, 3-petaled trillium, sprays of tiny star-flowered solomonseal, and solitary queens cup. By late August, expect ripe blue and red huckleberries along the way.

After 0.6 mile the trail forks. Both paths traverse relatively tedious lodgepole pine and mountain hemlock woods to the lake basin, but the right-hand fork gets there a bit quicker, so branch right on the South Rock Creek Trail. In another 1.8 miles you'll reach a delightful isthmus between the Heavenly Twin Lakes. This is a great place to let kids explore the shores of these shallow lakes, and it offers the area's only mountain view — of Luther Mountain and Devils Peak at the far northern end of the Sky Lakes Basin. If you're backpacking, remember that camping is banned within 100 feet of lakeshores, so this isthmus is off limits.

When you're ready to continue the loop, backtrack from the isthmus and veer left along the shore of the larger Heavenly Twin for 0.4 mile. At the far end of this lake, turn left on the Isherwood Trail for 0.8 mile to reach the shore of dramatic, half-mile-long Isherwood Lake. The smooth, curved bedrock shore was polished by glaciers that capped the Cascade Range during the Ice Age. Look closely for scratch marks showing the direction the ice flowed as it slowly carved the Sky Lakes Basin. Then continue along the trail 0.6 mile, passing lima-bean-shaped Lake Elizabeth and deep, blue-green Lake Notasha.

At a junction just beyond Lake Notasha, turn right for 0.3 mile. Then complete the loop by forking left onto the Cold Springs Trail for the final 2.4-mile walk back to your car.

Other Hiking Options

Backpackers can continue north from the Heavenly Twin Lakes for 1.9 miles to Trapper Lake, and from there explore a different part of the long Sky Lakes Basin, described in Hike #50.

Luther Mountain from Heavenly Twin Lakes.   *Opposite: Lodgepole pine cone.*

50 Sky Lakes via Nannie Creek

Easy (to Puck Lakes)
4.8 miles round-trip
760 feet elevation gain
Open mid-July through October
Use: hikers, horses

Difficult (to Margurette Lake)
12.8-mile loop
1560 feet elevation gain

Difficult (around Luther Mountain)
16.7-mile loop
2240 feet elevation gain

This lake basin deep in the heart of the Sky Lakes Wilderness is dominated by the cliffs of Luther Mountain—a landmark named to provide a religious opponent for nearby Devils Peak. For an easy hike, head for the large but shallow Puck Lakes. If you continue to deep, picturesque Margurette Lake, you can return on either of two loops: a short tour to Trapper Lake or a much longer trek around Luther Mountain for a grandstand view of the entire basin. Note that visitors in the Wilderness are limited to a group size of eight people and 12 stock animals. Mosquitoes can be plentiful in late July and early August.

To start, drive east of Medford 6 miles on Highway 62 and turn right on Highway 140 toward Klamath Falls for 43.5 miles. (If you're coming from Klamath Falls, head west on Highway 140 for 25 miles.) Between mileposts 43 and 44, turn north on paved Westside Road for 12.2 miles, and then turn left on gravel Road 3484 for 5.2 miles to a parking lot at road's end.

The Nannie Creek Trail switchbacks up through a forest of mountain hemlock and Shasta red fir for 1.6 miles, and then descends slightly for 0.8 mile to an unmarked Puck Lakes turnoff on the right. This side path leads 100 yards to a shaley beach. It's a great place to lounge in the pink heather below the shore's

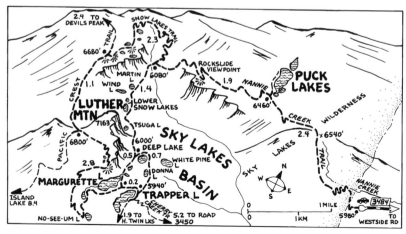

Margurette and Trapper Lakes.   Opposite: Luther Mountain from Lower Snow Lakes.

lodgepole pines while the kids look for tiny Cascade toads or wade in the relatively warm lake. A fainter trail continues left around the shore 0.3 mile to the northern Puck Lake. All that's missing at these lakes is a mountain view.

If you're continuing on the Nannie Creek Trail, you'll descend gradually for 0.9 mile to an open rockslide with a view that sweeps from Pelican Butte (on the left) to Mt. McLoughlin (above Luther Mountain's shoulder), and Devils Peak (on the right). After another downhill mile, veer left at a junction. Nearly level, the next 1.9 miles to Margurette Lake pass a series of scenic pools reflecting Luther Mountain's cliffs. Blue and red huckleberries ripen here by late August.

When you reach a T-shaped trail junction beside Margurette Lake you'll face a decision. For the shortest loop back, turn *left* 0.2 mile to large but less dramatic Trapper Lake and turn left again past shallow Donna and green Deep Lake, where you'll rejoin the route back to your car.

For a longer loop with better views, however, turn *right* at the Margurette Lake junction. This route climbs past two small lakes to a dramatic, glacier-smoothed clifftop overlooking Margurette Lake, Trapper Lake, and distant Upper Klamath Lake. Scratches in the bedrock here reveal the direction Ice Age glaciers moved while scouring this lake basin from the mountainside. Continue up the trail to a pass and turn right on the Pacific Crest Trail for 1.1 mile to another cliff-edged viewpoint. Beside a large cairn where the PCT leaves the rim, turn right on the Snow Lakes Trail. This spectacular path passes a dozen rimrock tarns before switchbacking down through the woods to the Nannie Creek Trail, where a left turn will take you back to your car.

North Fork Little Butte Creek. *Below: Brown Mountain from Fish Lake.*

51   Fish Lake

Easy (to Fish Lake Resort)
6.6 miles round-trip
100 feet elevation gain
Open mid-May to mid-November
Use: hikers, bicycles

Moderate (High Lakes Trail)
9.3 miles one way
500 feet elevation gain

A bicycle-friendly trail links Fish Lake with Lake of the Woods, passing the lava flows of the Cascade summit on the way. The lakes on either end of the broad new High Lakes Trail are probably Southern Oregon's most popular — each has campgrounds, picnic areas, boat launches, and a rustic, old-timey resort. If the 9.3-mile, packed-gravel High Lakes Trail sounds too long, try the ungraveled 3.3-mile trail along Fish Lake's shore instead. Because the two trails connect end-to-end, adventurous hikers (or bicyclists) can do them both.

The Fish Lake Trail is easy enough for hikers with children. To find it, drive Highway 140 east of Medford 35 miles (or west of Klamath Falls 40 miles). Between mileposts 28 and 29, turn south on paved Road 37 at a "North Fork Campground" pointer. After half a mile turn left into the trailhead parking pullout, just opposite the campground entrance.

The Fish Lake Trail sets off along North Fork Little Butte Creek — a beautiful stream that begins as a glassy, meandering, meadow-edged river but soon shifts to a rushing whitewater torrent. Fir trees grow 4 feet thick along the path, with an understory of hazel and a few wildflowers. Look for white, 3-petaled trillium, fuzzy pink spirea, and lavender lousewort. At a trail junction after 0.6 mile, the main trail turns left away from the creek, but a spur continues straight 100 yards to the base of Fish Lake's dam. Arduously built in 1921-22 by men hauling rocks in horse-drawn railroad cars, the dam tripled Fish Lake's size. The original lake was created a few thousand years ago by a natural rock dam — the Brown Mountain lava flow visible across the creek. The Medford Irrigation District draws down the enlarged reservoir each summer to water orchards.

After leaving the creek, the Fish Lake Trail makes a tedious 0.8-mile detour to avoid private summer homes. But then the path sticks to the lakeshore for 1.9 miles, skirting two campgrounds and a picnic area before reaching the Fish Lake Resort. The dock, cafe, and general store here make a good turnaround point.

If you're planning to bicycle (or hike) the new High Lakes Trail to Lake of the Woods, it's probably best to start at the Fish Lake Campground. To find this trailhead, drive Highway 140 east of Medford 35 miles (or west of Klamath Falls 38 miles). Between mileposts 30 and 31, turn south at a "Fish Lake Recreation Area" sign and keep left for 0.4 mile to the start of the High Lakes Trail on the left. There's no room for parking here, however, and the nearby Fish Lake Resort has no parking for trail users either, so you'll have to drive on 100 yards to the Fish Lake Campground and pay a $5 day-use parking fee. Then walk (or ride your bike) back to the trail.

From Fish Lake, the well-graded, 8-foot-wide High Lakes Trail climbs through ancient lava flows that have grown over with forest. The trail is often within 100 yards of noisy Highway 140. At the 1.8-mile the path skirts a sinkhole where water from the 20-foot-wide Cascade Canal vanishes underground. Irrigators built the canal to shunt Fourmile Lake's outlet creek toward the Fish Lake reservoir. To their chagrin, the canal's water vanished into a lava tube here. Then they realized the tube carries the water underground to Fish Lake anyway.

Just beyond the sinkhole, the path crosses the Pacific Crest Trail (closed to bikes; see Hike #52). Then the High Lakes Trail climbs another 1.7 miles along the edge of a fresh-looking lava flow to the Cascade summit and descends 3.1 miles to the shore of Lake of the Woods, 200 yards behind the Forest Service's visitor center on Highway 140. If you continue 0.8 mile, you'll cross two bridges at the marshy end of the lake (with views, ducks, and mosquitoes) before reaching a trail junction at Aspen Point's north picnic area. A fee is charged if you park a car here. If you keep left at trail junctions and cross two roads, however, you'll follow the High Lakes Trail 1.8 miles around a vast, grassy plain to trail's end at the Great Meadow Recreation Site. To bring a shuttle car to this free parking lot, drive Highway 140 to between mileposts 37 and 38.

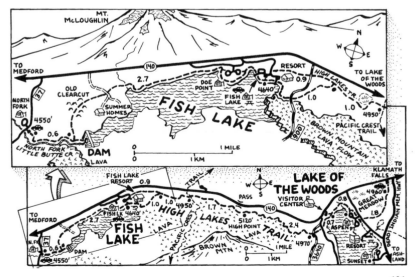

52 Brown Mountain Lava Flow

Easy (to view at high point)
5.8-mile loop
550 feet elevation gain
Open June to mid-November
Use: hikers, horses

The lava flows on Brown Mountain are so rugged that trail builders had to dynamite the jumbled basalt surface and lay a tread of crushed red cinders. Perhaps the most expensive portion of the 2400-mile Pacific Crest Trail, this spectacular section is now easy to hike. From Highway 140, the path climbs gently to viewpoints of Brown Mountain, Fish Lake, and Mt. McLoughlin.

From Medford, take Highway 62 east 6 miles and turn right toward Klamath Falls on Highway 140 to the Cascade crest. Between mileposts 32 and 33, turn north at a "Summit Sno-Park" sign and drive to the far end of the huge paved parking area. The trail that starts here crosses a grassy, open fir forest for 0.2 mile and crosses a footbridge to the Pacific Crest Trail. Turn left, following the canal 0.4 mile to a crossing of noisy Highway 140. Of course you could start your hike at this unmarked crossing (Highway 140 does offer a small parking pullout at the end of a guardrail by milepost 32), but the walk alongside Cascade Canal can be quite pleasant. The canal was built to divert Fourmile Lake's outlet to the west side of the Cascade summit for Medford irrigators. When full, the rushing 20-foot creek provides a stark contrast to the lava ahead.

Beyond the highway crossing 0.2 mile, the PCT crosses the packed-gravel High Lakes Trail (see Hike #51). Shortly afterward, the PCT enters a moonscape of black boulders, with views ahead to Brown Mountain, the lava's source. Brown Mountain is called a shield volcano because of its low profile, built up by count-less flows of runny black lava. About 2000 years ago a cinder cone erupted on the summit, adding a brown peak with a little crater. Shortly afterward, the lava

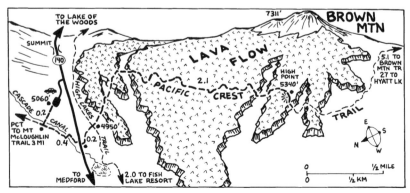

Mt. McLoughlin from the lava flow.   Opposite: Chinkapin flowers and fruit.

you're crossing vented from the cinder cone's base. The flow's crust cooled first and jumbled when the lava underneath kept moving.

A surprising variety of life has gained a foothold here. Where the rocks aren't disturbed, they're crusted with gray, green, and black lichens — a combination of fungus and algae that gets all the nutrients it needs from the rain and the air. Another pioneer, chinkapin, forms 10-foot-tall bushes along the trail, with sprays of white flowers in summer and spiny fruit (known as "porcupine eggs") in the fall. Some animals live in lava to escape predators. Watch for orange-bellied Douglas squirrels and listen for the *meep!* of guinea-pig-shaped pikas.

At the 2.9-mile mark, by a cairn with the last best view of Mt. McLoughlin's huge cone, the PCT reaches a high point and begins heading downhill through Douglas fir woods. This makes a good turnaround point, although long-distance hikers can continue 5.7 miles to the Brown Mountain Trail crossing, 7.6 miles to a spring at the South Brown Mountain Shelter, or 9.6 miles to a parking area near milepost 27 of the Dead Indian Memorial Highway.

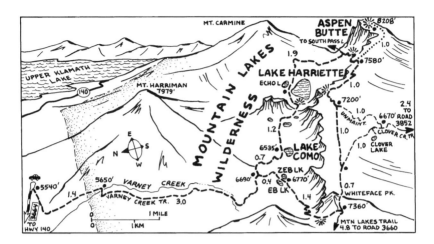

53   Mountain Lakes

Moderate (to Eb and Zeb Lakes)
9.6 miles round-trip
1230 feet elevation gain
Open mid-July to early November
Use: hikers, horses

Difficult (to Harriette Lake)
12.6 miles round-trip
1800 feet elevation gain

Difficult (Mountain Lakes loop)
17.1-mile loop
2720 feet elevation gain

Precisely 6 miles square, this pocket Wilderness towers above Upper Klamath Lake like a misplaced chunk of the High Cascades. In its center, a gorgeous 8.3-mile loop trail tours a string of hidden lakes and mountain passes. The price of admission is a 4.4-mile climb through the woods to the start of the loop.

Geologists once thought this isolated highland might be the remains of a huge volcano that exploded in Crater Lake fashion. But the area's outline is a lopsided square, not a circle, suggesting a cluster of at least four smaller volcanoes instead. Did one of them explode? It's hard to tell. Any caldera would have vanished in the Ice Age when five glaciers gutted these highlands, leaving lake basins, headwall cliffs, and several exposed lava plugs.

The Mountain Lakes Wilderness was one of eight Oregon areas protected by the original 1964 Wilderness Act. All seven of the other areas have been expanded since then, and more than two dozen new areas have been designated, but this preserve retains its original square boundary—exactly one township. The maximum group size for visitors here is ten people, or if you have pack stock, ten hearts. Campers can't be closer than 100 feet to lakeshores, and horses can't be closer than 200 feet except on trails.

Three paths climb to the central loop, but the Varney Creek Trail requires the least elevation gain. To find it, drive Highway 140 west of Klamath Falls 21 miles (or east of Medford 54 miles). Between mileposts 46 and 47 turn south onto Road 3637 at a large brown "Varney Creek Trailhead" sign. Follow this gravel road straight 1.8 miles and turn left on Road 3664 for 1.9 miles to the road's end.

The trail starts by contouring around a *lateral moraine*—a jumble of rocks and sand pushed aside by a valley glacier. Ponderosa pine and thickets of white fir now forest the slope. After 1.4 mile the path crosses mossy, gurgling Varney Creek and heads up the valley floor. Sparse lodgepole pine and Shasta red fir allow views of Mt. Harriman's broad, forested cone.

The trail forks at the 4.4-mile mark—the start of the central loop. If you're tired, turn right for 0.4 mile to make your goal Eb and Zeb Lakes, a pair of shallow but swimmable little lakes just 100 yards apart. The shores have pink heather, red huckleberries, and views of Whiteface Peak's bright rockslides. If you're up to a longer hike, however, skip Eb and Zeb. Instead turn left at the junction and descend 0.7 mile to Lake Como, a deeper, bigger, blue-green pool with better swimming and lots of small, jumping fish. But don't turn back yet. If you continue another 1.2 miles you'll climb to a rocky pass with a terrific view and descend to Lake Harriette—the largest, deepest, and prettiest lake of all.

Backpackers can complete the scenic central loop. Beyond Lake Harriette the path climbs 1.5 miles to a pass. If you've time for a detour, a spur trail to the left here deadends in 1.6 miles at South Pass Lake. Otherwise veer right and climb 0.4 mile to the crest of a cliffy rim. For a very dramatic detour, bushwhack left along the open ridgecrest 1 mile through stunted whitebark pines to the former fire lookout site atop Aspen Butte—the best viewpoint in the Wilderness. To continue, however, follow the loop trail right along the rim 1 mile, ignore an unmaintained left-hand spur trail (which heads toward small, disappointing Clover Lake), go straight through mountain hemlock woods 1.7 miles to a pass beside Whiteface Peak, and turn right for 1.8 miles to complete the loop, passing viewpoints and the twin lakes of Eb and Zeb along the way.

Eb Lake.   Opposite: Lake Harriette.

Eastern Siskiyous

Campgrounds

		Campsites	Water	Flush toilet	Open (mos.)	Rate range
1	**CANTRALL-BUCKLEY.** This county campground on the Applegate River near Ruch has coin-operated showers.	30	●	●	V-IX	$16
2	**CARBERRY.** On a creek beside the upper end of Applegate Reservoir, this forested camp has some walk-in sites, and no services in winter.	10			IV-IX	$8
3	**EMIGRANT LAKE.** Near I-5, the county park at this shadeless reservoir has swimming, a water slide, and coin-op showers. Res: 541-774-8183.	74	●	●	IV-X	$20-30
4	**HART-TISH.** On Applegate Reservoir, this shady camp has a boat launch, boat rentals, and trails nearby (see Hike #64).	15	●	●	V-IX	$15
5	**JACKSON.** In a historic gold mining area among ponderosas, this camp includes a swimming hole on the Applegate River. No services in winter.	12	●	●	●	$10
6	**MT. ASHLAND.** Carry your tent a few yards to primitive campsites with Mt. Ashland views. Pacific Crest Trail access (see Hike #56).	9			VI-X	free
7	**SNAKE MONSTER (SQUAW) LAKES.** Summer reservations are *required* at these lovely forest-rimmed lakes. Expect to carry your gear 0.1 mile downhill. No fees in winter. Res: 877-444-6777 (*www.recreation.gov*).	17	●			$10
8	**WATKINS.** On a small, exposed hummock beside Applegate Reservoir, this camp has walk-in sites. No fees or services in winter. See Hike #64.	14			●	$8
9	**WRANGLE.** This remote, primitive camp is in a high glade near the Pacific Crest Trail at Wrangle Gap's pass.	5			VI-X	free

◁ *The Iris Inn in Ashland.*

Cabins, Lookouts & Inns

		Rental units	Private bath	Breakfast	Open (mos.)	Rate range
1	**ASHLAND MOUNTAIN HOUSE.** A bed and breakfast in an old farmhouse at an 1852 stage stop just south of Ashland at 1148 Old Hwy 99 S. Reservations: 866-899-2744 or *www.ashlandmountainhouse.com*.	4	●	●	●	$179-219
2	**ASHLAND'S BLACK SWAN**. This B&B in an 1896 Victorian is a block from downtown Ashland at 111 Third Street. Three rooms have Jacuzzis and fireplaces. Res: 541-488-3070 or *www.ashlandsblackswaninn.com*.	6	●	●	●	$109-189
3	**BAYBERRY INN.** In a 1925 house 4 blocks from Ashland's Plaza, this B&B is at 438 N. Main St. Res: 800-795-1252 (*www.bayberryinn.com*).	8	●	●	●	$100-225
4	**IRIS INN**. This 1905 Victorian house with antiques and gardens has been a bed & breakfast inn since 1981. It's 4 blocks from Ashland's Plaza at 59 Manzanita Street. Reservations: 800-460-7650 (*www.irisinnbb.com*).	5	●	●	●	$100-193
5	**JACKSONVILLE INN.** President Bush stayed in this 1861 brick hotel in downtown Jacksonville (175 E. California St.). The hotel has 8 rooms and 4 cottages with hot tubs. Res: 800-321-9344 (*www.jacksonvilleinn.com*).	12	●	●	●	$159-465
6	**McCULLY HOUSE.** From 1860, Oregon's oldest home used as a B&B (240 E. California St., Jacksonville). Res: 800-367-1942 (*www.mccullyhouseinn.com*).	5	●	●	●	$169-299

Top right: Pilot Rock (Hike #55).

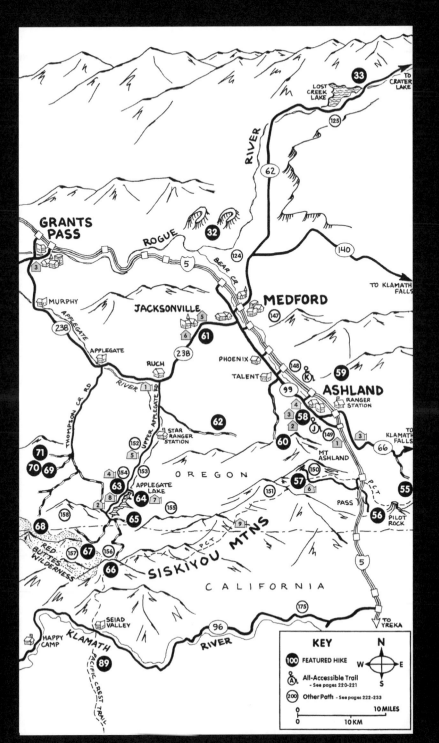

54 Soda Mountain

Moderate (to Soda Mountain)
4.2 miles round-trip
810 feet elevation gain
Open June to mid-November
Use: hikers, horses

Moderate (to Little Pilot Peak)
4.6 miles round-trip
660 feet elevation gain

Difficult (to Boccard Point)
10 miles round-trip
1200 feet elevation gain

The Cascade-Siskiyou National Monument near Ashland not only commands dramatic views, but it also contains an intriguing mixture of plants. The Soda Mountain Wilderness, in the heart of the monument, stands at the junction of three biologic regions, where fir forests from the Cascades mingle with sagebrush from the High Desert and droopy incense cedars from the Siskiyous.

The lookout atop Soda Mountain is the area's most popular goal, but adventurous hikers can discover to two stunning viewpoints nearby: Little Pilot Peak and Boccard Point.

From Ashland exit 14 of Interstate 5, head east on Highway 66 toward Klamath Falls for 15 winding miles. Just 200 feet before the highway pass at Green Springs Mountain Summit, turn right on Soda Mountain Road 39-3E-32.3. Follow this one-lane gravel road 3.8 miles. The second time the road crosses under a set of big powerlines, park in a grassy pass just beyond the powerlines (*GPS location N42°05.117′ W122°28.9′*). Small brown posts on either side of the road mark the Pacific Crest Trail's crossing.

Take the PCT to the right under the powerlines through a meadowed slope full of June wildflowers: purple larkspur, red paintbrush, pink onion, and yellow composites. When the trail levels off in a grand fir forest after 1.1 mile, watch for a rock cairn marking a side trail that switchbacks up to the left. This unmaintained path climbs past two telephone poles for 0.2 mile to a dirt road.

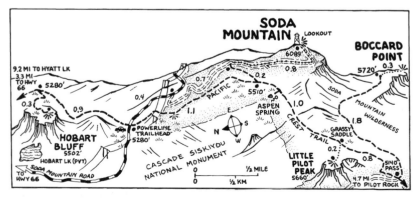

Mt. Shasta from Boccard Point. Opposite: Soda Mountain lookout.

Turn right on the steep road 0.8 mile to Soda Mountain's summit.

The 1933-vintage fire lookout tower atop the peak is staffed from early June to early October. Labels above the windows identify dozens of landmarks in each direction, but you won't need any help spotting snowy Mt. Shasta above the Klamath River canyon. Note the river's Irongate Reservoir, and broad Shasta Valley to the right. Farther to the right are Mt. Eddy (with a snow patch), the Trinity Alps, the Marble Mountains, and nearby Pilot Rock's knob.

On your way down it's slightly shorter — and less scenic — to follow the road all the way to your car. If you'd rather explore deeper into the Soda Mountain Wilderness, skip the lookout altogether. Instead follow the PCT south from the powerline trailhead for 1.3 miles, where you'll find campsites near a lilypad pond and a spring with quaking aspen. Continue another 0.8 mile on the PCT to a grassy saddle with an old road in the woods to the left. Leave the trail here and explore 300 yards up to the right through a sagebrush meadow to the cliff-edge viewpoint of Little Pilot Peak *(GPS location N42°03.833′ W122°29.807′)*.

For the longer hike to Boccard Point, continue on the PCT past Little Pilot Rock 0.8 mile down to a pass where half a dozen trails and roads connect. Turn left on the second abandoned dirt road to the left, where boulders block vehicle access to the Wilderness. The correct road goes level to the left for 50 feet, crosses a cattle guard, and then forks. Take the uphill fork to the left for 1.8 miles to its end. Then take a faint trail to the right along a broad ridgecrest 0.3 mile to Boccard Point *(GPS location N42°02.349′ W122°28.973′)*, a windswept crag with junipers and stonecrop overlooking Mt. Shasta and Northern California.

Other Options

For a shorter viewpoint hike from the powerline trailhead, take the PCT south 0.9 mile and turn left for 0.3 mile to Hobart Bluff.

55   Pilot Rock

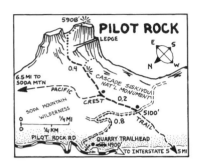

Moderate
2.8 miles round-trip
1010 feet elevation gain
Open late May through November

Pioneers once looked to Pilot Rock to find the easiest pass across the Siskiyous from California to Oregon. Today Interstate 5 may miss this mountaintop Gibraltar by a few miles, but the landmark's sweeping viewpoints and dramatic columnar basalt cliffs are just a short hike away in the new Soda Mountain Wilderness of the Cascade-Siskiyou National Monument. The Pacific Crest Trail skirts the base of the crag. From there, agile hikers can tackle a very steep scramble route to the top.

Geologically, Pilot Rock is a remnant of a 30-million-year-old lava flow. Whenever basalt lava cools slowly enough, it fractures into hexagonal pillars perpendicular to the cooling surface. The sheer cliffs on Pilot Rock's south and west faces are entirely composed of these 6-sided stone columns. It's a popular practice spot for serious rock climbers.

The area also has a history as a wild hideout. Oregon's last grizzly bear,

Columnar basalt atop Pilot Rock.

Pilot Rock from the southwest.

Old Reelfoot, was felled near the base of Pilot Rock in 1891. In 1923, after the D'Autremont brothers killed three men in a bungled train robbery at the end of the Siskiyou tunnel, they camped under a fallen log near Pilot Rock—and managed to elude a four-continent manhunt.

To find the trailhead from Interstate 5, take Mt. Ashland exit 6 and follow a "Mt. Ashland" pointer onto old Highway 99, paralleling the freeway south. After 0.7 mile go straight under the freeway, following the old highway another 1.2 miles. Beyond the Siskiyou summit 0.4 mile turn left onto Pilot Rock Road 40-2E-33. After 1 mile on this very bumpy one-lane gravel road, ignore a Pacific Crest Trail crossing. After another 1 mile, pull into a huge parking area in an old quarry on the right *(GPS location N42°02.194' W122°34.246')*.

Since the designation of the Soda Mountain Wilderness in 2009, the trail begins at the quarry. The path ahead—actually an old road blocked by boulders—climbs past small incense cedars, Jeffrey pines, and blue elderberry bushes. After 0.8 mile the Pacific Crest Trail crosses the roadbed. Turn left on the PCT for 300 yards and then fork to the right on a wide, unmarked path toward Pilot Rock. Wildflowers along this rocky, braided route include fuzzy mint, yellow Oregon grape, gooseberry, wild rose, and strawberry.

If you're just out for an easy hike, declare victory at the base of Pilot Rock's cliffs, where the view opens up across Shasta Valley to Mt. Shasta. If you're ready for a scramble, head left up a dusty scree chute along the cliff's base. After another 100 yards, you may be tempted to follow a ledge angling up to the right—but that slippery route deadends at a cliff. Instead go straight up a very steep chute, using hands and feet to climb past a tricky spot.

At the top the view of Mt. Shasta steals the show. Look to its right to spot Mt. Eddy (with a patch of snow) and the jumbled, distant peaks of the Trinity Alps. Close by to the west is Mt. Ashland, with the white dot of a radar dome on top. If you face north you'll see I-5 snaking between Ashland and Emigrant Lake, while Mt. McLoughlin's cone guards the horizon to the right.

Mt. Ashland from the Pacific Crest Trail.   Below: Siskiyou fritillary wildflower.

56   Mount Ashland Meadows

Moderate
6.8 miles round-trip
600 feet elevation gain
Open mid-June to mid-November
Use: hikers, horses

There's no handier spot for a quick stroll through subalpine wildflower meadows than along the Pacific Crest Trail at Mt. Ashland. Starting from a paved road just ten minutes from Interstate 5, this nearly level hike traverses the side of the Siskiyous' tallest peak, with views south to majestic Mt. Shasta. To make the trip even easier, you can shuttle a car or bicycle to Grouse Gap and hike this 3.4-mile section of the PCT one way.

To start, drive I-5 toward the Siskiyou summit and take Mt. Ashland exit 6. Following "Mt. Ashland Ski Area" pointers, parallel the freeway for 0.7 mile and turn right on Mt. Ashland Road 20. After 7.2 miles—just 400 yards beyond milepost 7—park at a pullout on the right. Then walk across the road to the trail, identified by a triangular Pacific Crest Trail marker on a tree.

The trail sets off through a forest of grand fir (with flat needles) and Shasta red fir (with upcurved needles). At the half-mile mark the path breaks into the

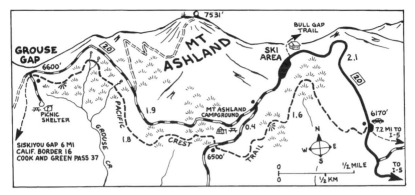

first of five large meadows on the route. In July these slopes blaze with huge blue lupine, fuzy lavender mint, tall purple larkspur, and red paintbrush. By August the show includes yellow daisy-like Bigelow's sneezeweed, petalless brown coneflower, purple aster, white yarrow, and the tiny yellow trumpets of monkeyflower. Look for deer and even black bear in these fields during the early mornings and evenings.

Beyond the second meadow the trail rounds a dry ridge where speckled granite bedrock has been weathered into rounded shapes. Yellow sulphur flower and two kinds of manzanita bushes grow here. After crossing a narrow gravel road at the 1.6-mile mark, you'll get your first views up to Mt. Ashland's summit. A white Doppler radar dome built atop the peak in 1995 resembles an eerie rising moon.

A mile beyond the gravel road the PCT enters a final, broad meadow that wraps around an alpine bowl to Grouse Gap. Joining the flower show here are a few surprising plant visitors from desert country—pungent sagebrush and white-barked quaking aspen. Turn back when the PCT crosses the road to the Grouse Gap picnic shelter. To bring a shuttle car (or bicycle) here from the first trailhead, simply drive 2 miles to Mt. Ashland ski area's huge parking lot and continue straight 2 miles on what becomes a narrow gravel road.

Mt. Shasta from the Pacific Crest Trail at Grouse Gap.

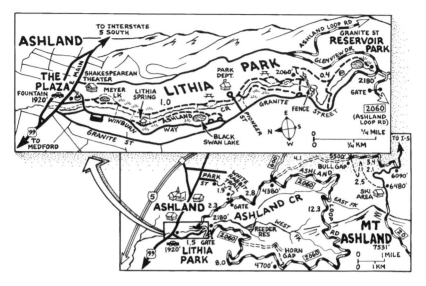

57   Lithia Park

Easy (Lithia Park)
2.8 miles round-trip
260 feet elevation gain
Open all year
Use: hikers

Difficult (Ashland Loop Road)
28.4-mile loop
3180 feet elevation gain
Open April through November
Use: bicycles

Before settling down to a play at Ashland's Shakespearean Festival, theater-goers often stretch their legs with a stroll through Lithia Park, a woodsy canyon with duck-filled lakes and the tumbling little falls of bouldery Ashland Creek. But there's room here for more than just a stroll. A hiking trail continues upstream 1.5 miles to a swimmable reservoir. And if you're on a mountain bike, you can tackle a challenging 28-mile loop that circles the entire Ashland Creek watershed to the edge of Mt. Ashland itself. Dogs are banned only in Lithia Park.

After gold rush miners found gold near Jacksonville in 1851, they found a different treasure here—water. By 1852, Southern Oregon's first lumber mill was using Ashland Creek's power to saw boards for the mines. In 1893, when the Chautauqua movement began bringing lectures and plays to rural areas of Oregon, the creek's campable woods became a regular stop. In 1908, the esteemed architect who designed San Francisco's Golden Gate Park was hired to lay out the curving paths, pools, picnic lawns, and gardens of Lithia Park. In 1935, local college professor Angus Bowmer converted an abandoned Chautauqua building into a replica of Shakespeare's open-air Globe theater and launched the tradition of performing plays beside the park.

To drive here from Medford, take Interstate 5 to Ashland exit 19 and follow signs 2.5 miles into town to a "Lithia Park" sign on the right. If you're driving here from the south, take Ashland exit 14, turn left into town on Ashland Street and Siskiyou Boulevard for 2.7 miles, cross a bridge on the far side of downtown, turn left at a "City Center" pointer, and curve back a block to the Plaza.

A fountain in the triangular Plaza serves up samples of Lithia Water—a bubbly, bitter combination of sodium, calcium, iron, bicarbonate, "and other healthful minerals" piped here from natural springs nearby. After tasting this restorative drink, walk across Winburn Way to Lithia Park (see upper map). Footpaths meander everywhere here, but if you stick to the left-hand bank of Ashland Creek you'll follow increasingly quiet trails for a mile upstream to a fence. To continue, take a small switchback trail uphill to the left. Then turn right on an upper path that leads 0.4 mile up to Granite Street Reservoir—a 200-foot-wide lake with a small sandy beach where swimming is allowed all year, at your own risk.

Hikers should turn back at the reservoir. To explore more of the park on the return trip, retrace your steps 0.2 mile, fork left across the creek, and then follow Lithia Park paths along the left-hand side of the creek where possible.

If you're tackling the 28.4-mile Ashland Loop Road by mountain bike (see lower map), remember that bicycles aren't allowed inside Lithia Park. So skirt the park, climbing from the Plaza along Winburn Way and then Granite Street for 1.5 miles to the Granite Street Reservoir, where the road turns to gravel. Turn left on Glenview Drive for 0.5 mile and then turn right on Ashland Loop Road for 4.7 grueling uphill miles to Four Corners, a 4-way junction with Road 600. (Many tourers skip the 2460-foot elevation gain of this first, difficult section by cajoling a friend to drive them to Four Corners in a shuttle car.) From

Lithia water fountain in The Plaza.   Opposite: Ashland Creek.

there the loop route turns right, following gravel Road 2060 at a much easier, rolling up-and-down grade for 12.3 miles to Horn Gap, where a thrilling 9.5-mile downhill run shoots you back to the Plaza. To trim 1.1 mile off this final downhill stretch, take a marked shortcut trail from Horn Gap to a lower bend of the loop road. The gravel, one-lane Ashland Loop Road is almost entirely within the watershed for Ashland's water supply, so camping, fires, off-road travel, and private vehicles are banned. Because Forest Service vehicles do use the road, however, bicyclists should keep an eye out for traffic.

58   Mike Uhtoff Trail

Easy (To bench viewpoint)
1.7 miles round-trip
500 feet elevation gain
Open all year
Use: hikers, bicycles

Moderate (entire trail)
4.7-mile loop
1350 feet elevation gain

Popular with hikers, dog walkers, and mountain bikers, this convenient trail network in Ashland's hills connects with paths to Lithia Park (Hike #57) and Mt. Ashland (Hike #56).

After two local philanthropists, Vincent Oredson and John Todd, donated ten acres here in 1983, Ashland businessman Mike Uhtoff led a fundraising campaign with the Southern Oregon Land Conservancy that enabled Ashland to buy the adjoining 270 acres in 1992.

Dogs need to be on leash. Mountain bikes are allowed on the White Rabbit Trail and some of its spurs, but not on the Mike Uhtoff Trail or the loop to Clay Creek's waterfall.

From exit 14 of Interstate 5 (the second Ashland exit), head west into town 0.2 mile on Main Street and turn left at the first light onto Tolman Creek Road for 1.2 miles. Beyond Siskiyou Boulevard 0.5 mile, turn right on Green Meadows

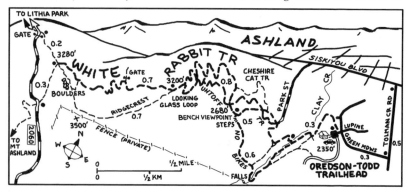

Grizzly Peak from Ashland's White Rabbit Trail.   Opposite: Sign along the route.

Way for 0.3 mile and take the first left at Lupine Drive to a small parking area for the Oredson-Todd Trailhead. (If you're driving here from downtown Ashland, start by taking Siskiyou Boulevard 2.8 miles south and turning right on Tolman Creek Road.)

At a mapboad before the parking spots, set out to the right on a bark dust path alongside a lawn. This path crosses a gravel driveway and turns left along the rim of a creek canyon. The woods here include oak, madrone, Jeffrey pine, poison oak, and Oregon grape.

At an X-shaped trail crossing, follow "White Rabbit Trail" signs down to the right. Cross Clay Creek, go up wooden steps to the left, and keep uphill at the next few junctions to find the start of the White Rabbit Trail, at a big junction at the end of Park Street. The White Rabbit Trail starts as a steep old road that's open to bicycles. If you're on foot, however, you should instead go uphill to the left on the Mike Uhtoff Trail. This hiker-only path switchbacks uphill and crosses the White Rabbit Trail twice. Then continue up on the White Rabbit Trail to its end at a big 4-way junction on a ridgecrest.

At this viewpoint bench you face a decision. If you're ready to head back, turn left down some steps and keep downhill at all junctions for 0.3 mile to a footbridge beside a small pool with a 10-foot waterfall slide. Cross the bridge and follow the trail down the creek 0.3 mile to a junction that should be familiar from the start of your hike; go up to the right to find your car.

If you're still going strong at the bench viewpoint, however, continue 1.5 miles up the White Rabbit Trail to its end at a big 4-way junction on a ridgecrest.

Admittedly, this isn't all that scenic a destination, because the ponderosa pine woods block views and the trails ahead are mostly used by mountain bikers zooming from Mt. Ashland down to Lithia Park. So just tap the sign to acknowledge that you made it, and head back. For variety on the return trip, keep right at junctions. This scenic route will take you on the Lookingglass Loop and to Clay Creek Falls without adding much distance.

59   Grizzly Peak

Easy
5.4-mile loop
750 feet elevation gain
Open mid-May to late November
Use: hikers, horses, bicycles

Wildflowers, woodpeckers, and viewpoints highlight the loop around this high plateau near Ashland. The route traverses a fir forest with meadowed openings. A 2002 wildfire raced through the western third of the area, cleaning out smaller trees, opening new views, and leaving snags for woodpeckers.

Drive Interstate 5 to south Ashland exit 14, turn east toward Klamath Falls on Highway 66 for 0.7 mile, and turn left on Dead Indian Memorial Highway for

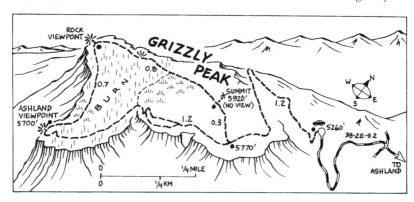

6.7 miles. Turn left on Shale City Road for 3 miles, and then turn left on gravel Road 38-2E-9.2. After 0.8 mile, keep straight at a three-way fork, continuing uphill another 0.9 mile to the trailhead at road's end *(GPS location N42°16.329' W122°36.377')*.

The parking lot has the area's best view east, sweeping from the snowy cone of Mt. McLoughlin to the distant Three Sisters. The trail itself switchbacks gradually up through a forest of Douglas fir and grand fir. Wildflowers carpet the forest floor in May and June: three-petaled white trilliums, yellow violets, and the large, ornate leaves of waterleaf.

Turn right at a fork after 1.2 miles, following a "Summit" pointer. But don't get excited about summiting this peak. When the path crests in another 0.3 mile, you simply walk 100 feet to the right to a small, viewless rockpile *(GPS location N42°16.175' W122°36.988')*. The summit's chief attraction is a surprise collection of pink wild onions, blooming from the gravel.

The rest of the hike has much better views, so sally onward along the loop trail. Soon you'll pass a large meadow, enter the fire zone, and begin tracing the rim of a broad plateau. The first views are north to Medford. Then a rock outcrop to the right overlooks Wagner Butte (Hike #60). The last viewpoint is the best of all, sweeping from the city of Ashland (on the right) to Mt. Ashland, Emigrant Lake, thumb-shaped Pilot Rock (Hike #55), and the ghostly cone of Mt. Shasta (on the left).

Follow the trail another 1.2 miles to complete the loop, and then keep right on the 1.2-mile path down to your car.

Ashland from Grizzly Peak.   Opposite: Wild onion on Grizzly Peak's summit.

60   Wagner Butte

Difficult
10.4 miles round-trip
2200 feet elevation gain
Open mid-June to mid-November

The best view of the Ashland area isn't from Mt. Ashland, but rather from this lesser-known 7140-foot peak nearby. With binoculars, hikers atop Wagner Butte can pick out most of the individual buildings in Ashland, a vertical mile below. The demanding trail to the top offers other rewards as well—old-growth firs, an interesting landslide regrowing with wildflowers, a cold spring, sagebrush meadows, and an unusual quaking aspen grove.

The butte's name recalls Jacob Wagner, an early Talent settler who served in the 1853 Indian War and ran the flour mill at Ashland's Plaza. After a 1910 forest fire burned much of Ashland Creek's canyon and threatened Ashland, the Forest Service agreed to set up a fire lookout atop the butte. Staff made do with an open-air observation post until a cupola-style building could be built in 1923. Winter storms blew parts of the structure off the mountain. The building was finally replaced in 1961, but by then airplanes were taking over fire surveillance. Abandoned after just a few summers, the tower was intentionally burned by smokejumpers in 1972, leaving only foundation piers, melted glass, an iron railing, and the extraordinary view.

From Interstate 5 south of Medford, take Talent exit 21, head west on Valley View Drive for 0.4 mile, turn left on S. Pacific Highway for 0.4 mile, turn right on Rapp Road for 1.1 mile to the second stop sign, and continue straight on Wagner Creek Road. After following this road for 4.7 paved miles and another 2.5 miles of one-lane gravel, fork left on (possibly unsigned) Road 22 for the final 3.6 miles, still keeping left at forks. The trailhead has a trail sign on the left

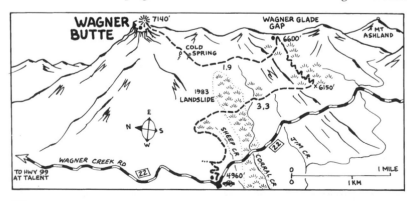

Piers remain from Wagner Butte's lookout tower.   Opposite: Bigelow's sneezeweed.

and a large parking area on the right.

The trail starts out climbing steeply for 0.9 mile through a second-growth forest with ponderosa pines, beargrass clumps, orange paintbrush, and speckled granite rocks. Then the path climbs more gently, traversing old Douglas fir woods with occasional meadowed slopes. The largest of these meadows is the Sheep Creek Slide, where a May 1983 thundershower sent 400,000 tons of soil, trees, and granite from Wagner Butte sliding 4 miles to the Little Applegate River. The Forest Service has since seeded the slide with grass and opened it to cattle grazing, but a wealth of native flowers also thrive here. In summer look for blue lupine, petalless brown coneflower, bulbous yellow sneezeweed, and sweet-smelling mint.

At the 2.4-mile mark the trail suddenly begins switchbacking up a steep sagebrush meadow for 0.9 mile to Wagner Glade Gap. Then the path ambles along for the final 1.9 miles, passing wind-gnarled mountain mahogany, white-barked quaking aspen, and a cold, piped spring before clambering up a stack of car-sized granite boulders to the summit. From here, the strip of urban development between Medford and Ashland looks like white confetti strewn along Interstate 5, with the dark squares of orchards on either hand. To the right stretch the forests of the Ashland's watershed valley, topped by Mt. Ashland and its white Doppler radar dome. Farther to the right look for snowy Mt. Shasta, the distant Marble Mountains, Red Buttes, flat-topped Preston Peak, and broad Grayback Mountain.

61 Jacksonville

Easy
3.3-mile loop
350 feet elevation gain
Open all year
Use: hikers, bicycles

This well-preserved gold mining boomtown from the mid-1800s is more than just a living museum; it's an active cultural center with shops, a first-rate summer music festival, and miles of hiking trails through recently-acquired parklands.

Miners on their way back from California's more famous Gold Rush discovered gold here in Rich Gulch in 1852. The tent-and-plank town that sprang up was briefly Oregon's largest. After the easy gold was panned out, giant hydraulic hoses washed away acres of land in search of gold dust. When the new railroad line through Southern Oregon bypassed Jacksonville in favor of Medford in 1886, the city slipped into a kind of suspended animation, lacking the money to remodel or even to tear down buildings. The entire city was declared a National Historic Landmark in 1966, and a reawakening began.

For a walking tour of the town and its surrounding woodlands, start at an 1891 railroad depot converted to a visitor center on Oregon and C streets. If you're coming from Interstate 5, take Medford exit 30 and follow signs 7 miles to Jacksonville on Highway 238. At a "Britt Parking" sign opposite the Jacksonville Museum, turn right on C Street for four blocks to its end at the visitor center.

Start at the far end of the parking lot, where a sign announces the entrance to Jacksonville Woodlands Park. Cross the highway on a crosswalk and climb a set of stairs into the Britt Gardens. Stone walls here mark the site of the home of Peter Britt, a Swiss-born miner, painter, vintner, and photographer whose acclaimed pictures documented early Southern Oregon.

The Britt House burned in 1960. A walkway to the left leads to the amphitheater where the Britt Festival's open-air concerts are held on summer evenings. For the loop hike, however, turn right instead, following a pointer for the Sara Zigler Interpretive Trail. After just 150 feet you'll pass a 4-foot-diameter sequoia planted by Peter Britt in 1862 on the day his son Emil was born. Then the path enters a forest of Douglas fir, madrone, white oak, and ponderosa pine.

After half a mile, turn right across a footbridge over Jackson Creek, continue upstream to a parking area, and turn left across another footbridge. Then follow signs for "Rich Gulch" and "Panoramic Viewpoint," taking a left turn followed by two right turns and two lefts, to find a knolltop bench *(GPS location N42°18.638' W122°58.748')* overlooking the town and Mt. McLoughlin.

After admiring the view, continue 100 yards to a trail junction, turn right, and then keep straight at all junctions to descend through Rich Gulch. Trailside

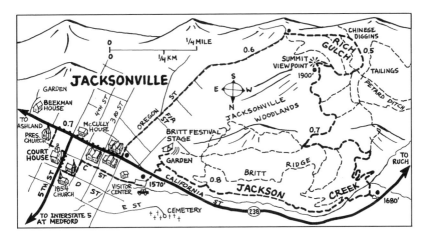

signs describe the flumes and giant hydraulic hoses that washed gold from this valley, leaving cobble tailings.

When you reach paved Oregon Street, turn left for 0.6 mile to the town's historic center. If you're ready for coffee, you might stop at the Good Bean Coffee Company, on the right just before California Street. If you'd prefer nachos and local microbrews, look on the far side of California Street for the restored 1856 Bella Union Saloon.

To continue the walking tour, turn right along California Street four blocks, passing the clapboard 1860 McCully House. Turn left at the Victorian Gothic 1881 Presbyterian Church on Sixth Street to find the 1883 county courthouse, once the site of the Jacksonville Museum. Then zigzag to Fifth and D Streets to see two rival Protestant and Catholic churches from the 1850s before returning along C Street to your car.

California Street in Jacksonville.   Opposite: Jacksonville trolley.

62 Sterling Ditch Tunnel

Easy (to tunnel)
4.7-mile loop
550 feet elevation gain
Open all year
Use: hikers, horses, bicycles

Difficult (entire trail)
17.1 miles one way
700 feet elevation gain

Three years after the 1851 discovery of gold at Jacksonville, miners struck paydirt in Sterling Creek. After the easy ore was panned out, quite a bit of gold dust remained in the ancient river gravels stranded on dry slopes high above the creek. But how could miners get water up there to wash the gold loose?

That question launched one of Southern Oregon's most remarkable engineering projects—a 26.5-mile ditch carrying water from the Little Applegate River to the Sterling Creek hills. Hand-dug by nearly 400 Chinese laborers in 1877, the 3-foot-deep ditch remained in use until the 1930s.

Today the Sterling Mine ditch lives on as a 17.1-mile recreation trail winding through the oak grasslands and pine forests of the upper Applegate country. While much of this route is best appreciated from the saddle of a mountain bike or a horse, hikers can sample the trail's highlights on an easy, 4.7-mile loop to an explorable 100-foot tunnel where the ditch ducks through a ridge.

To drive here from Medford, follow signs west to Jacksonville and continue straight on Highway 238 for 8 miles to the settlement of Ruch. (If you're coming

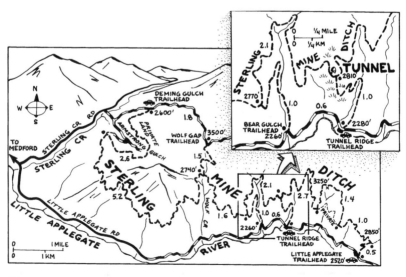

154

Giant madrone tree on the Sterling Mine Ditch's rim.   Opposite: Tunnel entrance.

from Grants Pass, follow signs south to Murphy and continue straight on Highway 238 to Ruch, between mileposts 25 and 26.) In Ruch, turn south toward the Upper Applegate area for 2.9 miles. Then turn left on Little Applegate Road for 9.7 miles to the Tunnel Ridge Trailhead parking pullout on the right. The trail climbs through oak woodlands mixed with Douglas fir, ponderosa pine, and Douglas maples. Expect wildflowers in May and June: pink clarkia, tall blue ookow, lilac-like deerbrush, and the pinkish, ball-shaped blooms of wild onion. Watch out for poison oak's triple leaflets. After 1 mile the path reaches the old ditch at the tunnel. Just 4 feet high, the tunnel is tight for adults but easy enough for children to hike through.

To continue the loop, walk left along the dry ditch's rim for 2.1 miles, passing huge madrone trees and a collapsed trestle along the way. Then turn left at a trail sign on a ridge end, take a 1-mile path down Bear Gulch to Little Applegate Road, and follow this gravel road left for 0.6 mile to your car.

If you're planning to tour the entire 17.1-mile ditch trail, you'll want to drive past the Tunnel Ridge Trailhead 1.8 miles to the Little Applegate Trailhead, marked by a sign on the left. From there, a trail climbs 0.5 mile before turning left on the ditch itself. After a mile, the ditch path detours up a hillside for 1.4 miles to avoid private land. Beyond that, it's 2.7 miles along the ditch to the tunnel and another 3.7 miles to Wolf Creek, where a side trail climbs 1.5 miles through a patch of old-growth Douglas fir to the Wolf Gap Trailhead. If you continue on the ditch, you'll contour 5.2 miles to an unmarked left-hand spur that leads to Armstrong Gulch Road. The main trail continues along the ditch another 2.6 miles (through private land and clearcuts) to trail's end at Deming Gulch Road.

To find the Deming Gulch Trailhead, drive back along Little Applegate Road to milepost 3, turn north on paved Sterling Creek Road for 2.1 miles, turn right on Armstrong Gulch Road 39-2-17 for 0.3 mile, and fork left on Deming Gulch Road for 0.7 mile to the ditch crossing where the trail begins. To find the Wolf Gap Trailhead, simply drive another 1.7 miles, keeping right at all junctions.

63   Mule Mountain

Easy (to Mule Creek)
3 miles round-trip
720 feet elevation gain
Open all year
Use: hikers, horses, bikes

Moderate (to gnarled oak ridge)
4 miles round-trip
1120 feet elevation gain

Difficult (entire loop)
10.6-mile loop
2800 feet elevation gain
Open April to mid-December

Little Grayback Mountain from Mule Mountain.

You're unlikely to see other people on this route through the oak savannah foothills of the Applegate Valley, but you can count on meeting hawks and ground squirrels. One trail fork crosses a ridge to Mule Creek's small mossy pools. The other fork climbs to a viewpoint on a ridge of gnarled white oaks.

Adventurers can combine the two trails on a difficult 10.6-mile loop, but be forewarned that this includes several miles along Mule Creek where the faint tread is crowded with poison oak. Although motorcycle use is allowed, it's infrequent and pretty much confined to the first half mile near the trailhead.

To drive here from Medford, follow signs west to Jacksonville and continue straight on Highway 238 for 8 miles to the settlement of Ruch. (If you're coming from Grants Pass, follow signs south to Murphy and continue straight on Highway 238 to Ruch, between mileposts 25 and 26.) In Ruch, turn south on paved Applegate Road for 12.2 miles.

Slow down after passing milepost 12. The trail begins just 0.1 mile farther, at a four-foot-wide metal gate in a wire fence down to the left. But there is no parking here. So drive another 0.1 mile to a wide, gravel shoulder on the right with room for cars. Park by a wire fence there, walk back 500 feet, and cross the highway carefully to the trailhead gate *(GPS location N42°05.467' W123°05.811')*.

Latch the metal gate behind you and follow a fenceline up to the right through

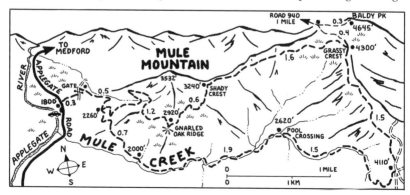

Baldy Peak from the oak savannah on Mule Mountain.

a grassy oak grove. Ground squirrels thrive on acorns here. The screaming hawks you see wheeling overhead thrive on squirrels.

When you reach a dirt road, turn left through a gate 30 feet to a sign marking the Mule Mountain Trail on the right. This path climbs through oak woods with Jeffrey pines and some big Douglas firs. Stay on the trail because the underbrush in the forest includes poison oak.

After another half mile you'll climb to an oak ridge with 15-foot-tall manzanita bushes. Here you'll reach a signed fork and face a choice.

For the easier hike to Mule Creek, fork to the right. This route starts out level, but then descends across a brushy slope for 0.7 mile, where the path starts following Mule Creek upstream through a shady fir forest. By late summer the creek doesn't always flow above ground, leaving only a string of small, cool, mossy pools. There are enough flat areas for a campsite. Still, this creek canyon is not that great for camping or for children because of the poison oak. Wear long pants and step carefully to avoid the plant's characteristic triple leaflets.

If instead you turn uphill to the left at the ridgetop fork, you'll find better views and far less poison oak. A good goal is to climb 1.2 miles to a ridge-end amidst gnarled oaks *(GPS location N42°05.087' W123°04.639')*. This lunch spot has the last view of the Applegate Valley and the first view ahead to Baldy Peak. Blue lupine and yellow balsamroot bloom here in late spring. In summer orange butterflies sip nectar from the fuzzy blooms of purple mint.

If you're willing to tackle the difficult loop, march onward and upward past the gnarled oak viewpoint. Long pants are essential because the trail becomes a little brushier. After 0.6 mile you'll reach a shady ridgecrest with fir trees. Then the trail climbs another 1.6 miles along the ridge to a faint junction atop a high, grassy divide on the shoulder of Baldy Peak. Keep right, following the ridge slightly downhill 1.5 miles.

When the trail ends at a dirt road, follow the road to the right 300 feet to a three-way fork. Don't take any of these roads. Instead angle down to the right on the Mule Creek Trail, marked only by a brown post *(GPS location N42°04.395' W123°02.169')*. This faint, rough trail descends 3.4 miles along Mule Creek before climbing up to the right 0.7 mile to rejoin the Mule Mountain Trail and the route down to your car.

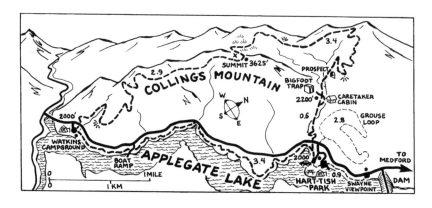

64 Collings Mountain

Easy (to Bigfoot Trap)
1.2 miles round-trip
200 feet elevation gain
Open all year
Use: hikers, horses, bicycles

Moderate (to Watkins Campground)
6.9 miles one way
1700 feet elevation gain
Open except in winter storms

Left: Bigfoot trap.

Hikers in this part of the Siskiyous have been reporting sightings of Bigfoot since 1895. So when a private research group resolved to catch the mythic apeman outright in 1973, they built their trap here. Today an easy half-mile trail from Applegate Lake leads to the abandoned contraption. If you believe more in exercise than in Sasquatch, consider following the woodsy trail another 6.3 miles, across Collings Mountain to the far end of Applegate Lake's reservoir.

To drive here from Medford, follow signs west to Jacksonville and continue straight on Highway 238 for 8 miles to the settlement of Ruch. (From Grants Pass, follow signs south to Murphy and continue straight on Highway 238 to Ruch, between mileposts 25 and 26.) In Ruch, turn south toward the Upper Applegate area for 15.9 miles. When you've driven 1 mile past Applegate Dam turn left into the Hart-Tish Recreation Area. Expect a $5 day-use fee.

Park in the picnic area parking lot on the right, walk to a large "Applegate Lake" sign at the upper end of the lot, and veer left on a level trail into the woods. After 200 yards, cross the highway to find a path that switchbacks down into a gulch and follows a mossy creek up through a forest of Douglas fir, white pine, madrone, and bigleaf maple. Keep an eye out for poison oak.

After 0.6 mile the path splits around the dilapidated caretaker's cabin, a shake-sided 9-by-12-foot shack. From here, a spur trail to the left climbs to the Bigfoot trap, a formidable 10-foot-tall cell with thick walls and a guillotine-like steel door. Poison oak is thick here.

If you decide to continue, return to the main trail and follow it up the canyon 0.3 mile to a prospector's adit—a short tunnel built to check for ore. Beyond this the trail climbs steeply up a hillside of scrub oak and madrone, with glimpses out to Applegate Lake. Then the path follows a broad ridge 2 miles before switch-backing past a grassy opening that is Collings Mountain's summit. Although this mountaintop lacks views, the open woods host a surprising variety of June wildflowers: beargrass plumes, fuzzy white lupine, trumpet-shaped purple penstemon, tall blue ookow, pink clarkia, and white iris.

Beyond the summit, the trail descends 2.9 miles through the woods before crossing the paved road to the Watkins Campground parking area. Ideally you'll have left a shuttle car or bicycle here for a quick ride back to the starting trailhead. If not, walk to the far left end of the parking lot and take the Da-Ku-Be-Te-De Trail, a path that parallels the reservoir's shore (and the road) for 3.4 miles back to your car.

65 Applegate Lake

Easy (around peninsula)
6.4-mile loop
400 feet elevation gain
Open all year
Use: hikers, bicycles

Difficult (around entire lake)
17.8-mile loop
300 feet elevation gain

Right: Ookow.

This reservoir is wreathed not only by the forests of the Siskiyou Mountains, but also by a convenient network of trails. Admittedly, low water levels expose the brown bathtub ring typical of reservoirs, but noisy speedboats are banned and the overall setting remains fairly wild. Expect to see fish-hunting osprey, wildflowers in grassy openings, and glimpses of Siskiyou peaks. For an easy loop hike along the shore, explore the trails on a peninsula beside French Gulch. For a longer, level bike ride, circle the entire lake on a 17.8-mile route that's two-thirds on trail and one-third on paved roads.

To find the trailhead from Medford, follow signs west to Jacksonville and continue straight on Highway 238 for 8 miles to the settlement of Ruch. (From Grants Pass, follow signs south to Murphy and continue straight on Highway 238 to Ruch, between mileposts 25 and 26.) In Ruch, turn south toward the Upper Applegate area for 14.9 miles. Then turn left across Applegate Dam for 1.2 miles to the French Gulch Trailhead parking area on the right.

The trail passes the walk-in campsites of French Gulch Campground and follows the lakeshore through a patch of wildflowers. In April look for pink shooting stars and calypso orchids. In June expect pink clarkia, fuzzy white lupine, tall blue ookow, and the 6-petaled, yellow-and-purple-striped blooms

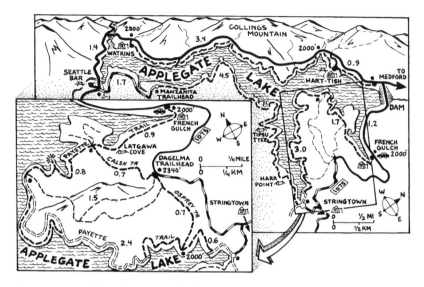

of pretty face. Then the path sallies into the open, second-growth woods that ring the lake with Douglas fir, white pine, and madrone. Keep an eye out for the triple leaflets of poison oak.

After 0.7 mile the trail crosses the decommissioned Latgawa Cove Campground. Just beyond, at a 5-way junction, ignore a "Viewpoint" pointer to the right that leads to a disappointing deadend. You'll find better views by simply continuing straight on the Payette Trail along the shore. In another 0.8 mile, at the tip of the peninsula, the Payette Trail becomes an old road. For much of the next 2.4 miles the path follows this abandoned chromium mining track around the lake, passing prospects of green ore. Then, to complete the peninsula loop, turn left on the Osprey Trail. This path climbs through an oak grassland 0.7 mile to the parking lot at the Dagelma Trailhead. Here, veer left onto the Calsh Trail for 0.7 mile. Then turn right on the Payette Trail to return to your car at

Stein Butte from Applegate Lake.   Opposite: Knobcone pine cones.

French Gulch.

If you'd like to circle the entire lake on a mountain bike, start out from the French Gulch Trailhead as described above, but follow the Payette Trail a total of 9.2 miles. When the trail ends at the Manzanita Trailhead, continue 1.7 miles on a gravel road to the Seattle Bar picnic area. Keep right for 1.4 miles on pavement, but then pull into Watkins Campground, where the Da-Ku-Be-Te-De Trail begins. Follow this path, wedged between the lakeshore and the paved road, for 4.3 miles to its end at the Swayne Viewpoint parking pullout just before Applegate Dam. Then cross the dam and follow the paved road 1.2 miles back to your car.

66   Stein Butte

Difficult
9.4 miles round-trip
2400 feet elevation gain
Open April through December
Use: hikers, horses, bikes

Motorcycle trails rarely appeal to other users, but the well-built path to this lookout site above Applegate Lake is an exception. After a strenuous climb through the woods, the path traces a ridgecrest with strange knobcone pines and birds-eye views of a dozen Siskiyou peaks.

From Medford, follow signs west to Jacksonville and continue straight on Highway 238 for 8 miles to the settlement of Ruch. (From Grants Pass, follow signs south to Murphy and continue straight on Highway 238 to Ruch, between mileposts 25 and 26.) In Ruch, turn south toward the Upper Applegate area for 18.8 miles. When you reach a T-shaped junction at the far end of Applegate Lake, turn left on Applegate Road for 0.9 mile to the Seattle Bar Trailhead and

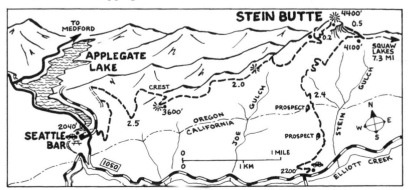

picnic area on the right. The entire driving route is paved.

From the parking area, walk across a lawn and duck under the highway bridge to find the trail. The path promptly crosses a gravel road and launches uphill at a steady grade through a dry forest. Trees here include Douglas fir, long-needled Jeffrey pine, madrone (with red, peeling bark), black oak (with large, pointy leaves), and canyon live oak (with small, pointy leaves). Also watch for poison oak bushes (with leaflets in threes).

After a wearying 2.5 miles the path finally gains the ridgecrest. Look here for knobcone pine—an odd, spindly species with knobby cones clustered on its trunk. You're also likely to see black bear droppings. Bears like to eat the tough berries of the 12-foot-tall manzanita bushes on this ridge—and the manzanita prospers because its berries only sprout after being passed by a bear.

A scenic 2-mile walk along the ridge brings you to a 0.2-mile spur trail to Stein Butte's rocky summit. This final trail segment is open to hikers only.

The Civilian Conservation Corps built a lookout tower atop Stein Butte in 1936, but only the foundation and the view remain. On the horizon to the left of Applegate Lake rises the broad hump of Grayback Mountain. A string of rocky Siskiyou peaks extends to its left. The reddest and nearest of these is Red Buttes. Hovering farther to the east are the Cascade snowpeaks, Mt. Shasta and Mt. McLoughlin.

Other Hiking Options

A shorter, but steeper and less scenic route up Stein Butte starts from Elliott Creek Road 1050. This path passes a couple of 100-foot prospecting tunnels near the Oregon-California border. If you can arrange a short car shuttle, you can hike both trails one way. To find the other trailhead from Seattle Bar, continue on Applegate Road for 0.3 mile to a big gravel intersection. Then go straight on Road 1050 for 2.8 miles to a small sign on the left for the New London Trail.

67   Red Buttes

Moderate (to Lilypad Lake)
8.2 miles round-trip
1440 feet elevation gain
Open June to mid-November
Use: hikers, horses

Lakes are relatively rare in the Siskiyous, but the Pacific Crest Trail passes near two as it skirts this rocky, double-topped mountain—the ruddy landmark of the Red Buttes Wilderness.

The buttes are made of peridotite, a red, iron-rich rock created when seafloor sand and mud are baked together inside the earth. The 200 million-year-old rock tells a lot about the history of this range. The Siskiyous formed as the

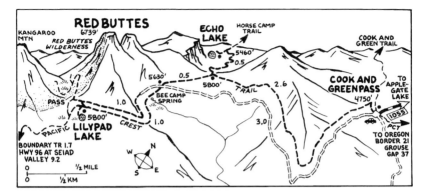

RED BUTTES
6739'

KANGAROO MTN

RED BUTTES WILDERNESS

ECHO LAKE

HORSE CAMP TRAIL

COOK AND GREEN TRAIL

5630'   0.5

5460'
0.5

5800'

PASS   5800'   1.0

BEE CAMP SPRING

TRAIL   2.6

COOK AND GREEN PASS   TO APPLE-GATE LAKE
4750'

1055

PACIFIC CREST   LILYPAD LAKE   1.0

3.0

PCT

TO OREGON BORDER 21
GROUSE GAP 37

BOUNDARY TR 1.7
HWY 96 AT SEIAD VALLEY 9.2

W   N   E   S

0   ½ MILE
0   ½ KM

North American continent crunched westward over the Pacific plate, scraping off seafloor sediments and volcanic island chains like cake batter on a spatula.

Patches of white marble on the side of Red Buttes are the remains of seashells, cooked and contorted by pressure. Outcrops of greasy-looking, greenish-black serpentine rock along the Pacific Crest Trail are the lubricant that formed between the sliding plates of continent and seafloor. An old road paralleling the PCT was built by miners searching for gold, chromium, and other heavy metals churned up by the titanic collision of crustal plates.

To find the trailhead from Medford, follow signs west to Jacksonville and continue straight on Highway 238 for 8 miles to the settlement of Ruch. (From Grants Pass, follow signs south to Murphy and continue straight on Highway 238 to Ruch, between mileposts 25 and 26.) In Ruch, turn south toward the Upper Applegate area for 18.8 miles. When you reach a T-shaped junction at the far end of Applegate Lake, turn left on Applegate Road for 1.2 miles to a big gravel intersection. Continue straight on one-lane Road 1050 for 0.9 mile and then fork to the right on Road 1055. Follow this narrow gravel road—not suitable for low-slung passenger cars—for 10 miles, climbing to Cook and Green Pass and a trailhead parking area on the right.

Lilypad Lake.   Opposite: Red Buttes from the Pacific Crest Trail.

Two trails start on the right-hand side of this parking area. Of these, take the Pacific Crest Trail up a forested ridge to the left. The shady woods of fir and tanoak soon give way to a rocky red scrubland of manzanita brush and beargrass with a few incense cedars and white pines. Expect views not only of Red Buttes, but also south across the Klamath River's dark canyon to the Marble Mountains and Mt. Shasta's ghostly white cone.

After 2.6 miles, at a trail junction in a brushy pass, detour 100 yards to the right to a spectacular viewpoint of green Echo Lake backed by red cliffs. If you have the time, scramble another 0.5 mile down this steep, rocky side trail to Echo Lake's shore and a wildflower meadow with blue gentians.

Then return to the PCT and continue 1.5 miles to another trail junction in Lilypad Lake's scenic alpine bowl. This smaller, shallower pond is packed with yellow pond lilies. The surrounding meadow has mint, yellow sneezeweed, coneflower, and unfortunately, cow pies. As in the Swiss Alps, the background music here is often the tinny clank of cowbells.

From the junction near the lake, turn uphill to the right 100 yards to find the end of the old mining road in a pass overlooking much of the Red Buttes Wilderness. To return on a loop, follow this abandoned roadbed back 1 mile to a barricade near Bee Camp Spring. High clearance vehicles can drive to this point from Cook and Green Pass, but seldom do. Walking this drivable portion of the old road is no fun either, so angle left on the PCT for the final 3.1 miles back to Cook and Green Pass.

68 Frog Pond

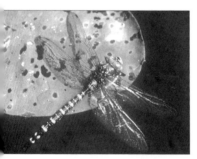

Easy (to Middle Fork Applegate crossing)
2.4 miles round-trip
400 feet elevation gain
Open except in winter storms
Use: hikers, horses

Moderate (to Frog Pond)
7.9-mile loop
1800 feet elevation gain
Open mid-May through November

The first of these two hikes is an easy stroll along the Middle Fork Applegate River to a swimmable pool, some log cabin ruins, and a scenic footbridge in an old-growth forest. The second, steeper trail loops past Frog Pond through subalpine Wilderness meadows. Backpackers can connect the two paths for a more challenging tour.

To drive here from Medford, follow signs west to Jacksonville and continue straight on Highway 238 for 8 miles to the settlement of Ruch. (From Grants Pass, follow signs south to Murphy and continue straight on Highway 238 to Ruch, between mileposts 25 and 26.) In Ruch, turn south toward the Upper Applegate area for 18.8 miles. At the far end of Applegate Lake, turn left on Applegate Road for 1.2 miles to a big gravel intersection. Then turn right on one-lane gravel Road 1040 for 5.1 miles to a signed junction.

From this junction you can find the easy riverside trail by simply driving

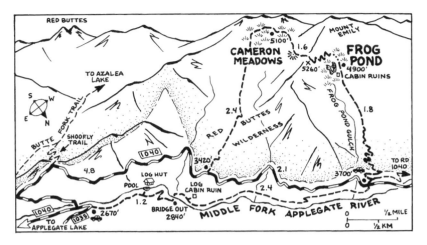

straight on Road 1035 for 300 yards to the Middle Fork Trailhead on the left. To drive to the upper Frog Pond Loop Trailhead instead, turn left at the junction and continue 6.9 miles on narrow Road 1040 to the *third* trailhead on the left, 0.2 mile after the road splashes across an easy ford in Frog Pond Gulch.

If you're setting out on the Middle Fork Trail, you'll start by tracing a canyon slope above the river. Douglas firs grow up to 4 feet thick in these shady woods. Vine maple and alder dapple the riverbank with bright green. Tanoak and madrone strew the drier slopes with crackly leaves. After 0.6 mile a steep spur to the left scrambles 100 feet down to a chilly but swimmable green river pool below a little waterfall, with a primitive log hut on the far shore.

After another 0.6 mile the Middle Fork Trail a bridgeless river crossing with a small gravel beach among riverside boulders. If you've brought children, this makes a good turnaround point. If you manage to cross the river and continue 200 yards up the trail you'll find a ruined log cabin on the left. Beyond this point the Middle

Frog Pond.   Opposite: Dragonfly on a lilypad.

Fork Trail mostly stays out of sight of the river for 2.4 miles to Road 1040 and the upper Frog Pond Loop Trailhead.

A pond may not sound like a spectacular Wilderness destination, but the Frog Pond Loop is actually one of the prettiest tours in the Red Buttes area. Unfortunately, it's not quite a loop. The path has two trailheads on Road 1040. To connect them you'll end up walking on the road 2.1 miles or shuttling a car.

Start the Frog Pond Loop from the upper trailhead. This wide spot in Road 1040 has a message board on the left reminding visitors that groups in this Wilderness are limited to eight persons. Hike past this sign and keep left on a steep, uphill path through the woods. Look here for pink rhododendron blooms, foot-long sugarpine cones, and the dusty blue berries of Oregon grape. Also notice witch's broom, an odd tree affliction that has channeled the growth of some local Douglas firs into clumps of greenery.

After 1.8 miles the path enters a meadow of mint and asters at Frog Pond, a sinuous pool with lilypads, water boatmen, and dragonflies. Nearby is the ruin of a 1920s prospector's cabin built using the trunks of eight living incense cedars. The trail peters out here, but angle to the right to the meadow's far upper end. There, a large "X" sign on a tree marks the resumption of the path. The trail then switchbacks over a ridge, ambles past viewpoints of Red Buttes and distant Mt. McLoughlin, descends through Cameron Meadows' grassy alpine bowl, and dives down a broad wooded ridge to Road 1040. If you haven't left a shuttle car at this lower trailhead, walk left 2.1 miles to complete a 7.9-mile loop.

69 Azalea Lake

Difficult
13 miles round-trip
2030 feet elevation gain
Open mid-June to mid-November
Use: hikers, horses

Showy pink mountain azaleas and white beargrass plumes fringe this lake deep in the Red Buttes Wilderness. The trail to the lake passes a Siskiyou crest viewpoint overlooking green Phantom Meadow and groves of two odd trees—knobcone pine and Brewer's weeping spruce.

To find the trail from Grants Pass, follow signs south 6.5 miles to Murphy and continue straight on Highway 238 another 11.5 miles to a green steel bridge just before the town of Applegate. (From Medford, follow signs for Jacksonville 5 miles west and continue straight on Highway 238 to the bridge at milepost 18.) At the Applegate bridge turn south on Thompson Creek Road for 11.9 miles of pavement and another 2.8 miles of gravel. Then, following "Azalea Lake" or "Fir Glade" pointers, turn right across a bridge, immediately fork left on Road

Phantom Meadow.   Opposite: Figurehead Mountain from Azalea Lake.

1030 for 5.1 miles, turn left on Road 400 (which becomes Road 1040) for 4.7 miles, and finally fork right onto rough, rocky Road 800 for 0.6 mile to a turnaround.

The trail starts in a second-growth fir forest with incense cedar, tanoak brush, and hazel. In the first 1.3 miles you'll pass a 40-foot pond, the California line, and several small meadows of brown coneflower, yellow sneezeweed, and grazing cows. Then the path switchbacks down beside Fir Glade, a larger meadow that also hosts blue lupine and red paintbrush. Next the path gradually climbs through sparsely wooded brushfields for 2.7 miles to a rocky pass above Phantom Meadow. Views here extend west to square-topped, snowy Preston Peak. Nearly all of the trees on the left side of this pass are Brewer's weeping spruces, whose cones dangle from strangely drooping branch tips. The trees on the drier, right-hand side of the pass are even odder—they're knobcone pines, whose cones cluster along skinny trunks like bumps on flagpoles.

After crossing a second pass the path switchbacks down to a 0.6-mile loop trail through the lodgepole pine and white pine around shallow Azalea Lake.

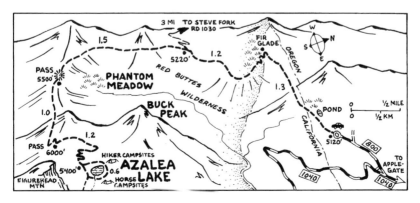

Camping and fires are banned within this lakeshore loop. Backpackers are supposed to tent in the sloping area west of the loop, while equestrian campers are directed to the flatter area east of the loop.

70   Sturgis Fork

Moderate
4.8 miles round-trip
1350 feet elevation gain
Open mid-June to mid-November
Use: hikers, horses, bikes

In this beautiful but often overlooked corner of the Siskiyous you can trace a mountain brook to a forested pass, and then follow the Boundary Trail through a huge meadow to a nameless viewpoint peak. Backpackers can continue for days in any of three directions: north to Grayback Mountain, south into the Red Buttes Wilderness, or west to the Oregon Caves National Monument. Incredibly, motorcycles are allowed in this fragile subalpine area; fortunately, they are rare.

From Grants Pass, follow signs south 6.5 miles to Murphy and continue straight on Highway 238 another 11.5 miles to a green steel bridge at milepost 18, just before the town of Applegate. (From Medford, follow signs for Jacksonville 5 miles west and continue straight on Highway 238 to the bridge at milepost 18.) At the Applegate bridge turn south on Thompson Creek Road for 11.9 miles.

Where pavement ends at a pass, veer right onto gravel Road 1020. After 4.2 miles, turn right to stay on Road 1020, following a "Sturgis Fork Trail" pointer. When the road forks after another 0.4 mile, ignore Road 500 to the right. The road forks again after another 3.3 miles, but this time turn steeply up to the right on rough, rocky Road 600 for 0.6 mile. Then fork uphill to the left for 200 yards to road's end at a trailhead turnaround (*GPS location N42°04.658' W123°20.819'*). If you have a low-slung passenger car, you might prefer to walk the final 0.7 mile from Road 1020.

The trail begins in a grove of 4-foot-diameter grand fir, beside a meadow of hellebore (corn lily), vanilla leaf, mountain bluebells, and yellow violets. Right after the snowmelt in early June, expect two lilies: white 3-petaled trilliums and yellow 6-petaled fawn lilies.

Climb alongside the creek 0.7 mile to a T-shaped junction with the Boundary Trail atop a broad, forested ridgecrest. Turn right for 0.3 mile to another junction in a small meadow. The Oregon Caves are 4.8 miles to the left, but for the viewpoint, head up to the right. This route promptly traverses a gigantic meadowed slope of hellebore (with big boat-shaped leaves), fragrant mint, blue lupine, and purple larkspur.

The Boundary Trail crosses a meadow of hellebore (corn lily). Opposite: Phlox.

After 0.8 mile you'll reach a barren pass that's often visited by motorcycles. Go straight, following the Boundary Trail up a granite slope where patches of snow linger until late June. When the path crests after 0.6 mile, walk 100 feet to the right to a rocky summit where lavender phlox blooms on black lichen-encrusted rocks *(GPS location N42 05.287 W123 20.190)*. Here you can see the entire route of your hike, as well as every major peak in the Siskiyous.

Other Hiking Options

If you're not ready to turn back at the viewpoint peak, you can continue north on the Boundary Trail 3 miles to Grayback Mountain (Hike #71). Or you could turn around and follow the Boundary Trail south as far as you like. It's 7.4 miles to the shelter at Sucker Creek Gap, but trails continue through the Red Buttes Wilderness to Azalea Lake (Hike #69) and the Pacific Crest Trail (Hike #67). Yet another option is to hike west to a lesser view atop Mt. Elijah, the meadows at the shallow Bigelow Lakes, or the Oregon Caves (Hike #72).

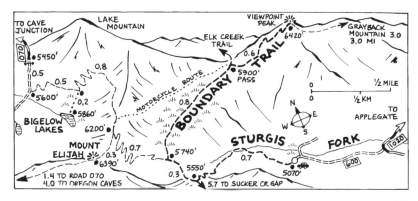

71   Grayback Mountain

Moderate (to cabin and meadow)
2.6 miles round-trip
1100 feet elevation gain
Open mid-June to early November
Use: hikers, horses, bikes

Difficult (to summit)
6.2 miles round-trip
2450 feet elevation gain

A historic cabin and a glorious wildflower meadow adorn the slopes of this landmark peak. The trail ends short of the summit, but adventurers can scramble on to the panoramic view at the top.

This mountain looks like the broad, gray back of an elephant when viewed from the Applegate Valley, but it was named for a much smaller animal. Miners in Southern Oregon's 1850s gold rush christened the peak after their worst bugaboo—the itchy lice commonly called graybacks.

To drive here from Grants Pass, follow signs south 6.5 miles to Murphy and continue straight on Highway 238 another 11.5 miles to a green steel bridge at milepost 18, just before the town of Applegate. (If you're coming from Medford, follow signs for Jacksonville 5 miles west and continue straight on Highway 238 to the bridge at milepost 18.) At the bridge turn south on Thompson Creek Road for 11.9 miles. Where pavement ends at a pass, turn sharply to the right past an "O'Brien Creek Trail" sign onto Road 1005. Follow this bumpy gravel road 0.3 mile, fork left, and continue another 2 miles to a fork. The unmarked lower O'Brien Creek trailhead is uphill to the right of the creek. Stop here if you're towing a horse trailer; otherwise turn right and drive uphill another 1.7 miles to the road's end at an upper trailhead. This final rough stretch has a patch of sharp rocks that can cause flat tires, so drive slowly.

From the upper trailhead, the path climbs along an ancient roadbed for 0.2 mile before charging steeply up through dense, cool woods of old-growth

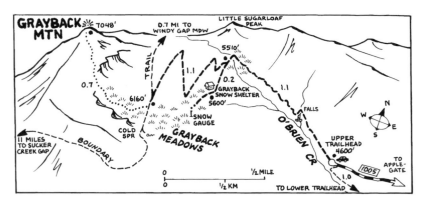

Grayback Mountain's snow shelter.   Opposite: Inside the cabin.

Douglas fir and incense cedar. At the upper end of a gully of wildflowers the path crosses O'Brien Creek.

Keep left at a fork for the level path 0.2 mile to the Grayback Snow Shelter, a funky 10-by-14-foot cabin with a wood floor, rustic table, folding chairs, three glassless windows, and an unlocked door. Use a knife or thin stick to lift the door's latch. The roof is tight and the loft has bunks for two. The cabin's stove should not be used in summer due to forest fire danger, so bring a backpacking stove if you want to cook. Notes at the cabin report that hikers often find a foot of snow here in mid-December. In winter, snow survey crews reserve the cabin for their work the last weekend of each month. In June of 2009 a visitor named Aleksander wrote, "Only 11 years old. My dad drug me up here."

Just beyond the cabin is Grayback Meadows, abloom each summer with purple aster, goldenrod, yellow sneezeweed, orange paintbrush, and big-leaved hellebore. A campsite and snow gauge pole mark the site of a burned cabin.

If you'd like to climb Grayback Mountain, you could just bushwhack straight up this meadow, but it's probably easier to walk back to the fork in the trail and switchback uphill 1.1 mile on a path through the woods. When you reach the Boundary Trail, go left 200 feet to the meadow, and then bushwhack straight uphill to the right. Scramble through a gap in the cliffs, follow a ridgecrest, and push your way through the manzanita brush for 0.2 mile to the rocky summit.

Here a 360° panorama encompasses a startling shiny swath of the Pacific Ocean near Crescent City. To the right is the woodsy Illinois Valley with the peaked ridges of the Kalmiopsis Wilderness beyond. To the left are the spires of the Siskiyou Wilderness (with M-shaped Preston Peak the tallest). Farther left are Red Buttes, snowy Mt. Shasta, Mt. McLoughlin's cone, Crater Lake's rim (above Medford), Mt. Thielsen's spire, and the Applegate Valley's ranches.

Western Siskiyous

Campgrounds

		Campsites	Water	Flush toilet	Open (mos.)	Rate range
1	**BIG PINE.** A path leads to one of the world's tallest ponderosa pines (see Hike #84) from this lovely camp beside Meyers Creek.	12	●		V-X	$5
2	**BOLAN LAKE.** In deep woods by a high mountain lake (boat ramp, no powerboats), this camp has a trail to a lookout (see Hike #75).	12			VII-X	$5
3	**BRIGGS CREEK.** At the Illinois River Trailhead (see Hike #82), this camp's trees burned in 2002. Look for a side path to a river gravel bar.	3			III-X	free
4	**CAVE CREEK.** A 2-mile trail leads from this creekside camp in a dark, old-growth forest to the Oregon Caves (see Hike #72).	18	●		V-IX	$10
5	**GRAYBACK.** Along a creek 8 miles from the Oregon Caves, this camp has a footbridge to a nature trail.	39	●		V-IX	$10
6	**INDIAN MARY.** A hit with Rogue River rafters, this county park has showers and 2 rental yurts ($30; reservations *www.reserveamaerica.com*).	92	●	●	●	$19-22
7	**LAKE SELMAC.** Wooded county park at a reservoir has wind-surfing, showers, and 2 rental yurts ($30; *www.reserveamerica.com*).	93	●	●	●	$15-20
8	**SAM BROWN.** This camp on Briggs Creek (see Hike #85) has big trees, a meadow, and corrals for 2-4 horses at each site.	19	●		V-X	$5
9	**SCHROEDER & WHITEHORSE.** These two county parks on the Rogue River (west of Grants Pass 3 miles and 7 miles) have boat ramps, ballfields, playgrounds, showers, and rental yurts.	93	●	●	●	$19-22
10	**WOLF CREEK.** Quiet, but conveniently close to I-5, this camp has a trail up London Peak (see Hike #176).	7	●	●	V-IX	$19-20

◁ *The Bolan Mountain lookout.*

Cabins, Lookouts & Inns

		Rental units	Private bath	Breakfast	Open (mos.)	Rate range
1	**BOLAN MOUNTAIN LOOKOUT.** Rent this 1953 lookout and get a gate key (Hike #75). No water or stove. Res: 877-444-6777 *(www.recreation.gov)*.	1			VII-IX	$40
2	**CLAY HILL LODGE**. Access only by boat or Rogue River Trail (Hike #87). Per person price includes meals. Res: 503-859-3772 *(www.clayhilllodge.com)*.	5	3	●	V-X	$150
3	**KERBYVILLE INN.** Near Lake Selmac (see above) this inn has a deck, gardens, and 2 rooms with spas. Res: 877-273-4843 *(www.bridgeviewwine.com)*.	5	●	●		$64-110
4	**OREGON CAVES CHATEAU**. Grand 1934 lodge at the National Monument (Hike #72). Res: 877-245-9022 *(www.oregoncaveschateau.com)*.	23	●	●	●	$109-185
5	**PARADISE LODGE.** Access only by boat or Rogue River Trail (Hike #87). Per person price includes meals. Res: 888-667-6483 *(www.paradise-lodge.com)*.	12	●	●	V-XI	$150-160
6	**PEARSOLL PEAK LOOKOUT.** Primitive 1954 cabin atop Kalmiopsis Wilderness peak, accessed by a 7-mile hike. Info: 541-618-2200.	1			VI-IX	free
7	**WOLF CREEK INN**. Restored 1883 stagecoach inn has good food and access to I-5 (Hike #176). Res: 541-866-2692 *(www.historicwolfcreekinn.com)*.	9	●	●	●	$95-135

Top right: The Rogue River at Mule Creek Canyon (Hike #87).

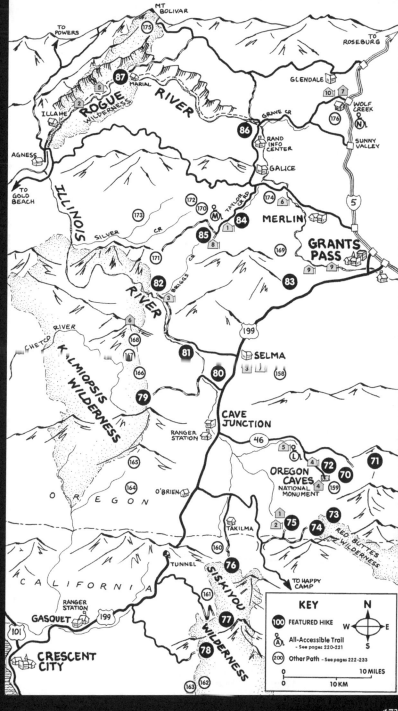

72   Oregon Caves

Easy (cave tour)
1.3-mile loop
220 feet elevation gain
Open late March to early November

Moderate (to Big Tree)
3.7-mile loop
1125 feet elevation gain
Open late April to early December

Poet Joaquin Miller's praise of the "great Marble Halls of Oregon" helped promote National Monument status for Oregon Caves in 1909. Visitors today can join a guided tour for about $8.50 ($6 for children 16 and under), exploring narrow passageways and stairs to hidden rooms of cave formations. For a free hike above ground try the Big Tree Loop, crossing a forested Siskiyou mountainside to one of Oregon's largest Douglas firs. Pets are banned on all park trails.

The caves' marble began as tropical island reefs in the Pacific Ocean. About 190 million years ago the advancing North American continent scraped up the island sediments to form this part of the Siskiyous. At first the land here was so wet that percolating ground water dissolved parts of the marble, forming pockets. When the land rose and the caves drained, dripping water gradually deposited calcite inside — much as a dripping faucet can stain a sink. Drips in the cave first form "soda straws," thin tubes hanging from the ceiling. When the tubes get plugged, water runs down the outsides and forms thicker stalactites. If the drip is fast, it carries dissolved calcite to the cave floor to form a stalagmite.

Hunter Elijah Davidson discovered the cave in 1874 when his dog chased a bear into the entrance.

Davidson lit matches to follow. When the last match died he found his way out of the darkness only by crawling along a cave-floor stream. After word spread of his find, early entrepreneurs damaged the cave by encouraging visitors to break off stalactites as samples, sign their names on the walls, and hug the white dripstone columns, darkening the rock. A cave operator who took over in the 1920s hoked up his tours with ghost stories, colored lights, and hidden growling men in lion skins—the origin of the Grants Pass caveman mascot. To preserve the cave, the National Park Service now urges visitors not to touch anything in the cave. Lighting is dim to discourage the moss and algae that grow near artificial lights.

To drive here, take Highway 199 south from Grants Pass 29 miles (or north from Crescent City 57 miles) to Cave Junction and follow "Oregon Caves" pointers east on Highway 46 for 20 miles to a turnaround. Unless you have lodge reservations, park here and walk the road 0.2 mile to the gift shop and cave entrance.

Cave tours leave about every half hour from 9am to 6pm in summer, and about every hour from 10am to 4pm in spring and fall. There are no tours between November 5 and late March due to hibernating bats, and there are no tours mid-week in late April or November. Children under six must be 42 inches tall to join the tour. Don't bring a flashlight or a backpack, but because it averages 42° F in the cave year-round, you'll want warm clothes.

The 90-minute cave tour climbs 0.6 mile through the cave to an upper exit. From there the quickest return route is a 0.3-mile trail to the right.

If you'd rather hike to Big Tree, walk through the visitor center's breezeway arch and fork to the left. This path climbs a slope of marble outcroppings and manzanita bushes before entering old-growth fir woods with rhododendron, vanilla leaf, and incense cedar. Expect lots of golden-mantled ground squirrels, chipmunks, and dark blue Steller's jays with pointy black topknots. At Big Tree (a Douglas fir over 13 feet in diameter) the loop trail switchbacks up to the right. Keeping right at junctions you'll pass high meadows of aromatic mint, orange paintbrush, purple larkspur, and cow parsnip before descending through a grove of Port Orford cedars to the gift shop by the cave entrance.

Other Hiking Options

For a longer hike, either start two miles below the cave at Cave Creek Campground (see map), or continue up from the Big Tree Loop 2.3 miles to a viewpoint atop Mt. Elijah (see Hike #70).

Inside the caves (National Park Service photo).   Opposite: Big Tree.

The 1930s Sucker Creek Shelter was restored in 2001. Below: Swan Mountain.

73   Sucker Creek

Easy (to cirque lake)
3.8 miles round-trip
730 feet elevation gain
Open early June to mid-November
Use: hikers, horses

Difficult (to Swan Mountain)
7.2 miles round-trip
1780 feet elevation gain

At the headwaters of Sucker Creek a rustic shelter stands in a meadow ringed with huge incense cedars. The shelter is a perfectly good hiking goal, but nearby are two attractions that are less well known—a hidden lilypad lake in a cliff-rimmed glen and a viewpoint atop trailless Swan Mountain.

Sucker Creek won its gullible-sounding name in the 1850s gold rush, when miners from Illinois (proudly known to Midwesterners as the "Sucker State") christened both the Illinois River and this tributary, Sucker Creek.

To drive here, take Highway 199 south from Grants Pass 29 miles (or north from Crescent City 57 miles) to Cave Junction and follow "Oregon Caves" pointers east on Highway 46 for 13.3 miles. Beyond Grayback Campground 1.8 miles, where the highway switchbacks to the left, turn right onto narrow, paved Road 4612. Set your odometer to zero here to keep track of mileage. At the 2-mile mark pavement ends and the road forks; keep right on Road 4612. At the 6.1-mile mark, follow Road 4612 as it forks to the right. When the road forks again at the 9.9-mile mark, keep straight on Road 098. At the 13.5-mile mark ignore a fork to the left. Then drive 1.6 miles farther to road's end at the trailhead.

The path sets off through a mixed forest of tanoak, Douglas fir, grand fir, and incense cedar. Early in summer you'll see the yellow clusters of Oregon grape, the state flower. The large three-part leaves along the trail are vanilla leaf, which puts up a little stalk of tiny white flowers in June. Its roots were sometimes mashed by pioneers as a vanilla substitute.

After 0.7 mile the path crosses Sucker Creek and then climbs steeply for half a mile to a meadow of yellow violets, fawn lilies, and purple larkspur, surrounded by incense cedars. The path becomes faint here, but climb to the left side of the meadow, where the tread reappears. Then look for the shelter down to your left *(GPS location N42°00.390' W123°20.950')*. Rebuilt in 2001, the 3-sided shake structure no longer leaks.

To find the other attractions nearby, continue up past the shelter 300 yards to a signpost marking a 4-way trail junction in Sucker Creek Gap, a broad pass. First go straight, following a pointer for the Steve Fork Trail. This path climbs 200 yards to a low rise and then descends 150 yards to a sharp left-hand corner. Leave the path here, following a fainter trail to the right 100 yards to a lovely, secret lake, wedged between cliffs and a bunchgrass meadow with purple aster and yellow sneezeweed *(GPS location N42°00.123' W123°20.899')*. Like most lakes in the Siskiyous, this one fills a cirque—a high, bowl-shaped valley carved at the head of a vanished glacier. Siskiyou cirque lakes are small because only small glaciers formed in these sunny mountains during the Ice Age.

For a more strenuous viewpoint goal, return to the 4-way junction in Sucker Creek Gap and turn right on the (possibly somewhat overgrown) Boundary Trail. After 1.4 miles the trail passes a Wilderness boundary sign in a ridgecrest pass. Continue 200 yards until the trail veers away from the ridge. Then leave the trail and bushwhack straight ahead up the ridgecrest meadow. Wear long pants for this adventure because you'll have to wade through some manzanita brush. After climbing 0.6 mile you'll reach the top of Swan Mountain *(GPS location N42°01.811' W123°21.838')*, where the 360° view swivels from Mt. Shasta to Cave Junction.

Other Hiking Options

If you're coming from Medford, it's quicker to hike to Sucker Creek Gap from the Steve Fork Trailhead instead. To find it, drive through Jacksonville on Highway 238 to the town of Applegate. Just beyond a green steel bridge at milepost 18, turn left on Thompson Creek Road for 11.9 miles of pavement and another 2.8 miles of gravel. Then, following "Steve Fork Trail" pointers, turn right across a bridge and immediately fork left onto Road 1030 for 11 miles to a large parking lot at road's end. From here the 3-mile trail to the pass gains 860 feet.

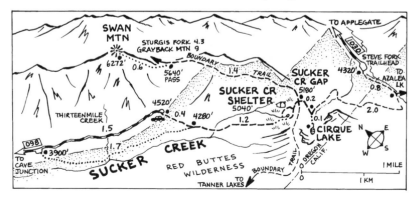

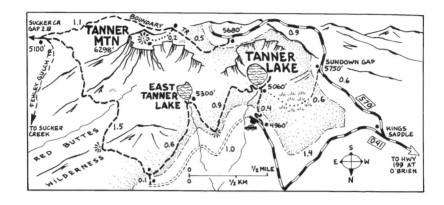

74 Tanner Lakes

Easy (to the lakes)
2.6 miles round-trip
350 feet elevation gain
Open late May through November
Use: hikers, horses
Map: Oregon Caves (USGS)

Difficult (to Tanner Mountain)
8.3-mile loop
1700 feet elevation gain
Open early June to mid-November

This pair of green mountain lakes set in side-by-side, cliff-rimmed cirques makes a clever destination for hikers with children. If the kids seem tired when they reach lake number one, declare victory there. If they're still antsy, push on to the huckleberry fields at lake number two. And if you're hiking without children, the ticket is to continue up Tanner Mountain for a birds-eye view of the lakes and the whole Siskiyou range. The mountain and the lakes were named for Illinois Valley miner Ezra Sherman Tanner after his death in 1877, but were mistakenly labeled "Tannen" by the Forest Service from the early 1900s to 2012.

To start, drive Highway 199 south of Grants Pass 35.5 miles (or north of Crescent City 50.5 miles). South of Cave Junction 7 miles, between mileposts 35 and 36, turn east on Waldo Road. Follow this route 5 miles to a crossroads, go straight on paved Happy Camp Road for 12.5 miles to a high pass, and turn left at a "Tanner Lakes" pointer onto a one-lane gravel road. Watch your odometer from here, because junctions are poorly marked. After 0.8 mile, fork to the right. After another 0.6 mile keep left at a fork. At a junction 0.4 mile farther on, turn right. In another 2.4 miles ignore the Bolan Campground turnoff, and instead keep right for 3.3 miles to a fork in Kings Saddle. Then keep left for 1.4 miles to a parking area where the road ends at a washed out culvert. Walk back 100 feet along the road to the trailhead.

The trail angles up through a forest of big Douglas firs with orange paintbrush,

East Tanner Lake from Tanner Mountain.   Opposite: Tanner Lake.

blue Oregon grape, incense cedar, and acorn-bearing tanoak bushes. After a mere 0.4 mile you'll reach Tanner Lake, a large but fairly shallow round pool in a steep-walled, forested amphitheater. Several gaps in the shore's alder brush provide good lake access.

Head left across Tanner Lake's outlet creek to find a 0.9-mile trail through nice huckleberry patches to East Tanner Lake, a smaller but scenic twin with lots of small jumping fish. Thick alder brush allows only one small access path to the shore itself, where you can look across the lake to the cliffs of Tanner Mountain.

To climb Tanner Mountain, continue past East Tanner Lake for 2.1 nearly level miles to a ridge end, turn right on the Boundary Trail, and climb steeply 1.1 mile to the trail's crest in a small grassy meadow of yellow sulphur flowers. Leave the trail here and walk up through the meadow to the right 300 yards to Tanner Mountain's rocky summit. The view here includes (from right to left), East Tanner Lake, the Illinois Valley, a patch of Pacific Ocean, M-shaped Preston Peak, the crumpled canyons of the lower Klamath River, the Marble Mountains' highlands, snowy Mt. Shasta, and Red Buttes' double-humped summit.

To return on a loop, continue on the Boundary Trail 0.5 mile to a trailhead on Road 570. Ideally, a shuttle car will be waiting for you here. (To drive here from the other trailhead, simply return 1.4 miles to Kings Saddle, and turn left on Road 570 for 1.5 miles.) If you don't have two cars you could simply turn right and walk 2.9 miles along the road to your car. But if you've brought a compass and some route-finding skills, there's a shortcut. Walk just 0.9 mile along the road to a pullout at Sundown Gap, turn right past a boulder, and follow an abandoned roadbed 0.2 mile into a meadow. When the old road peters out, follow your compass due east down through the meadow (and some woods) for 0.4 mile to the Tanner Lake Trail. Then turn left to return to your car.

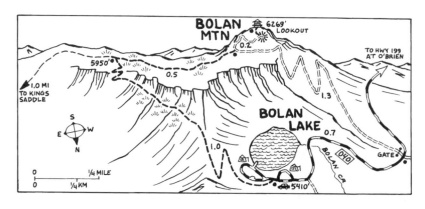

BOLAN
MTN
6269'
LOOKOUT
0.2
5950'
0.5
1.0 MI
TO KINGS
SADDLE
TO HWY 199
AT O'BRIEN
1.3
BOLAN
LAKE
0.7
1.0
GATE
BOLAN CR.
H2O
5410'
S
E — W
N
0   ¼ MILE
0   ¼ KM

Bolan Lake from Bolan Mountain.   Opposite: Bolan Mountain's lookout.

75 Bolan Mountain

Moderate
3.4 miles round-trip
860 feet elevation gain
Open early June to mid-November
Use: hikers, horses, bicycles

A well-graded trail from a campground at a quiet mountain lake climbs past patches of wildflowers to a lookout atop this panoramic Siskiyou summit.

The names of Bolan Mountain and nearby Bolan Creek date to Southern Oregon's 1853 gold rush, when cagey entrepreneurs sought to lure gold dust from entertainment-starved miners by building a bowling alley at the confluence of Sucker Creek and *Bowling* Creek (as it was then called). Indians burned the entire establishment to the ground, but the determined bowlers returned in 1857, carrying 30 balls and 20 pins on their backs over a mountain trail. To drive here, take Highway 199 south of Grants Pass 35.5 miles (or north of Crescent City 50.5 miles). South of Cave Junction 7 miles, between mileposts 35 and 36, turn east on Waldo Road. Follow this route 5 miles to a crossroads, go straight on paved Happy Camp Road for 12.5 miles to a high pass, and turn left at a "Bolan Lake Campground " pointer onto a one-lane gravel road. Take the uphill fork at the first two junctions you meet along this poorly signed road, but go downhill to the right at the 1.8-mile mark. After another 2.4 miles a "Bolan Lake Campground " arrow points left onto Road 040. Follow it 1.8 miles down to the lake and keep left through the campground for 200 yards to a trailhead message board on the left. Park just beyond at a wide spot in the road.

The trail climbs through a forest of flat-needled grand fir. Notice that the trunks are draped with three kinds of lichen: a shaggy black variety, the bright yellow *Letharia*, and the gray-green matted hair of *Alectoria*, or witch's hair. Lichens don't sap trees, but instead collect nutrients solely from the air and rain. This explains why they cannot live below the winter snowpack—which must be 5 feet deep here, judging from the height of lichen on these trees.

After 0.4 mile the forest shifts to mountain hemlock. Small rocky meadows bloom with purple asters, orange paintbrush, and lavender penstemon. The trail switchbacks up a cliffy rim to a junction at the 1-mile mark in a field of yellow sulphur flowers. Turn right for a nearly level half mile to the Bolan Mountain Road and follow it 400 yards left to the summit lookout. The towerless cabin has a railed deck that makes a good lunch spot. The view includes not only Bolan Lake, but nearly all of the Illinois Valley, a large swath of Pacific Ocean, most Siskiyou peaks, and distant Mt. Shasta.

The cabin can be rented for $40 a night from July through September (see page 172 for details). In summer the cabin's access road is locked, and only renters are given the key.

Private Lake.   Below: Black Butte.

76   Polar Bear Gap

Moderate (to Polar Bear Gap)
5.2 miles round-trip
1000 feet elevation gain
Open mid-June to mid-November
Use: hikers, horses

Difficult (to Private Lake)
14.3-mile loop
3600 feet elevation gain

This corner of California's Siskiyou Wilderness is so remote it's accessed via Oregon. A well-graded trail traverses Black Butte's dry forests to Polar Bear Gap, a bare saddle strewn with bright red, green, and white rocks. Views extend east to Mt. Shasta. For a grander adventure, however, continue on a much rougher loop trail across Twin Valley to a rarely visited cirque lake surrounded by the crags of The Lieutenants. If you plan on using a campfire, be sure to pick up a permit from the Forest Service ranger stations in Cave Junction or Gasquet.

To find the trailhead, drive Highway 199 south of Grants Pass 35.5 miles (or north of Crescent City 50.5 miles). South of Cave Junction 7 miles (and between mileposts 35 and 36), turn east on Waldo Road. Follow this route 5 miles to a crossroads, turn right on Bridgeview-Takilma Road for 3.7 miles to the end of pavement, fork left on one-lane Road 4904 for 1.6 miles, and fork to the right across a bridge onto one-lane gravel Road 4906. Then simply follow the largest road at junctions for 9.6 miles until you reach the trailhead, where you'll find parking pullouts on both shoulders.

The Black Butte Trail starts at a small message board on the right. The path sets off along a broad, dry ridge of serpentine—a shiny greenish rock that creates such mineral-poor soils that only a scattering of small Douglas fir, incense cedar, and Jeffrey pine can survive. Ahead looms the massive dark plug of Black Butte. Before long the trail traverses the mountain's slopes through cooler woods of Shasta red fir, droopy-limbed Brewer's weeping spruce, and Port Orford cedar. In all, this area has quite an odd jumble of tree species.

After 1.8 miles keep left at a fork marking the start of the long loop. In another 0.4 mile you'll pass a patch of huge, blue gentian blooms and come to a miraculously cold, clear, delicious spring that gushes out of the ground 6 inches wide. Then continue 0.4 mile to Polar Bear Gap, a stark saddle beneath the craggy tower of Polar Bear Mountain. Far to the east, Marble Mountain looks like a white brick dropped onto the horizon beside Mt. Shasta.

Polar Bear Gap makes a good turnaround point, but if you're geared for a longer loop on faint, rugged trails, sally onward into the Wilderness. The path switchbacks gently downward six times before giving up and tumbling straight down the hill. Following feeble rock cairns, skirt Twin Valley's grassy upper meadow and continue down to the lower meadow, where the trail gives out altogether. Expect to search a bit for the continuation of the trail—and expect to be disappointed when you find it. From the right-hand side of the middle of this long, lower meadow, the path launches straight up a steep, rocky hillside to the right, as graceless as a bobsled run in a quarry.

After 2.1 more miles of up-and-down hiking—and just 250 yards beyond a meadow with a marshy pond—look for a large rock cairn. Here, veer left on a faint trail for 200 yards to lovely, swimmable Private Lake. The commanding crags surrounding this first-class pond are The Lieutenants, standing guard for El Capitan to the south.

To complete the loop, return to the main trail, turn left, and then keep right at all junctions. You'll cross a pass, descend to an old road , follow it right 0.2 mile, turn right for 0.5 mile alongside grassy Youngs Valley, and turn right at a "Black Butte Trail" pointer for a relatively easy 2.4-mile hillside tour back to the start of the loop. Then turn left for 1.8 miles to your car.

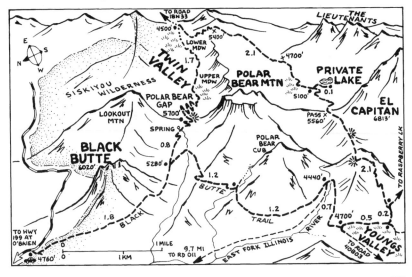

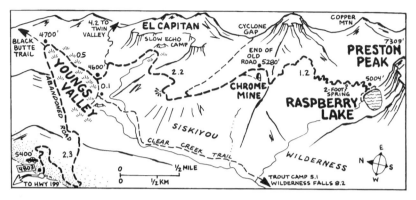

Raspberry Lake.   Opposite: Youngs Valley.

77   Raspberry Lake

Difficult
12.4 miles round-trip
2300 feet elevation gain
Open mid-June to mid-November

Nestled against the cliffs of the Siskiyou Wilderness' highest peak, this deep lake is fringed with sweet-smelling mountain azalea blooms in July. A massive marble outcropping on one shore makes a dramatic base for fishing or chilly swimming.

Such a beautiful spot would be more crowded if the hike were easier. The first 5 miles of the route follow an ancient roadbed to the ruins of an old chrome mine. From there a rugged path scrambles 1.2 miles to the lake. Black bears are common, so remember to hang food 10 feet high at night. Permits are required only for campfires or camp stoves, and are available at the Gasquet Ranger Station 18 miles east of Crescent City.

To find the trailhead, drive Highway 199 south of Grants Pass 48 miles (or north of Crescent City 33 miles). South of the Siskiyou summit tunnel 3.5 miles (at milepost 30.12), turn east on Knopki Creek Road 18N07. Follow this one-lane, gravel road 13.7 miles to a T-shaped junction. Then turn right on Road 4803 for 1.1 rough miles to a parking area at road's end.

Start hiking down a barricaded old road. Colorful rocks strewn along the route include green serpentine, red peridotite, and white marble. Despite poor soils and the high elevation, the struggling forest here includes Douglas fir, grand fir, Shasta red fir, and white pine. The underbrush of tanoak and manzanita bushes is well adapted to tolerate fierce winters and bone-dry summers. Across the valley rise the landmarks of the Siskiyou Wilderness: El Capitan (on the left) and Preston Peak (on the right, with snow).

After a 2.8-mile downhill march, the road/trail curves around flat, grassy Youngs Valley for half a mile. Wild roses and incense cedar trees rim this broad field. The road forks at the meadow's far end. Veer left here and follow the increasingly rocky road another 2.2 miles as it climbs past the cliffs of El Capitan. Ignore small side trails to Twin Valley and Cyclone Gap.

The road ends at the old Cyclone Gap chrome mine with tailings piles, collapsed shacks, tunnel entrances, and ore cart rails. Keep left to continue on a narrow, rocky, up-and-down trail. After a mile on this maddeningly rugged path, listen for the gurgle of a spring just below the trail. Surrounded by big orange tiger lilies and lady ferns, an amazing, delicious fountain bubbles out of the ground and flows just 2 feet before vanishing without a trace.

Beyond the spring 0.2 mile the path crashes down to Raspberry Lake, a mountain paradise that makes it all worth while. Although no raspberries grow here, wild ones do ripen along the trail at Youngs Valley in September.

78 Devils Punchbowl

Easy (to Buck Lake)
3.6 miles round-trip
500 feet elevation gain
Open June to late November

Difficult (to Devils Punchbowl)
10.8 miles round-trip
1650 feet elevation gain

The color of sapphires and emeralds, Devils Punchbowl Lake is surrounded by a breathtaking, cliff-walled coliseum of stone. The trail to this Shangri-La, however, is breathtaking in other ways as well. After hiking four miles and switchbacking up an exceedingly steep ridge, visitors have to follow cairns across an eerie, bedrock granite valley. This is why many people opt instead for the simpler stroll to Buck Lake, a less dramatic goal.

If you insist on tenting in the Devils Punchbowl's bare granite basin, be sure to bring a stove so you're not tempted to scavenge scarce, scenic wood for a fire. Also bring plastic bags to pack out toilet paper, because it can't be buried in solid rock. This fragile area's popularity may bring more restrictions. So far, permits are required only for campfires. The permits are available at the ranger station in Gasquet, 18 miles east of Crescent City.

To find the trailhead, take Highway 199 north of Crescent City 28 miles (or south of Grants Pass 53 miles). South of the Siskiyou summit tunnel 9 miles (at milepost 24.85), turn east on Little Jones Creek Road 17N05. Stick to this one-lane paved road for 10 miles. Then turn left and keep left on gravel Road 16N02, following "Doe Flat" pointers 3.5 miles to a gravel parking area at road's end *(GPS location N41°48.850' W123°42.425')*.

The trail sets off across a cliffy slope, down an abandoned roadbed that has been narrowed by rockslides to a trail. Views extend to the peaks of the high Siskiyous. Trees here include largish Douglas fir, Port Orford cedar, and vine maple. After 0.6 mile the roadbed ahead has been blocked by boulders, but a

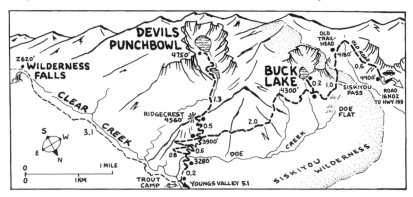

Devils Punchbowl Lake.   Opposite: Buck Lake.

nice new trail contours to the right. The understory here includes thimbleberry, wild hazel , and vanilla leaf.

After a mile on the new trail you'll climb to a junction. Up to the right 0.2 mile is Buck Lake — a good goal if you've brought kids. Backed with cliffs and ringed by forest, the lake has woodsy campsites, a gravelly beach, blooming mountain azaleas along the shore, and a fair supply of jumping fish.

For the more spectacular goal of the Devils Punchbowl, however, keep straight past the Buck Lake junction. This route contours 2 miles to a trail junction on a rocky ridge. Turn right for a steep, switchbacking, half-mile climb to a ridgecrest. Here the path sets off across a bare landscape of speckled granite — much of it cooked by tectonic pressure to stripey gneiss and then polished smooth by Ice Age glaciers. Following rock cairns, you'll pass a small lake before reaching trail's end at a large lake that's so deep and clear the boulders in its depths look like looming whales.

Other Hiking Options

A longer hike leads to a swimmable pool at the base of 50-foot Wilderness Falls. At the junction for the steep ridge trail to Devils Punchbowl, switchback downhill 0.8 mile, continue 0.2 mile past Doe Creek, and turn right on the Clear Creek Trail. This path promptly crosses the bouldery creek (an easy hop in summer) and ambles down through creekside woods 3.1 miles to the falls. Save energy for the 7.7-mile return trip to your car, because it's uphill.

Some old-growth trees on the shore of Babyfoot Lake survived the 2002 Biscuit Fire.

79   Babyfoot Lake

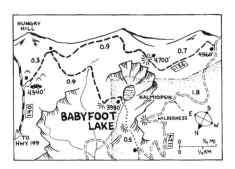

Easy (to Babyfoot Lake)
2.4 miles round-trip
360 feet elevation **loss**
Open May to mid-December
Use: hikers, horses

Moderate (also to viewpoint)
4.2-miles round-trip
760 feet elevation gain

A sprawling land of rugged canyons, rare plants, and ancient gold mines, the remote Kalmiopsis Wilderness was overswept in 2002 by one of the largest wildfires in Oregon's history. In most places the fire merely burned away the brush, poison oak, and small trees, leaving the forest healthier and tidier than before. Some valleys were skipped by the flames altogether.

Here on the Wilderness' eastern rim the fire roared up the ridgecrests, killing virtually every tree. The short trail to Babyfoot Lake starts at a sad clearcut, where poorly supervised "salvage" loggers mistakenly cut 17 acres of this protected botanical area in 2005. Then the path traverses a much healthier, naturally recovering forest of silver snags and young seedlings. The lake itself is a green oasis, where a pocket of cool, damp air saved a narrow circle of ancient cedars. For a broader view, climb to a clifftop above the lake, where you can see the patchwork of trees left by the fire.

To start, drive Highway 199 south of Grants Pass 24 miles (or north of Cave Junction 5 miles). At milepost 24, turn west onto Eight Dollar Road, following a pointer marked "Kalmiopsis Wilderness Area 17." After 0.9 mile you might stop to hike a short boardwalk to a bog of pitcher plants (Hike #80). Then continue on the main paved road, which narrows, crosses the Illinois River at the 3-mile mark, and then climbs for another 12 gravel miles. At a fork in a pass, veer left on Road 140 for 0.7 mile to a well-marked gravel parking lot on the right *(GPS location N42°13.475' W123°47.579')*.

The trail sets off along a slope with Douglas fir stumps and lots of robust volunteer seedlings. Soon you enter the zone of snags from the 2002 fire. The blooms of beargrass, vanilla leaf, and Oregon grape are prospering in the extra sun.

After 0.3 mile fork to the right, and in another 0.9 mile reach Babyfoot Lake. This green pool, ringed with cream-colored mountain azaleas in May, preserved an odd assortment of trees: long-needled Jeffrey pines, Brewer's weeping spruces (with weirdly drooping branches), and three varieties of cedars (Port Orford, incense, and western red).

Clearcut at the trailhead.

If you'd like a longer hike to a higher viewpoint, walk back 0.9 mile toward your car, turn right at a signed junction in a pass, and follow a fainter path up a ridgecrest 0.9 mile. As you climb this rocky ridge, panoramic views open up from the snowy Siskiyous in the south to the patchwork forests of the Kalmiopsis in the north. Make your goal a clifftop overlooking Babyfoot Lake.

Other Options

Adventurers with routefinding skills (and a global positioning device) can bushwhack past Babyfoot Lake on a 5.4-mile loop. When you first reach the lake turn right along the shore, cross the outlet creek 100 feet from the lake, and bushwhack onward, keeping level for 0.5 mile to a dirt road *(GPS location N42°13.507' W123°48.558')*. Turn left on this mining track 1.8 miles to a rock cairn and a sign on the left marking a trail *(GPS location N42°12.760' W123°48.809')*. Follow this path straight up a steep slope to the left for 0.7 mile to a clifftop viewpoint above Babyfoot Lake. Continue 1.2 miles to return to your car.

Viewpoint above Babyfoot Lake.

80 Eight Dollar Mountain

Easy (boardwalk trail)
0.6 miles round-trip
100 feet elevation gain
Open all year

Easy (Little Illinois River Falls)
0.9-mile loop
160 feet elevation gain

Almost perfectly conical, 3-mile-wide Eight Dollar Mountain looks like a young volcano, but it's actually an erosional remnant that includes some of Oregon's oldest rocks. The reddish peridotite and greenish serpentine here began as seafloor rock more than 200 million years ago. These rocks produce a soil so infertile that plants have struggled to adapt. As a result, Eight Dollar Mountain is an island of botanical diversity, home to odd bogs and rare flowers.

The mountain's name dates to the 1850s gold rush, and most likely recalls a nugget unearthed along the Illinois River at the mountain's base.

With the purchase of 650 acres by the Oregon Parks and Recreation Department in 2008, all of Eight Dollar Mountain is now in public or nonprofit ownership. One recreation proposal would build an 8-mile loop trail around the peak. In the meantime, the mountain's two best trails are a boardwalk to a viewpoint and a loop to a churning chute on the Illinois River. If you like, you can connect the two walks by taking a 1.4-mile path along the river.

To find the boardwalk trail from Grants Pass, follow signs toward Crescent City 24 miles on Highway 199. At milepost 24 (beyond Selma 4 miles), turn right on Eight Dollar Road for 0.9 mile to a large parking area on the left. Then walk up a paved road to the right 200 yards to find the start of the 0.2-mile boardwalk. (If you have a disabled parking permit, you can drive to this upper trailhead.)

The landscape here is strange in many ways. Although Eight Dollar Mountain receives more than 60 inches of rain a year, the rock has so few nutrients that the Jeffrey pine trees here are sparse and stunted. Some slopes resemble a desert.

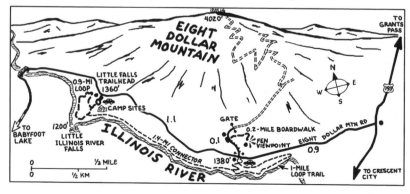

The cone-shaped mountain has virtually no creeks. Instead runoff oozes downhill through vast fens, boggy slopes punctuated with the baseball-bat shapes of *Darlingtonia* pitcher plants. The viewpoint at trail's end overlooks a fen with these plants. *Darlingtonia* lures insects into its hooded throat and dissolves them to provide nitrogen and other nutrients that the soil lacks.

For another short hike in this area, return to your car and drive 1.1 mile farther west on Eight Dollar Mountain Road. Turn left at a sign for the Little Falls Trailhead, park, and walk down the paved loop of a small campground. The three campsites here are $10 a night, but have no water.

Take a trail at the right-hand side of the campground loop and keep right at junctions for the 0.9-mile hike. This route passes a *Darlingtonia* fen and then parallels the green-pooled Illinois River through a rocky chasm, A 100-foot side trail to the right descends to Little Illinois River Falls, a five-foot drop at the head of the gorge. A stone's throw upstream is a small sandy beach — the best river access. If you swim here, however, beware of the falls downstream!

Other Options

To learn more about the area, sign up for a class or an outing with the Siskiyou Field Institute. Allied with the Southern Oregon University Foundation, this nonprofit group runs the nearby Deer Creek nature study and research center. To find it, drive Highway 199 to the flashing yellow light in Selma (4 miles north of Eight Dollar Mountain Road or 20 miles south of Grants Pass), and turn west on Illinois River Road for 1.4 miles. For course offerings, tuition rates, and lodging prices at the nature center, check *www.thesfi.org* or call 541-597-8530.

Little Illinois River Falls.   *Above:* Darlingtonia.   *Opposite:* Boardwalk trail.

81   Illinois River Beaches

Easy (Kerby Flat and Star Flat)
4.3-mile loop
560 feet elevation gain
Open all year

Easy (3 other beaches)
3 miles round trip
890 feet elevation gain

When summer heat sears Southern Oregon, many people flee here, to the sandy beaches, swimmable green pools, and shady trails of the Illinois River. This dramatic canyon has other attractions as well—weird bogs, whitewater falls, and a spectacular suspension footbridge.

To drive here from Interstate 5 at Grants Pass, follow "Crescent City" signs south on Highway 199 for 20 miles to Selma. At a flashing yellow light, turn right on Illinois River Road for 4.3 paved miles to the well-marked Kerby Flat Trailhead, a paved pullout on the left *(GPS location N42°16.785' W123°41.065')*.

The trail starts at the far right-hand end of a railed viewpoint and descends along a dry, rocky ridge. After 0.6 mile you'll reach a trail junction on a plateau with stunted Douglas firs and Jeffrey pines. To start the loop, turn right. This path descends past viewpoints for another 0.4 mile. Then turn sharply left on a trail that follows the Illinois River upstream, passing swimmable green pools along the way.

After 0.6 mile along the river you'll reach a lovely but shadeless sand-and-gravel beach with the hike's best river access, by the mouth of Deer Creek. It's a nice spot for lunch. When you're ready to continue, follow an abandoned dirt road alongside Deer Creek. After 0.4 mile, look for a trail that climbs the hillside

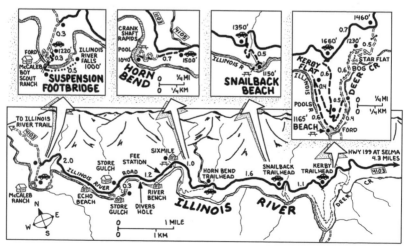

The Illinois River at Kerby Flat.   Opposite: Suspension Footbridge.

to the left. This is the loop route back to your car. But before heading back it's worth continuing along the road to see Star Flat's bog of insect-catching pitcher plants. To find the bog, walk another 0.6 mile along Deer Creek to a large road junction and walk back to the right through a grassy meadow 100 feet.

For the next beach hike, drive another 1.1 mile east on Illinois River Road from the Kerby Flat Trailhead to the Snailback Beach Trailhead, a pullout on the left. The half-mile path here climbs a few feet at first, but then descends a shady ridge and switchbacks down to Snailback Creek's confluence with the Illinois River. There are two beaches here, each with a picnic table and a swimmable pool. The beach to the left is backed by a cliff, while the beach to the right borders a river rapids with a six-foot drop.

One of the river's quietest beaches and best swimming holes is at Horn Bend. To find it from the Snailback Beach Trailhead, drive another 1.6 miles east on Illinois River Road to the Horn Bend Trailhead, a parking pullout on the left. The trail parallels the road for 0.4 mile through woods burned in the 2002 Biscuit Fire. Then you turn left down a steepish cat road, braided at times with bits of trail, for 0.3 mile to two picnic tables shaded by tanoaks beside a broad sandy area. Cross the sand to find the river access, where 15-foot-deep green pools with tiny, darting fish surround rock coves, ledges, and islands.

The final recommended hike is a short path to a suspension footbridge high above the river. To find it from the Horn Bend Trailhead, drive east on Illinois River Road another 4.2 miles (and 2 miles past the crowded Store Gulch picnic/camping/swimming area). Where pavement ends, follow a pointer for the Fall Creek Trailhead straight down dirt Road 087. After 0.2 mile on this rough track, turn left into a large parking area. The trail here switchbacks down 0.3 mile to rejoin Road 087 at the dramatic, 240-foot-long, railed suspension footbridge. Although it is also possible to drive here, the road is rough and parking is tight.

82   Illinois River Trail

Easy (to York Creek)
5 miles round-trip
450 feet elevation gain
Open all year
Use: hikers, horses

Moderate (to Pine Flat)
10.6 miles round-trip
1650 feet elevation gain

Difficult (to Bald Mountain)
20.6-mile loop
4125 feet elevation gain
Open late April to early December

The Illinois River rages through a Wilderness canyon so rugged that the Illinois River Trail has to climb over a 3975-foot mountain just to get through. Following this trail up Bald Mountain is a classic backpacking adventure through some of the wildest country in Oregon. But day hikers can sample the trail's scenery, too—either with an easy walk to York Creek or with a longer hike to Pine Flat, where the green river boils over aptly-named Boat Eater Rapids.

The massive 2002 Biscuit Fire began with a lightning strike at Florence Creek in the midst of this hike's route. Surprisingly, although the blaze overswept the entire area, many of the large trees survived. Even in the small areas where the fire burned so hot that it left only snags, the trees have sprouted back with a vengeance. The pines reseeded naturally. Deciduous trees such as scrub oak, tanoak, and madrone simply sent up fresh shoots from the roots.

From Grants Pass, follow "Crescent City" pointers south on Highway 199 for 20 miles to a flashing yellow light in Selma. Then turn right on Illinois River Road 4103 for a total of 18.6 miles to the road's end and a primitive campground in a patch of severely burned woods at the Briggs Creek Trailhead. Be warned that although this road starts out paved, it turns to gravel after 11 miles and becomes so rough that passenger cars have to be driven quite slowly for the final 7.6 miles.

The trail begins with a 140-foot steel footbridge across bouldery Briggs Creek.

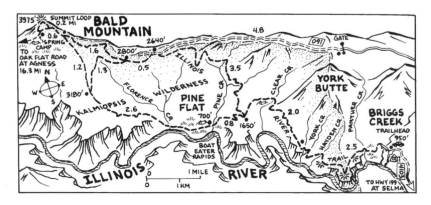

The Illinois River Trail.   Opposite: The Illinois River Trail.

Rusting model T parts and a grassy opening remain from an old homestead. In May and June look for the blooms of pink clarkia ("farewell to spring") and blue, 6-petaled elegant brodiaea. After crossing Panther Creek on a footbridge, the path traverses a slope 300 feet above the Illinois River's roaring gorge. Views continue until the trail's 1.9-mile mark. In another 0.6 mile you'll reach York Creek in a red canyon that's full of sweet-smelling mountain azalea blooms in June. Explore 20 feet up the creek's first fork to find a patch of *Darlingtonia*, the insect-eating pitcher plants that resemble green baseball bats.

This is a good turnaround point for hikers with children. If you're continuing past York Creek you'll climb 2 miles to a ridgetop junction. Turn left here on a steep trail that drops 0.8 mile to Pine Flat, a broad riverside bench. The top attraction here is Boat Eater Rapids, where the Illinois splits around a granite island and drops 6 feet. To find it, strike off to the left 200 yards across a rock-strewn river bar. On hot days, green pools below the rapids invite swimming.

If you're headed to Bald Mountain, continue 0.7 mile to the far end of Pine Flat. After crossing Florence Creek, the path shoots uphill at a staggering grade, gaining 2300 feet in 1.5 miles. Then keep left to follow a ridge to a campsite and spring beside grassy Bald Mountain Prairie. From here a 0.2-mile loop trail visits the actual summit, a rocky area with 360° views. To complete the long loop back to your car on the well-graded Illinois River Trail, keep left at trail junctions as you descend from the summit.

Other Hiking Options

With a car shuttle you can hike the entire 27-mile Illinois River Trail one way. Beyond Bald Mountain the trail ambles past ridgetop bracken meadows for 3 miles before diving 4.7 miles down to scenic Silver Creek. The footbridge here burned in the 2002 fire but is scheduled for replacement. Then the path traces a slope high above the river for 4.4 miles to Indigo Creek and climbs across craggy Buzzards Roost 4.2 miles to the Oak Flat Trailhead near Agness. To drive the 94-mile car shuttle route from Briggs Creek to Oak Flat (via Selma, Grants Pass, and Galice), bring a Siskiyou National Forest map.

83 Grants Pass Nature Trails

Easy (Cathedral Hills)
3.4-mile loop
300 feet elevation gain
Open all year

Easy (Limpy Creek)
1-mile loop
120 feet elevation gain

Easy (Waters Creek)
3.4-mile loop
400 feet elevation gain

These three easy loop trails are close enough together that you could do more than one in a day. Almost within Grants Pass, the Cathedral Hills loop is best when the Indian warrior wildflowers bloom in spring. Limpy Creek has a little waterfall and a loop that's easy enough for kids. The Waters Creek loop extends from a meadow into a canyon of big Douglas fir trees.

To find the Cathedral Hills trailhead, take exit 55 of Interstate 5 at the south end of Grants Pass, follow "Redwood Highway" signs 2.3 miles, and turn left on Highway 238 toward Murphy for 2.8 miles. At a "Cathedral Hills" sign, turn left on Espey Road for 0.3 mile and fork left to stay on Espey Road another 0.3 mile to its end at a parking turnaround—the hub for a 10-mile network of hiking, biking, and equestrian trails.

Logged more than a century ago, the Cathedral Hills now host the state's largest knobcone pine (117 feet tall) and the largest whiteleaf manzanita (25 feet). The slopes here blaze with native wildflowers from April to June: Indian warrior (with clusters of red tubes), purple shooting stars, yellow iris, and orange painbrush. Poison oak is common too, so stay on the trail.

From the parking area, walk past the outhouse 50 feet and fork to the right to set out on a 3.4-mile tour, following "Outback Loop"

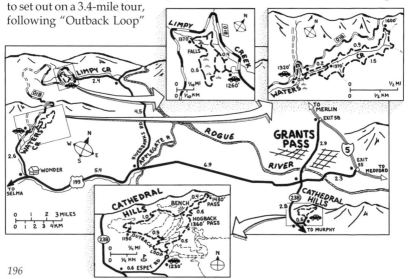

Madrone trees on the Outback Loop at Cathedral Hills.   Opposite: Waters Creek Trail.

signs at junctions. The route climbs 1.1 mile to a pass and turns left along a ridge 0.4 mile to a bench with a view of Grants Pass. Continue 1.9 miles to complete the Outback Loop back to your car.

To find the Limpy Creek trailhead from Interstate 5 at Grants Pass, follow signs for Crescent City on Highway 199 for 10 miles. At the far side of the Applegate River bridge, at milepost 7, turn right onto Riverbanks Road. After 4.5 miles, turn left on paved Limpy Creek Road (which becomes Road 018) for 2.4 miles to the Limpy Botanical Trail parking area on the left.

Limpy was the "white" name given to one of two Indian brothers whose families lived where Limpy Creek joins the Rogue River. Limpy and his brother Cholcultah were among the more than 1400 Takelma, Tututni, and Dakubetede tribespeople rounded up by the U.S. Army after the bloody 1856 Rogue River Indian War and sent to a reservation on the northern Oregon Coast. In 1996, an archeological excavation near the mouth of Limpy Creek found a 600-year-old Indian village with arrowheads, middens, and notched stone fishing net sinkers.

The Limpy Creek Trail starts beside an outhouse and climbs 50 feet to a junction at a kiosk. If you keep left at this and all other junctions, you'll complete a 1-mile loop. The route switchbacks up through a grove of incense cedars and Jeffrey pines to a dry hillside of bluish serpentine rock. Although serpentine is rich in magnesium and iron, it lacks so many other nutrients that it cripples vegetation. Spring wildflowers adapted to the stark slope include elegant brodiaea, fawn lily, shooting star, and yellow iris.

After 0.6 mile the loop trail passes an 8-foot waterfall. The final 0.4 mile back to the car descend along the creek, with lots of places where kids can play at little gravel beaches. If you go off trail, keep an eye out for poison oak .

To find the hike at Waters Creek, drive back to Highway 199 at the Applegate River bridge and turn right toward Crescent City for 5.4 miles. Half a mile past the store in the settlement of Wonder, turn right on Waters Creek Road for 1.9 miles of pavement and another 0.7 mile of one-lane gravel to the trailhead on the left*(GPS location N42°23.409' W123°32.649')*. Vandals often destroy signs here.

The trail follows the creek up to a culvert by a pond and then ambles through a white oak grassland with mint, balsamroot, and bachelor buttons. Keep left at junctions for the full 3.4-mile loop, a route that follows the creek up a canyon amid a forest with big Douglas firs five feet in diameter. The path loops back on the far side of the creek's canyon. Keep left to return to your car.

84 Taylor Creek

Easy (to Big Pine)
0.8-mile loop
60 feet elevation gain
Open all year
Use: hikers, horses, bikes

Moderate (to Tin Can Campground)
3.6 miles round-trip
1130 feet elevation gain

Difficult (entire trail, with shuttle)
10.1 miles one way
1700 feet elevation gain

Big Pine.

Conveniently located near Grants Pass, this all-year trail traces Taylor Creek to a forested pass and then descends past Big Pine Campground, home of the world's tallest ponderosa pine. Although the path is 10.1 miles long, it touches Taylor Creek Road every few miles, so most visitors sample shorter segments.

For an easy introduction to the area, try Big Pine Campground's collection of little loop trails—all less than a mile long. To drive there from Interstate 5, take Merlin exit 61 just north of Grants Pass, follow signs 3.6 miles to Merlin, continue straight 8.5 miles toward Galice, turn left onto Briggs Valley Road 25 for 12.5 miles, turn right at the Big Pine Campground entrance, and keep right for 200 yards to a day-use parking area and map board on the left.

From here a packed gravel path crosses 15-foot-wide Meyers Creek on a footbridge (see inset map). Keep straight for 200 feet to find Big Pine. This ponderosa's double top soars 252 feet high (although the sign says 259). It was one of many pine seedlings that sprouted after a major fire some 300 years ago. Douglas firs later grew up beneath them, and the firs' cooler shade fostered a host of smaller plants, including vanilla leaf, pathfinder, Oregon grape, and wild hazel. The world's tallest ponderosa, a 268-footer, is in a different, unmarked grove a few dozen miles south. From Big Pine you can either go left for a 0.4-mile loop back to your car, or you can turn right for 0.5- or 0.8-mile loops.

For a more substantial hike, start at the beginning of the Taylor Creek Trail. To

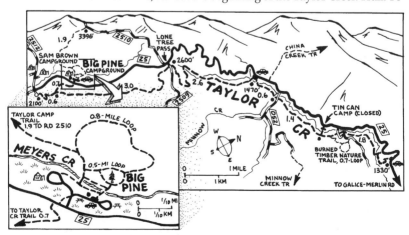

find this trailhead, drive as to Big Pine Campground, but go up Briggs Valley Road only 3.1 miles to a pullout on the left with a large "Taylor Creek Trailhead" sign. This route is known to mountain bikers as the Jedi Trail.

The path descends through a second-growth forest of Douglas fir, madrone, and live oak. Then it follows an ancient roadbed upstream along the creek past an old homestead meadow. At the half-mile mark the path crosses the creek on a 60-foot footbridge. Anchored logs in the streams are part of a project to create pools for fish habitat. Placer mining claim notices tacked to creekside alders and maples prove that the area's 1800s gold rush isn't entirely dead.

Next the trail traces the creek through a forested canyon for 1.3 miles to a footbridge that spans the creek to the site of the closed Tin Can Campground. This is a good turnaround point if you're hiking with children.

If you're continuing, the trail ambles along the creek 2 miles to the next trailhead, then promptly crosses two rushing forks of the creek and climbs 2.6 miles to another trailhead atop Lone Tree Pass. Beyond this, the trail follows a dry, wooded ridge 3 miles to a junction, where a spur to the right drops 0.7 mile to Big Pine Campground.

Other Hiking Options

Four side trails connect with the Taylor Creek Trail. The 0.7-mile Burned Timber Nature Trail is an easy interpretive loop on a hillside of meadows and recovering forest near the site of former Tin Can Campground. Three more difficult side trails (the China Creek, Minnow Creek, and Taylor Camp Trails) scramble faintly up steep, dry ridges to gravel logging roads.

85 Briggs Creek

Easy (to ford)
4.8 miles round-trip
210 feet elevation **loss**
Open all year
Use: hikers, horses, bikes

Moderate (to Onion Creek)
7.8 miles round-trip
Open except in high water
600 feet elevation **loss**

Briggs Creek ford.

Starting at a gold mining ghost town, the trail along this mountain stream west of Grants Pass passes old hydraulic mines and crosses a flume ditch on its way to an abandoned miner's cabin. And yet this is not just a path for mining history buffs. The valley's old-growth forest and lovely creekside scenery have survived the area's rough-and-tumble gold rush era surprisingly well.

From Interstate 5 just north of Grants Pass, take Merlin exit 61, follow signs 3.6 miles to Merlin, continue straight 8.5 miles toward Galice, and then turn left onto paved, one-lane Briggs Valley Road 25 for 13.4 miles. A mile after Big Pine Campground, turn right on Road 2512 for 0.3 mile. Then turn left into the Sam

Brown Campground entrance and keep left for 200 yards. Just before the two picnic shelters, pull into a large trailhead parking lot on the right.

The meadow here is all that remains of Briggs, a gold mining boomtown that

Sam Brown Campground.

once boasted a hotel, barber shop, brothel, and bar. A gravesite near the picnic shelters commemorates one of the first black men in Southern Oregon, Sam Brown, a barkeeper who was shot for allegedly "messing with miners' wives."

From the parking area, the trail sets off through creekside Douglas firs and big ponderosa pines. In early summer expect a carpet of inside-out flowers (delicate white blooms dangling from 6-inch stalks) and tiny 6- or 7-pointed white starflowers. Also notice pathfinder plant, whose arrow-shaped leaves have a silvery underside that points the way any off-trail traveler has gone.

After 0.4 mile hop across Dutchy Creek. In another 0.3 mile, join dirt Road 017 and follow it left for 600 yards. When the path resumes, it briefly crosses two old clearcuts before launching into uncut woods with 6-foot-thick Douglas firs, sweeping creekside red cedars, and twisted little yews. At the 2.1-mile mark, pass a campsite with rusty hydraulic mining equipment marking the Elkhorn Mine. Another 0.3 mile beyond, the trail fords Briggs Creek—a good turnaround spot if you don't want to take off your boots. The creek is cold, 30 feet wide, and calf-deep even in summer. After winter rainstorms, it's too deep to wade at all.

On the far shore, the trail climbs gradually through drier woods of tanoak and madrone for 1.3 miles before descending steeply past an abandoned flume ditch and several huge sugarpines to another ford of Briggs Creek. To the left 100 yards is a dilapidated one-room shake cabin—a good goal for a moderate hike. The mossy creekbank here, overhung with bigleaf maples, makes a nice lunch spot.

Other Hiking Options

Explorers will want to look behind the cabin's porch for a trail angling up the wooded hillside to the right. This path climbs 100 yards to a junction atop a rocky ridgecrest. To the left, orange dots on trees mark the Onion Creek Trail, which climbs to an abandoned flume ditch and follows it up the canyon 1.8 miles to Road 224, passing active placer claims along the way.

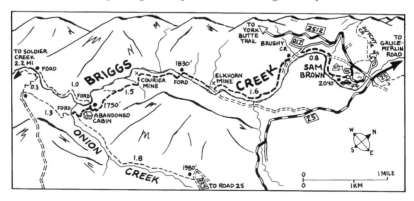

Easy (to Rainie Falls)
4.2 miles round-trip
180 feet elevation gain
Open all year

Moderate (to Whisky Creek)
7 miles round-trip
300 feet elevation gain

Difficult (Grave Creek to Marial)
23.2 miles one way
2800 feet elevation gain

The Whisky Creek Cabin.

At times the irascible Rogue River idles along in lazy green pools, but elsewhere it's misty mayhem, plunging over Rainie Falls or boiling through Mule Creek Canyon's Coffeepot. During the peak whitewater season from May 15 to October 15, the 40-mile stretch between Grave Creek and Illahe has become such a popular float trip for kayakers and rafters that a lottery is held to issue 120 permits a day from a total of 90,000 applications.

Why not hike through this spectacular canyon instead? Trails along the Rogue River offer the same scenery without the crowds or the permit hassles. Day hikers can sample the canyon's eastern end with an easy walk to the 15-foot cascade at Rainie Falls. A longer day hike reaches the Whisky Creek Cabin, a gold miner's shack from 1880 restored as a rustic museum. Backpackers continuing west on the 40-mile Rogue River Trail should bring stoves because campfires are only allowed within 400 feet of the river if they're kept in firepans. At night, hang food at least 10 feet high and 5 feet from a tree trunk to discourage black bears.

To find the eastern trailheads at the Grave Creek bridge, take Interstate 5 north of Grants Pass 4 miles to Merlin exit 61, follow signs 3.6 miles to Merlin, and continue straight for 18.5 paved miles down the Rogue River. Beyond the settlement of Galice 7 miles (and 4.5 miles past the Rand Visitor Center), park on the right just before a high bridge across the Rogue River at Grave Creek.

The easy Rainie Falls Trail starts on the left-hand side of the road just before the bridge. Although this 2.1-mile trail does not connect to the 40-mile Rogue River Trail, it's gentler and much shadier, so it's a better choice if you've brought kids or if the weather is hot.

After 0.3 mile on the Rainie Falls Trail you'll pass Grave Creek Rapids, a rock-walled chute where boaters flail. At a cliffy narrows at the 1.2-mile mark, look for a sign on the far shore marking the 1964 flood's astonishing high-water level, 55 feet above normal. Just beyond are the cement piers of Sanderson's Bridge, a miner's mule bridge from 1907 swept away by a 1927 flood. The trail ends at Rainie Falls, where most boats are lined around the falls through a channel blasted out of the rock on the far shore for migrating fish. A small sandy beach here makes a nice picnic spot.

For longer hikes you'll need to start on the river's north shore instead. When you're driving here from Merlin, continue across the high river bridge and turn left down to a boat ramp and parking area.

The Rogue River near Grave Creek.   Opposite page: Rogue River jet boat.

Mossy, gnarled canyon live oak trees provide a few spots of shade along this eastern portion of the Rogue River Trail. Western fence lizards do push-ups on rocks, warning other lizards away from their territory. Expect tall blue wildflowers in May: cluster lily and 6-petaled elegant brodiaea. Beware of poison oak along the trail.

Hike 1.8 miles to Rainie Falls—although this shore doesn't have as good a view as the south bank. Then continue on the main trail 1.6 miles, pass a cluster of popular campsites at a sandy beach, and cross Whisky Creek on a footbridge. Here a spur to the right leads up to the historic two-room log cabin, with its collection of rusty mining memorabilia. Note the 1890 flume ditch just uphill.

Backpackers continuing to Marial will find that the Rogue River Trail mostly traverses rocky slopes high above the river, but there are several attractions. Just 0.4 mile past Whisky Creek is Big Slide Camp, a quiet riverside tent area where a late 1800s landslide briefly dammed the Rogue, backing it up 15 miles. Attractions farther down the trail include Horseshoe Bend's dramatic river loop, Western author Zane Grey's 1926 log cabin at Winkle Bar, and the restored 1903 Rogue River Ranch museum beside the Marial trailhead.

If you'd like to stay in commercial lodges along this route, expect to pay about $150 per person per night, including meals. For the first night out, reserve well in advance at Black Bar Lodge (541-479-6507), and for the second night, aim for Marial Lodge (541-471-3262 in summer; otherwise 541-474-2057). Note that Black Bar Lodge is across the river, so you must arrange a time between 4pm

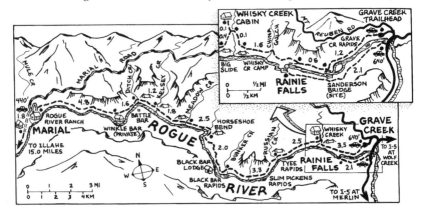

and 6pm for them to pick you up by boat.

Shuttling a car from the Grave Creek trailhead to Marial requires a 35-mile drive, described in Hike #87.

Other Options

If you'd really rather float the Rogue—usually a 3-day whitewater trip from Grave Creek to Illahe—you'll need a permit between May 15 and October 15. Applications are accepted between December 1 and January 31 at *www.blm.gov/ or/resources/recreation/rogue.* If you don't win a permit, you can plan a trip for the off-season's iffy weather or pay for a commercially guided trip (at least $500).

87 Rogue River Trail West

Easy (Marial to Paradise Lodge)
6.6 miles round-trip
200 feet elevation gain
Open April to December

Difficult (Marial to Illahe)
15.6 miles one way
950 feet elevation gain

At Inspiration Point, the trail through the Rogue River's wilderness canyon has been blasted out of sheer basalt cliffs. Hundreds of feet below, kayaks and rafts drift through green-pooled chasms toward the roar of Blossom Bar's whitewater. In other places the river trail ducks into forested side canyons with waterfalls. Sometimes the path emerges at grassy river bars with ancient ranch cabins and gnarled oaks. Hikers always share this wilderness gorge with the plentiful wildlife drawn by the river—kingfishers, black bears, deer, and eagles.

The eastern portion of the 40-mile Rogue River Trail is described in Hike #86. This western segment crosses the Wild Rogue Wilderness, with the river's wildest rapids and narrowest canyons. It also passes commercial lodges where hikers can stop for a meal or a night—or catch a jet boat to Gold Beach. A few warnings: Avoid August, when the rocky, exposed slopes often shimmer with 100° F heat. Poison oak is common. Backpackers should bring a stove because campfires are only allowed in no-trace firepans. At night, hang food bags at least 10 feet high and 5 feet from a tree trunk to discourage black bears.

The river's name comes from the Takelma and Tututni Indians, whom the early French trappers called *coquins* (rogues). When gold attracted white interlopers, the tribes retaliated in 1855 by massacring settlers. The Army pursued the Indians to this remote canyon, where the soldiers were besieged by a superior force of well-armed warriors. The Army's trenches are still visible above the trail at Illahe's Big Bend Pasture. Relief troops from the east turned back when Indians rolled rocks on them from the steep slopes above Solitude Bar. When soldiers from Gold Beach arrived, however, more than a thousand Indians were taken

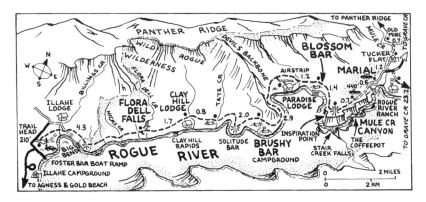

captive and forcibly moved 150 miles north to the Siletz Reservation.

Today hikers can sample the Rogue River Trail's most dramatic scenery on an easy 3.3-mile walk from Marial to Paradise Lodge. To find the trailhead from Interstate 5, drive 4 miles north of Grants Pass to Merlin exit 61, follow signs 3.6 miles into Merlin, and continue straight another 18.6 miles along the Rogue River through Galice. Beyond the Rand Visitor Center 4.6 miles, at the far end of a high bridge, turn briefly downhill to the left toward the Grave Creek Launch Site, but then fork uphill to the right on one-lane paved Mt. Reuben Road.

After climbing 4.3 miles on Mt. Reuben Road, pavement ends. Fork to the right on gravel Road 34-8-1 for 10.3 miles to a T-shaped junction, turn right for 0.6 mile to another T-shaped junction, and and turn left on paved road 32-8-31, following signs for Marial. After another 5 miles, fork left. The final 15 miles down to Marial starts out paved, but turns to gravel and narrows to one lane.

As you approach Marial, you might detour briefly left at a sign for the Rogue

Hikers at Inspiration Point.

THE ROGUE RIVER churns through Mule Creek Canyon
(Hike #87) toward The Coffeepot and Inspiration Point.

CRATER LAKE and Cloudcap from Sun Notch (Hike #29).

Townsend's chipmunk

Golden-mantled ground squirrel

CRATER LAKE NATIONAL PARK

Crater Lake fills the caldera of Mount Mazama, a volcano that collapsed in 5700 BC, blowing 14 cubic miles of rock into the sky. The deepest lake in North America, Crater Lake has no outlet but maintains its level by evaporation and seepage. The lake's purity and 1943-foot depth account for its stunning blue color. Klamath tribal legends claim the lake is the haunt of an evil spirit named Llao. Native Americans refused to speak of the lake, so explorers overlooked it for years.

CRATER LAKE LODGE (see Hike #26) was built for $50,000 in 1909-15 and renovated for $35 million in 1995.

ROCKING CHAIRS laced with rawhide overlook the lake from the back porch of Crater Lake Lodge.

GARFIELD PEAK (Hike #26) has perhaps the best view of Crater Lake.

PHANTOM SHIP

A small, craggy island at the foot of Dutton Cliff *(above)*, Phantom Ship is the 400,000-year-old core of ancient Mount Mazama. To see the island's many moods *(right)*, take the trail to Sun Notch (Hike #29).

LEFT: Skis or snowshoes are needed to tour the 33-mile Rim Road in winter.

MARGURETTE and Trapper Lakes, in the Sky Lakes Wilderness south of Crater Lake (Hike #50).

DEVILS PEAK from Cliff Lake, in the Seven Lakes Basin of the Sky Lakes Wilderness (Hike #44).

MT. McLOUGHLIN looms above lava fields along the Pacific Crest Trail (Hike #52).

PILOT ROCK, on the California border (Hike #55).

Blacktail Deer.

Black bear.

LOWER TABLE ROCK overlooks the Medford area (Hike #31).

DEVILS PUNCHBOWL lAKE, in the Siskiyou Wilderness just south of the Oregon border (Hike #78).

JACKSONVILLE'S historic downtown (Hike #61).

ILLINOIS RIVER footbridge (Hike #81).

MT. ASHLAND from the Pacific Crest Trail (Hike #56).

OREGON CAVES (Hike #72; NPS photo).

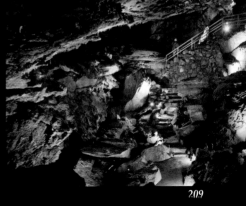

THE ROGUE RIVER TRAIL crests Inspiration Point, between The Coffeepot and Blossom Bar (Hike #87).

FLORA DELL FALLS on the Rogue River Trail (Hike #87).

RAFTING THE ROGUE

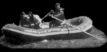

The 40-mile stretch of Rogue River between Grave Creek and Illahe is a world-class 3-day whitewater trip. It's so popular that boating permits are issued by lottery for the high season (May 15 to October 15), and only one in ten applicants wins. See page 203.

BLOSSOM BAR's treacherous boulder field resembles a giant pinball machine for boaters on the Rogue River.

THE COFFEEPOT swirls boats in Mule Creek Canyon.

SKY HIGH LAKES in the Marble Mountains (Hike #89).

CASTLE DOME in Castle Crags State Park (Hike #98).

LONG GULCH LAKE in the Trinity Alps (Hike #92).

MT. SHASTA from South Gate Meadows (Hike #100).

CARIBOU MOUNTAIN reflects from a tarn in the Trinity
Alps Wilderness of Northern California (Hike #96).

River Ranch to see this lovely farmhouse museum. Then continue on the main gravel road another mile to a parking area on the left just before Marial Lodge. Stop here if you are driving a low-slung passenger car. Otherwise continue 0.7 mile on a rough track to the Rogue River trailhead parking lot at road's end.

The trail ahead traces the edge of Mule Creek Canyon, a gorge so narrow that boaters sometimes bridge sideways or spin helplessly in a cylindrical maelstrom called The Coffeepot. After 0.7 mile the path crests at Inspiration Point, with a view across the chasm to Stair Creek's dramatic waterfalls. In another 1.4 miles the trail crosses Blossom Bar Creek, with campsites and a swimmable creek pool. Across a brushy lava flat to the left is the river's most treacherous rapids, a boulder field resembling a giant pinball game for boaters. Blossom Bar's rapids mark the upstream limit of jet boat traffic from Gold Beach.

In another mile the trail forks at Paradise Bar's grassy airstrip. The official trail skirts the woods to the right, but keep left along the river 0.2 mile to visit rustic Paradise Lodge, a good day-hike goal. Drop-in hikers are welcome at the bar and buffet restaurant. Book well in advance at *www.paradise-lodge.com* or 888-ON-ROGUE if you want a room; rates are $160 per person, including meals. if you want an overnight room (see page 172). Jet boats from Gold Beach (about $87 round-trip) make scheduled stops at Paradise Lodge from May 1 to October 15. Call Jerry's Rogue Jets at 800-451-3645 *(www.roguejets.com)* for reservations.

If you're hiking onward from Paradise Lodge, rejoin the main trail at the upper west end of the airstrip and turn left 2.9 miles to Brushy Bar, a forested plain with a large, official campground. In the next 2.8 miles the trail skirts the scenic cliffs of Solitude Bar and reaches Clay Hill Lodge, a rustic riverside inn with views and wildlife. Book well in advance at www.clayhilllodge.com for rooms. Meals are included in the per-person price of $150 for adults and $100 for kids. From Clay Hill Lodge it's 6 miles to the Illahe trailhead, passing lovely 20-foot Flora Dell Falls along the way.

To drive a shuttle car to Illahe from Marial, go back up the Marial road 15 miles. At an "Oregon Coast" pointer, turn left for 5 miles. At a 6-way junction, go straight on gravel Road 32-8-31 (which becomes Road 3348) for 22 miles. Then turn left on Road 33 for 15.6 miles toward Agness, and turn left toward Illahe for 3.5 miles to the trailhead spur on the right.

Mule Creek Canyon.

Northern California

Campgrounds

		Campsites	Water	Flush toilet	Open (mos.)	Rate range
1	**CASTLE CRAGS STATE PARK.** Reopened in 2013, this handy camp is near I-5 (see Hike #98). Res: 800-444-7275 or *www.reserveamerica.com*.	82	●	●	●	$15-30
2	**GRIDER CREEK.** The Pacific Crest Trail climbs from this camp into the Marble Mountains (Hike #179). Horse corrals and ramp available.	10			V-X	free
3	**HIDDEN HORSE.** Access the Trinity Alps from this camp (see Hike #92). Each site has corrals for 4 horses, but no stock troughs.	6	●		VI-X	$10
4	**INDIAN SCOTTY.** On the Scott River (swimming, kayaking), this camp has horseshoe pits and access to the Marble Mountains.	28	●		V-X	$10
5	**JUANITA LAKE.** Conveniently near Highway 97, this reservoir in the pines has stocked fish, two fishing jetties, and a 1.5-mile lakeshore trail.	23	●		V-X	$15-20
6	**KANGAROO LAKE.** By a scenic mountain lake (no motors) this camp has 5 walk-in sites, 2 all-accessible sites, and trails (see Hike #94).	18	●		VI-X	$15
7	**LAKE SISKIYOU.** This reservoir near I-5 is popular for motorboating, swimming, and cooling off on hot days. Cabins run $65-153. Reserve sites at the huge campground at 800-811-6748 *(www.reynoldsresorts.com)*.	350	●	●	IV-X	$20-29
8	**LOVERS CAMP.** At a Marble Mountain trailhead (Hike #89), this remote, high camp has horse corrals and walk-in campsites.	8			V-X	free
9	**PANTHER MEADOW.** Often full, these free, walk-in campsites have spectacular Mt. Shasta views (see Hike #100).	15			VI-X	free
10	**SARAH TOTTEN.** One of the few camps directly on the Klamath River, these sites are free from November through April, when the water is off.	8	●		V-X	$10
11	**TRAIL CREEK.** Near the PCT and the Trinity Alps (Hike #92), this camp is by the South Fork Salmon River.	12	●		V-X	$10
12	**TREE OF HEAVEN.** A lovely little camp with a birdwatching/nature trail on the Klamath River's bank, conveniently located just 7 miles from I-5.	20	●		V-X	$15

◁ *Mt. Shasta from Castle Lake.*

Cabins, Lookouts & Inns

		Rental units	Private bath	Breakfast	Open (mos.)	Rate range
1	**GIRARD RIDGE LOOKOUT.** East of Castle Crags, this lookout at 5500 feet elevation has views of Mt. Shasta and the Sacramento River Canyon. No water, no heat, 2 twin beds. Res: 877-444-6777 *(www.recreation.gov)*.	1			VI-X	$75
2	**HIRZ MOUNTAIN LOOKOUT.** On a 20-foot tower near Shasta Lake, this 1940 lookout has no water, stove, or heat, but 2 twin beds. Access by rough road and hike the last quarter mile. Res: 877-444-6777 *(www.recreation.gov)*.	1			V-X	$50
3	**MOUNT SHASTA RANCH.** A gabled 1923 bed & breakfast with a view (1008 Barr Rd., Mt. Shasta). Res: 877-926-3870 *(www.stayinshasta.com)*.	12	5	●	●	$60-130
4	**STRAWBERRY VALLEY INN.** This motel/bed & breakfast has a garden and quaint rooms (1142 S. Mt. Shasta Blvd., Mt. Shasta). Res: 530-926-2052.	15	●	●	●	$120-200

Top right: Trinity Alps at Caribou Lake (Hike #96).

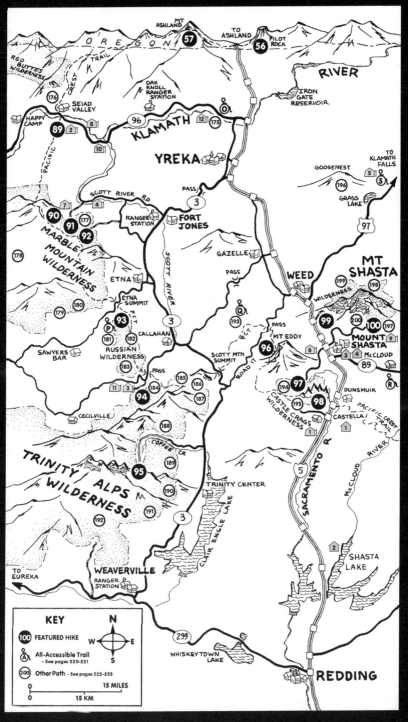

88 Paradise Lake

Moderate
3.8 miles round-trip
1400 feet elevation gain
Open mid-June to mid-November
Use: hikers, horses

Left: Paradise Lake.
Right: Marble Mountain.

This small but scenic lake high in the Marble Mountain Wilderness of Northern California is bordered by wildflower meadows and the cliffs of Kings Castle.

To find the trailhead, turn off Interstate 5 at the Fort Jones exit just south of Yreka and follow Highway 3 for 16 miles to Fort Jones. At the far end of town turn right on Scott River Road for 14.1 miles to a pointer for Indian Scotty Campground and Lovers Camp. Turn left on narrow, paved Road 44N45 for 5.6 miles to a junction. Following a pointer for Paradise Lake, go straight on gravel Road 44N44 for 6.9 miles to the Paradise Trailhead (avoiding a fork to the left through an open green gate at the 5.5-mile mark). Group size is limited to 25 and grazing of horses is banned in June. Free permits are required for overnight use or fires, and are available at the Scott River ranger station in Fort Jones.

The trail starts out dusty and rocky from heavy horse use, climbing steeply through a forest of spire-shaped Shasta red fir with Douglas fir, incense cedar, and a few 5-foot-diameter sugar pines. After 1.8 miles you'll reach a junction with the Pacific Crest Trail in a meadowed saddle. Flowers here are blue lupine, purple aster, yellow sulfur plant, hellebore, and tall, aromatic mint.

Turn right for 300 yards to Paradise Lake. This green pool is only a few feet deep, with a grassy island, waterdogs, polliwogs, and jumping fish. Blue, mottled orange, and black butterflies flit along the grassy shore.

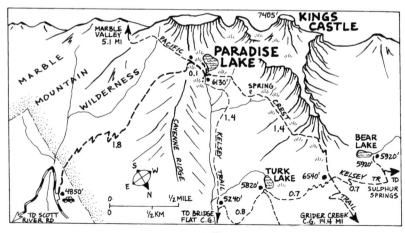

Other Options

If you're not yet ready to turn back, you can follow the PCT north 2.1 miles to Bear Lake or south 5.1 miles to Marble Valley (Hike #89). Athletic adventurers willing to work for a view can scramble straight up a very steep, brushy wildflower slope from the lake to Kings Castle, a hat-shaped rock outcrop on the horizon 1 mile away and 1275 feet up.

89   Sky High Lakes

Difficult
13.6-mile loop
2350 feet elevation gain
Open mid-June to mid-November
Use: hikers, horses

A mountain of white marble looms above the lakes and wildflower meadows of the two alpine basins on this spectacular loop. The flower show peaks in July. By mid-September, cattle are typically herded here to graze. Backpackers in the Marble Mountain Wilderness need to pick up a free permit from the Scott River ranger station in Fort Jones.

To find the trailhead, turn off Interstate 5 at the Fort Jones exit just south of Yreka and follow Highway 3 for 16 miles to Fort Jones. At the far end of town turn right on Scott River Road for 14.1 miles to a pointer for Indian Scotty Campground and Lovers Camp. Turn left on narrow paved Road 44N45 for 5.6 miles, and then turn left on paved Road 43N45 for 1.9 miles to its end at Lovers Camp's large parking area. Don't expect honeymoon suites in this romantically-named campground—just a few primitive walk-in sites without water.

The wide trail sets off from the left side of the parking lot, heads through the campsites, crosses a dirt road, and veers to the right into a cool old-growth forest. Some Douglas firs along the way are 7 feet in diameter. The woods are

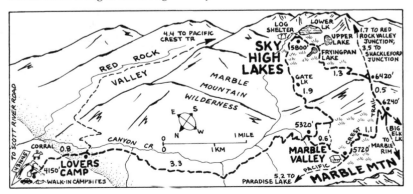

full of active chipmunks (with white eye stripes) and Douglas squirrels (without stripes). In early summer, white woodland flowers include 7- to 9-petaled queens cup, the double bells of twinflower, and sprays of star-flowered solomonseal.

If you keep right at all junctions for 4.7 miles you'll hike to the head of a broad, wooded canyon and climb through increasingly large meadows to Marble Valley. Beside the Pacific Crest Trail junction here you'll find a historic Forest Service guard station. It's locked, but the area makes a nice rest stop anyway, with views across a meadow of hellebore (corn lily), goldenrod, and aster to the huge white wall of Marble Mountain.

The mountain's white marble has the same geologic age and origin as the marble of the Oregon Caves (see Hike #72). Not surprisingly, the rock here is riddled with caves too. Bigfoot Cave, the largest of the area's nearly 100 known caves, was discovered in 1976 and has proven more extensive than the Oregon Caves. Because of dangerous dropoffs, endangered bat habitat, and extremely fragile dripstone formations, however, casual scramblers are urged to stay away from cave openings. Serious spelunkers should check with the Salmon/Scott Ranger District (530-468-5351) for information.

To continue the loop hike, turn left on the Pacific Crest Trail through a natural rock garden of blue larkspur, red paintbrush, pink fireweed, and white marble. After climbing 1.1 mile to a pass with a 4-way trail junction, turn left along a panoramic ridgecrest for 0.5 mile. Then fork left at a "Sky High Lakes" pointer and descend 1.3 miles through more alpine meadows to the basin's lakes. Go straight past Fryingpan Lake (aptly named for its shape) and an unmarked side trail to Upper Lake. Near the large, lower lake, the trail becomes badly braided in the meadows. Keep right to find Lower Lake's grassy shore.

For a worthwhile detour, follow Lower Lake's outlet creek 200 yards downstream and hop across the creek to Sky High Shelter—a shake-roofed, 3-sided

Sky High Lakes.   *Opposite: Cliff Lake.*

log shelter with a view of Marble Mountain. Then return to Lower Lake and turn right through the meadow to find the continuation of the loop trail. After 1.9 miles, turn right on the 4.1-mile trail back to Lovers Camp.

Other Hiking Options
   For a less visited 13.2-mile loop, hike to Marble Valley, and follow the Pacific Crest Trail left 3.3 miles. Then turn left to descend back to Lovers Camp through the Red Rock Valley—a quiet canyon named for its red peridotite bedrock.

90   Campbell Lake

Moderate (to Campbell Lake)
9.3-mile loop
1360 feet elevation gain
Open mid-June to mid-November
Use: hikers, horses

Difficult (to Cliff and Summit Lakes)
13.3-mile loop
2120 feet elevation gain

   Outcroppings of glacier-polished marble form dramatic borders to the popular mountain lakes at the head of Shackleford Creek. For a moderate loop hike, tour the wooded shore of Campbell Lake. For a longer loop, continue onward to the huge-walled cirque of Cliff Lake and the subalpine meadows at swimmable Summit Lake. Backpackers need to pick up a permit, available free at the Scott River ranger station in Fort Jones.
   To drive here from Interstate 5, take the Fort Jones exit (a mile south of Yreka) and follow Highway 3 for 20.5 miles. At a service station 4.5 miles beyond Fort Jones, turn right on Quartz Valley Road. Follow this paved road for 5.8 miles, making sure not to miss its left-hand zigzag after Mugginsville. Then turn left at a "Shackleford Trail" pointer onto gravel Road 43N21 for 7 miles to road's end. Park horse trailers in a lot to the left, while cars park on the right. Groups on the trail are limited to 25 and horse grazing is not allowed before July.

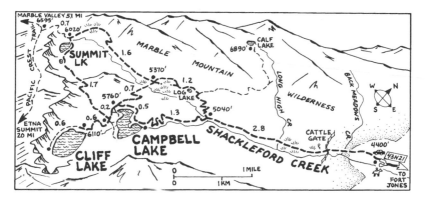

The Shackleford Trail follows a dusty, abandoned roadbed for its first half mile. Then the trail narrows and crosses a cattle gate at the 1-mile mark. From here on, the path passes small meadows full of huge-leaved hellebore (also known as corn lily), red-and-yellow columbine, fuzzy red spirea, red paintbrush, white yarrow, and blue aster. The meadows are also full of grazing cattle from mid-July through September. The cows wear tinny clanging bells to help cowboys find them. The calves don't need bells because each cow recognizes its offspring's bawl and stays close. Luckily, the cattle avoid the area's lakes.

After 2.8 miles, veer left at a fork and climb steeply through dense woods for 1.3 miles to Campbell Lake—a large lake with a many-bayed shore worth exploring. The main path parallels the shore for half a mile to a trail junction in the woods. If you're ready to take the shorter loop back, turn right past a "Shackleford Creek Trailhead" pointer, descend 0.7 mile to an X-shaped junction at a large meadow's edge, and go straight for 4 miles to your car.

If you'd like to take the longer loop, continue straight at the junction beside Campbell Lake—and continue straight through four other junctions in the next 400 yards. After 0.8 mile you'll climb to Cliff Lake, a deep pool rimmed on three sides by 1000-foot rock walls. Acres of bleached driftwood jam the outlet. The trail continues past a nice beach before ending at the lake's far end.

To continue the loop, head back from Cliff Lake 0.6 mile and turn left at a "Summit Lake" pointer. This path climbs over a hill to reach Summit Lake in 1.7 miles. Smaller and warmer, this lake is surrounded by pointy Shasta red firs, pink heather, colorful metamorphic rocks, and a cliffy mountain face. Beyond Summit Lake, follow the main loop trail downhill 1.6 miles to an X-shaped junction at a large meadow's edge. Turn left here and then go straight for 4 miles back to your car.

91   Paynes Lake

Moderate (to Upper Ruffey Lake)
4.2 miles round-trip
1200 feet elevation gain
Open late June to mid-November
Use: hikers, horses

Difficult (to Paynes Lake)
12 miles round-trip
2210 feet elevation gain

Left: Paynes Lake.

Hikers often drive past the Russian Wilderness on their way to its larger, more famous neighbors, the Trinity Alps and Marble Mountain Wilderness Areas. But this craggy chunk of the Salmon Mountains rivals those more crowded destinations in scenery. For a first-rate sample of the Russian Wilderness' charms, take the Pacific Crest Trail along a view-packed ridgecrest to Paynes Lake's dramatic granite basin. Car drivers for this trip will appreciate that the route to the trailhead is entirely paved. Backpackers using stoves or fires need to pick up a free burn permit from the Scott River ranger station in Fort Jones.

From Interstate 5, take the Fort Jones exit (a mile south of Yreka) and follow Highway 3 for 27 miles. Beyond Fort Jones 11 miles, where the highway turns left towards Callahan, go straight on Collier Way for 0.5 mile into the quaint village of Etna. In downtown Etna turn right on Main Street (which becomes Etna-Sawyers Bar Road) for a total of 10.5 miles, climbing this slow, twisty road to Etna Summit. Just 100 yards beyond the pass, turn left into an unmarked parking lot beside a radio tower.

From the parking area, walk 100 feet up a road beside the radio tower and veer right onto the Pacific Crest Trail. This path climbs gently past sparse, storm-battered Shasta red firs along a slope of red-limbed manzanita brush, yellow sulphur flowers, and schist scree. After half a mile the trail enters denser woods with firs up to 4 feet in diameter.

At the 1.7-mile mark the PCT crosses an old mining road. If you're wearing down, turn left on this road, which becomes an 0.4-mile path down to woodsy Upper Ruffey Lake—an acceptable day-hike goal. If you're headed for the craggier granite scenery at Paynes Lake, however, stick to the PCT for another 4.3 miles. Along the way you'll pass a cliffy slope with views across Smith Lake to distant Mt. Shasta, a saddle with a view west to Taylor Lake, and a series of granite steps with bouquets of goldenrod, blue aster, and red paintbrush. When you reach a junction by Paynes Lake's outlet creek, turn right to a large wooded area with dozens of campsites overlooking the lakeshore.

Other Options

Albert Lakes. Hike to the far end of Paynes Lake and climb to the far, upper end of a steep meadow to find a faint, boggy trail that leads 0.7 mile up through alder brush and wildflowers to a rugged alpine lake basin.

Paynes Lake Trail. This shorter, but steeper and fainter route to Paynes Lake gains 2100 feet in 2.1 rocky miles, mostly through old clearcuts. To find its trailhead, drive Highway 3 south past Etna 4.5 miles, turn right on French Creek Road, and follow signs for 9 increasingly rough miles.

Taylor Lake. Nearly as pretty as Paynes, this lake is a bit closer. To get there, drive past Etna Summit 0.4 mile, turn left on a very rough dirt road for 2.4 miles, and walk a very easy 0.3-mile path to the lake. Adventurers can also scramble down to the lake from the PCT, but the slope is very steep and rocky.

Smith Lake. A faint trail continues 1.7 miles past Upper Ruffey Lake to this rock-rimmed pool. A very steep scramble trail continues 0.3 mile up a rocky ridge to a switchback of the PCT, making possible a rugged loop.

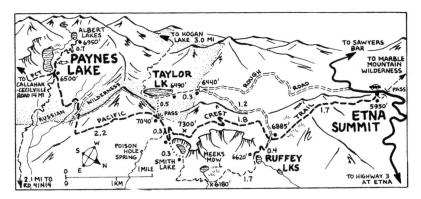

92 Trail Gulch Lake

Moderate (to Trail Gulch Lake)
3.6 miles round-trip
910 feet elevation gain
Open late June to mid-November
Use: hikers, horses

Difficult (to Long Gulch Lake)
9.6-mile loop
2280 feet elevation gain

Cars often pack the trailhead parking lots on the southern side of the popular Trinity Alps Wilderness, but here on the northern side, just an hour and a half's drive from the Oregon border, you can hike all day without meeting another group. Two of the Trinity Alps' prettiest lakes are hidden in a pair of subalpine canyons here. For a trip the whole family can manage, head for Trail Gulch Lake. For a longer loop, continue over a panoramic divide to cliff-backed Long Gulch Lake. Maximum group size is ten. If you plan to camp in the Wilderness, be sure to pick up a free permit at the Fort Jones or Weaverville ranger stations.

To drive here from Oregon, take Interstate 5 just past Yreka to the Fort Jones exit and follow Highway 3 west for 40 miles to the village of Callahan. (If you're coming from Redding, take I-5 north past Weed 2 miles, take Stewart Springs exit 751, follow signs north 7 miles on Highway 99 to Gazelle, turn left on Gazelle-Callahan Road 25 miles, and turn right on Highway 3 for 2 miles.) At a major junction just outside Callahan, turn off Highway 3 toward Cecilville. Follow this paved road 12 steep miles up to Carter Meadows Summit, continue 0.8 mile down the far side of the pass to a "Carter Meadows Trailheads" pointer, and turn left for 1.8 miles on a gravel road. Just beyond a creek culvert, park at a pullout and message board on the left for the Trail Gulch Lake trail.

The trail up Trail Gulch sets off through a forest of incense cedars and Shasta

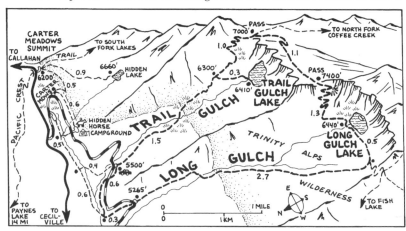

red firs with grassy openings of bracken, white yarrow, and granite rocks. The woods seem full of juncos, flashing their white tail-feather Vs as they swoop past. Midnight-blue Stellar's jays scold and tip their pointy topknots.

After 0.7 mile the path hops Trail Gulch Creek in a meadow. Then the trail climbs more steeply 0.8 mile to a fork. Veer right for 0.3 mile to Trail Gulch Lake, backed by a headwall of cliffs. The swimming's fine. If you're camping, pick a spot in the woods away from the shore.

If you're continuing on the loop, backtrack 0.3 mile from Trail Gulch Lake, turn right at the junction, and climb 1 mile to a pass. Just beyond the saddle, fork to the right on a new trail that traverses 1.1 mile to another picturesque pass. For a quick view of Mt. Shasta and the high Trinity Alps peaks, scramble 400 yards to the right up an open ridgecrest to a rocky summit. Then continue on the main trail across the pass, switchbacking 1.3 miles down a dramatic, cliffy amphitheater to Long Gulch Lake. A small bouldery island is evidence that a massive avalanche once skittered rocks onto the lake's winter ice.

The trail briefly becomes faint after crossing Long Gulch Lake's outlet creek in a meadow; head left through a campsite into the lakeshore woods. Then the trail is obvious for 3.2 miles down Long Gulch to a trailhead on the gravel road. Your car is 0.8 mile to the right, but rather than trudge back on the road, walk across it and return on a pleasant network of horse trails, following "Trail Gulch" pointers 0.9 mile to your car.

Long Gulch Lake.   Opposite: Trail Gulch Lake.

East Boulder Lake

Easy (to East Boulder Lake)
4 miles round-trip
930 feet elevation gain
Open early July through October
Use: hikers, horses

Moderate (to pass near PCT)
6.4 miles round-trip
1350 feet elevation gain

Difficult (along PCT)
9.8-mile loop
1920 feet elevation gain

This little known corner of the Trinity Alps Wilderness samples the best of the region—gorgeous lakes in scenic high country. But it also has the drawbacks of the region—rough trailhead access roads and cattle herds that damage alpine meadows. Note that group size for humans is limited to ten. Permits are required for campfires, stoves, or overnight use, and can be picked up at ranger stations.

To drive here from Oregon, take Interstate 5 just past Yreka to the Fort Jones exit and follow Highway 3 west for 40 miles to the village of Callahan. (If you're coming from Redding, drive I-5 north past Weed 2 miles, take Stewart Springs exit 751, follow signs north 7 miles on Highway 99 to Gazelle, turn left on Gazelle-Callahan Road 25 miles, and turn right on Highway 3 for 2 miles.)

In Callahan, between a highway bridge and the general store, turn south on paved South Fork Road. After 0.8 mile, fork up to the left on gravel Road 40N16 at a sign for "McKeen Divide." At a fork in another 0.4 mile, keep right on Road 40N17. Ignore private driveways along this rutted, rocky road for 1.9 miles to McKeen Divide. At this pass, fork uphill to the left for 2.9 miles to a junction. Then turn uphill to the left on Road 39N10 past signs warning "Dead End" and "Not Maintained For Travel." Passenger cars will have to drive slowly in first gear on this road for 2 miles to the trailhead parking area on the left, just beyond a creek culvert (*GPS location N41°15.129' W122°47.738'*).

Walk 100 feet farther up the road to find a messageboard marking the East

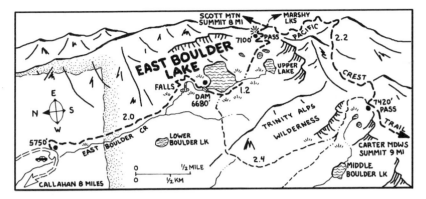

Boulder Lake Trail. This path climbs through shady mixed woods of grand fir, Shasta red fir, Jeffrey pine, and Douglas fir. Meadow openings gradually increase for 1.8 miles, when you switchback up a sagebrush slope beside a 15-foot waterfall. Wildflowers here include columbine, mint, and lupine.

Above the falls is a small stone dam at the outlet of East Boulder Lake, a large lake with lots of tadpoles. A few white pines provide shade at this destination.

For a longer hike, cross the dam and skirt the lakeshore for 0.3 mile, where the trail peters out in a meadow. Hop across the lake's inlet creek 100 feet from the lakeshore and look for a rock cairn across the meadow to find the continuation of the trail. The path climbs past three small upper lakes another 0.9 mile to a rocky pass with a view of Mt. Shasta and Mt. Eddy.

Turn back at this viewpoint unless you like adventure, because the loop ahead requires some route-finding ability. To be sure, it's easy to descend the far side of the pass 200 feet and turn right on the broad Pacific Crest Trail for 2.2 well-graded miles. But then, at a barren pass with a signpost, you'll need to turn uphill to the right on a smaller trail marked "Middle Boulder Lake."

This path soon descends half a mile to a pond popular with cattle, and then the route becomes faint. Beyond the pond 0.3 mile, look for an "East Boulder Lake" sign. Follow rock cairns marking the route to the right through sagebrush along the base of a rockslide. The path contours around a ridge for 1.6 mile, passing GPS locations *N41°13.147′ W122°47.770′* and *N41°13.881′ W122°47.728′* to complete the loop at East Boulder Lake (*N41°13.875′ W122°47.226′*).

East Boulder Lake.   Above left: The lake's outlet.

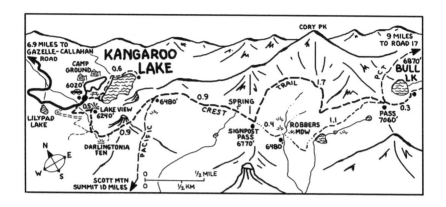

94   Kangaroo Lake

Easy (to Pacific Crest Trail)
2.8 miles round-trip
700 feet elevation gain
Open July through October
Use: hikers, horses

Moderate (to Bull Lake)
8.6 miles round-trip
1470 feet elevation gain

Hidden in the Scott Mountains on a paved road less than an hour from Interstate 5, this beautiful mountain lake has lots of secrets — one of the nicest little campgrounds in Northern California, a wheelchair-accessible picnic beach that's great for swimming on hot days, and an easy hiking path climbs past strange wildflower bogs to viewpoints. For a longer hike or a backpacking trip, continue on the Pacific Crest Trail to another little-known gem, Bull Lake.

To drive here from Oregon, take Interstate 5 south past Yreka 10 miles to Grenada exit 766. On the west side of the freeway, beside a Liquor Expo store, turn left on Old Highway 99 for 8.8 miles to Gazelle. (If you're driving here from the south, take I-5 past Weed to Stewart Springs exit 751, duck left under I-5, and take Highway 99 north 8 miles.)

In the middle of the little settlement of Gazelle, turn west on Gazelle-Callahan Road. After 16.5 miles (between mileposts 9 and 8) turn left at a sign for Kangaroo Lake. Follow this narrower road 6.9 miles to its end at a paved parking loop. Horse trailers aren't allowed to park here, but can use a gravel pullout 200 yards before the loop.

Your first order of business here should be to see the lake. From the campground messageboard at the end of the parking loop, a paved path leads 150 yards down to the right through a forested picnic area to a pebbly beach, with wheelchair-accessible spur paths on either side. Bald eagles hang out on clifftop snags. Motors aren't allowed on the lake, but canoes and inflatables are popular and fun. If the weather's hot in Weed, expect bikinis here despite the chilly water.

As for the adjacent 18-site campground, reservations aren't accepted, so it's hard to get a spot on weekends unless you arrive early.

When you've seen the lake and are ready for a hike, leave your car at the parking loop and walk back down the paved road 200 yards to a sign for the Fen Trail uphill to the left. This nature path switchbacks up past signs describing the area's *Darlingtonia* fens — odd bogs with insect-eating pitcher plants. Other flowers inlcude tiger lilies, mint, wild rose, beargrass, and columbine. After half a mile a short spur to the left leads to a clifftop viewpoint with a sweeping view of Kangaroo Lake.

If you've brought kids, you might declare victory at this viewpoint. If you're continuing, note that the trail makes a switchback at the viewpoint, angling up to the right past creeks and fens for 0.6 mile to a ridgecrest. Then the path gradually descends 0.3 mile to a Y-shaped junction with the Pacific Crest Trail. To find a scenic lunch spot near this junction, bushwhack to the left through scratchy manzanita brush 200 feet to an overlook of Kangaroo Lake.

If you're game for a longer hike, follow the Pacific Crest Trail to the left 2.6 miles to a pass overlooking Bull Lake and distant Mt. Shasta. A fork to the right descends 0.3 mile to the shore, where you'll find backpacking campsites in pine woods near the swimmable lake.

Kangaroo Lake from the viewpoint.   Opposite: Snag near the PCT junction.

95 Deadfall Lakes

Easy (to Middle Lake)
6 miles round-trip
400 feet elevation **loss**
Open July through October
Use: hikers, horses

Moderate (to Upper Lake)
8 miles round-trip
940 feet elevation gain

Difficult (to Mount Eddy)
11.6 miles round-trip
2170 feet elevation gain

Perhaps nowhere in Northern California can you see so many different kinds of wildflowers as when hiking to this string of alpine lakes below Mount Eddy. And if you're a fan of viewpoints, just keep following the trail up to the abandoned lookout on Mount Eddy's summit. At 9025 feet it's the highest point in the entire Klamath Mountains, with a breathtaking front-row view of Mt. Shasta.

Drive Interstate 5 south of Yreka 27 miles (or north of Weed 2 miles). Take Stewart Springs Road exit 751, head west on a highway for 0.5 mile, turn left onto Stewart Springs Road for 4.3 miles, and fork to the right on one-lane, paved Road 17. After another 9.3 miles, at a pass, pull into the Parks Creek Trailhead on the left. There is no limit to group size on the trail, but permits are required for campfires or stoves, and are available at the ranger station in Mount Shasta or the Cal Fire Station on Highway 97 in Weed.

Start your hike at the far end of the parking area, where the Pacific Crest Trail sets out just above the paved road ahead. The nearly level route traverses a slope with views of the distant Trinity Alps between occasional Jeffrey pine, prim Shasta red fir, and 5-needled white pine. Small springs along the way are lined with blue aster, and yellow monkeyflowers. Drier sagebrush slopes host yellow lupine, red paintbrush, and scarlet gilia.

After 2.8 miles you'll reach a fork—the first of many unmarked junctions in

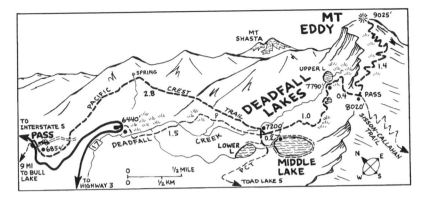

the lake basin, where user paths have proliferated. If you take the right-hand fork and stick to the PCT for 300 yards and then fork to the right again, you'll find the Lower Lake—a lovely pool, but no match for the other Deadfall Lakes.

So instead take the left-hand fork. After 50 yards turn briefly uphill on the large trail toward Mt. Eddy, and then fork to the right to discover Middle Lake, the largest and deepest of the group. This gem has a swimmer-friendly shore with gnarled mountain mahogany trees, rock outcroppings, and still more wildflowers. Campsites and lunch spots abound.

If you'd like to hike beyond Middle Lake, return 100 yards to the Mt. Eddy trail and follow it uphill to the right a mile to Upper Deadfall Lake, a small but gorgeous alpine pool reflecting the red metamorphic rock cliffs of Mt Eddy.

If you're climbing Mt. Eddy, continue 0.4 mile past the upper lake to a pass. Then turn left along the ridgecrest on a well-graded trail that switchbacks steadily up the mountainside. The only trees at this elevation are stunted whitebark pines, with limbs so supple they can be tied in knots. In addition to dwarf blue lupine and yellow sulphur flower, look for bladderpod, a bizarre locoweed relative that produces inch-long, mottled purple balloons as flowers.

At the summit, where scattered boards remain from an old lookout, you can stare eye-to-eye with Mt. Shasta. Notice the dark pyramid of Black Butte directly below Shastina's white cone. Also note Lake Shastina in the Shasta Valley to

Mt. Eddy (at right) from Upper Deadfall Lake.   *Above left: Signpost at the pass.*

the left, with Oregon's Mt. McLoughlin on the horizon. To the south, look for snowy Mt. Lassen. Far to the west are the snowcapped crags of the Trinity Alps.

Other Options

A shortcut trail to the Deadfall Lakes is steeper and rougher, but climbs through meadows full of wildflowers. To find it from the PCT trailhead at the pass, drive 1.3 miles east on paved Road 17, park inside a hairpin curve, and walk across the road to a "Deadfall Meadow" sign, where the trail strikes off through the fields. This path has boggy spots, so boots are a good idea.

96 Caribou Lake

Difficult
15.4 miles round-trip
3100 feet elevation gain
Open late July through October
Use: hikers, horses

Left: Caribou Lake from the pass.

In the spectacular heart of the Trinity Alps Wilderness, this huge blue lake sparkles in a vast granite bowl. Two difficult trails reach the Caribou Lake basin—an old steep path and a new, longer trail with a gentler grade. Both are better suited for a backpack than a day trip. Note that group size is limited to ten, and that overnight stays require a permit, available free at ranger stations in Fort Jones, Weaverville, or at the entrance to the Coffee Creek Road.

To drive here from Oregon, take Interstate 5 just past Yreka to the Fort Jones exit and follow Highway 3 through Fort Jones and Callahan for a total of 62 miles. Between mileposts 67 and 68, turn right onto Coffee Creek Road for 6.3

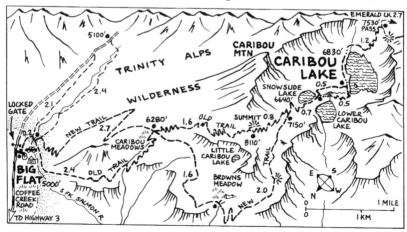

miles of pavement and an additional 13.4 miles of gravel. When you reach a locked green gate that closes the road ahead, turn right on Big Flat Campground's entrance road for 100 yards and park in a trailhead pullout on the left. The free campground by the trailhead has a dozen sites but no water.

If you're driving here via Redding, take Highway 299 west toward Eureka 49 miles to a "Trinity Center" pointer in downtown Weaverville, turn right on Highway 3 for 37 miles, and turn left on Coffee Creek Road for 19.7 miles.

The Caribou Lakes Trail descends 0.2 mile to a bridgeless crossing of the South Fork Salmon River. By August you can usually hop across on rocks dry-footed. On the far shore you'll find two trails: the new Caribou Trail to the left and the old Caribou Trail to the right. The old trail is slightly shorter, but includes scrambly steep pitches, so you're probably better off going left on the new, well-graded trail, even though it has long, shadeless switchbacks.

Either way, you'll reach an X-shaped junction at Caribou Meadows in a couple miles. Here again you'll face a choice. The old trail up to the left staggers up and over a mountain on its way to Caribou Lake. The new trail (to the right, this time) is genuinely easier, contouring around the mountain instead. The new trail also has the advantage of visiting Browns Meadow, the only possible campsite for those who cannot make it to Caribou Lake on the first day.

On the far side of Caribou Mountain the old and new trails join for keeps and switchback down to Snowslide Lake—a good spot to dive off a granite bank for a chilly swim. Beyond this point the trail often crosses bare rock, so it can be easy to lose. Keep left along the lakeshore, hop across Snowslide Lake's outlet, and keep left again to find a clear trail traversing a granite slope up to Caribou Lake. Remember to bring a stove because wood is too scarce here for campfires.

Other Hiking Options

Although the trail beyond Caribou Lake is faint, it's worth tracing it up to a 7530-foot pass. There a spur to the right scrambles out to a viewpoint of Emerald and Sapphire Lakes, in a snowy bowl beneath 9002-foot Thompson Peak.

97   Castle Lake

Easy (to Little Castle Lake)
2.4 miles round-trip
640 feet elevation gain
Open June to mid-November

Moderate (to Heart Lake)
3.4 miles round-trip
880 feet elevation gain

Right: Mt. Shasta from Castle Lake.

Wintu Indians believed this large, cliff-rimmed mountain lake was the fortress of Ku-ku-pa-rick, an evil spirit who made ominous rumbling noises here in winter. An 1851 gold rush brought swarms of white miners to these headwaters of the Sacramento, muddying the river below and destroying the Indian's supply

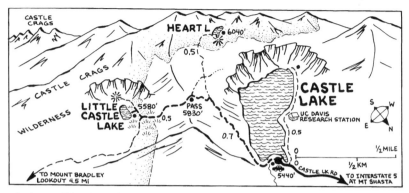

of salmon. The Wintu burned several of the intruder's cabins in response. Then they retreated to the bluffs above Castle Lake, where, with nothing but bows and arrows for defense, they were decimated by an impromptu army of heavily armed miners in the 1855 Battle of Castle Crags.

Today, easy paved access from Interstate 5 makes Castle Lake a popular summer picnic spot. For a short hike, take a 1.2-mile trail over a small, steep pass to a meadow at Little Castle Lake. For a better sample of the Castle Crags Wilderness—a landscape essentially unchanged since the days of the Wintu—track a faint trail to Heart Lake, a deep, swimmable pond in a high rock basin with a view across Castle Lake to Mt. Shasta and distant Mt. McLoughlin.

To start, drive Interstate 5 to the town of Mount Shasta, take the Central Mount Shasta exit, and follow "Siskiyou Lake" signs west for 3.5 miles through several forks and turns. Drive past the reservoir's dam 0.3 mile and turn left on Castle Lake Road for 7.3 miles to a large parking lot at road's end. Motorboats are discouraged on the still, 47-acre lake. Canoeists often launch from a small boat ramp beside the parking lot. And although camping is banned near the shore, there's an official campground 0.3 mile back down the road.

For the hike, walk left around the Castle Lake's shore through a forest of Shasta red fir and white fir. Look for dragonflies and fuzzy red spirea blooms along the bank. The path soon climbs away from the lake and steepens to a pass in open, high country with whitebark pines, orange paintbrush, white yarrow, and red-limbed manzanita bushes. The colorful jumble of rocks here are metamorphic—old serpentine and limestone that were cooked together and crystallized into veins when great bubbles of hot granite rose through the Earth's crust to form the Castle Crags.

Cross the pass, descend 0.5 mile to a meadow, and fork to the right to Little Castle Lake, a muddy-bottomed pond surrounded by spirea bushes and dramatic, July-blooming Cascade lilies. Scramble around the lake to a white granite cliff for the best views of Mt Shasta.

If you'd like a longer hike—and you have some pathfinding skills—consider a side trip to Heart Lake. From Little Castle Lake, walk back 0.5 mile to the pass. Just 5 steps beyond the summit, turn left on a faint path. After 150 yards you'll come to a confusion of faint trails on a barren rock tableland. Veer left, angling uphill toward a rocky ridgecrest for 0.3 mile. Then climb a short, steep trail to a little pass behind a small rock knoll. On the far side is Heart Lake, surrounded by bedrock, whitebark pines, Shasta red firs, and pink heather.

98   Castle Crags

Moderate (to Indian Springs)
3.6 miles round-trip
1040 feet elevation gain
Open except in winter storms

Difficult (to Castle Dome)
5.2 miles round-trip
2120 feet elevation gain

Right: Castle Dome.

Towering above Interstate 5 and the headwaters of the Sacramento, River, the granite spires of the Castle Crags are one of the most popular hiking goals of Northern California. For a quick bit of exercise, walk to Indian Springs, where cold water spurts from a cliff. For a tougher hike, continue up to Castle Dome, an enormous granite monolith with a panoramic view of the Mt. Shasta area.

The Castle Crags' granite domes look as though they rose straight up from the depths of the planet—and they did. For several hundred million years the North American continent has been crunching its way over the Pacific plate. In the process, the descending seafloor drags down a lot of sand and mud with it. When this relatively light sedimentary material gets deep enough it melts to form granite. Then it bubbles up through the continent toward the surface. Castle Dome, like Yosemite Valley's Half Dome, is the rounded top of a granite bubble that cooled underground and was later exposed by erosion.

In the late 1920s, photographs of these picturesque crags were used in the campaign to create California's state park system. Today the park includes a campground, several short nature trails, 7 miles of the Pacific Crest Trail, and a portion of the Castle Crags Wilderness. Dogs are not allowed on park trails.

Start by driving Interstate 5 south of Mount Shasta 14 miles (or north of Redding 48 miles). Take the Castella exit and follow "Castle Crags State Park" pointers 0.4 mile to the park's entrance booth. Expect to pay a day-use parking fee of about $8 a car. Also expect that a ranger will check yor car to make sure food and cooler chests aren't visible. Black bears in this park have become so savvy that they sometimes smash windows if they spot an easy meal.

Beyond the entrance booth, turn right and follow "Vista Point" signs through the campground 2.1 miles on a winding, paved road that's so narrow it's closed to trailers and motorhomes. Park in a lot at road's end. For a quick warm-up walk, take a 150-yard path from the far end of the parking lot through oak woods to Vista Point, a hilltop with views of Mt.Shasta and the Castle Crags.

Then walk back across the parking lot and down the road 50 yards to a sign for the Crags Trail on the right. This wide path climbs gradually through second-growth Douglas fir woods with incense cedars, dogwoods (white blooms in April), and some triple-leafletted poison oak. After 0.3 mile, keep left at a fork. Then cross the Pacific Crest Trail and continue straight, climbing steadily through viewless woods for 1.1 mile to the Indian Springs cutoff. Turn left for 0.2 mile to sample the delicious water that springs from a crack in a granite wall.

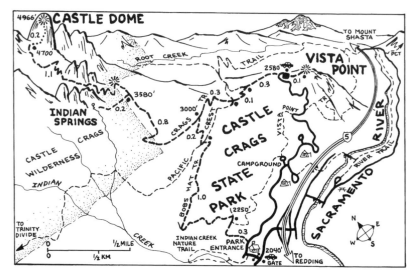

Red-and-yellow columbine blooms here in a glen of 6-foot-thick Douglas firs.

If you turn back here you'll miss the best views. So go back to the Crags Trail and continue uphill at least another 150 yards to catch the trail's first viewpoint of Castle Dome. Then, of course, it'll be hard to turn back. Although the trail steepens beyond this point, the views only improve as the path winds up past fantastic spires, clefts, and tilted crags. Finally the trail crosses a bedrock granite upland of manzanita bushes and peters out at the base of Castle Dome itself.

The final 300-yard climb to the summit of Castle Dome doesn't require technical climbing gear, but is too dangerous for most hikers. Confident scramblers should attempt it only when wearing shoes with good-gripping soles and only when the steep, slippery granite is dry. From the trail's end, scramble up to the right to reach the dome's bare granite face. From there, climbers have to use their hands while following faint ledges up the rock slope and then chimneying up large cracks to the top.

Mt. Shasta from Black Butte.   Opposite: Black Butte from Interstate 5.

99 Black Butte

Difficult
5.2 miles round-trip
1858 feet elevation gain
Open late May to mid-November

Wedged beside Interstate 5, this strange, steep-sided volcano boasts a close-up view of Mt. Shasta and a wide-angle panorama that stretches from the Sacramento Valley to Oregon. The convenient, well-graded trail to Black Butte's summit is perfect for a few hours of earnest exercise. Just don't forget your hat and water bottle in hot weather, because the route has no shade.

Black Butte looks like a cinder cone, but it was formed by a very different kind of eruption. When magma rose toward the surface here 10,000 years ago the rock didn't spray out as cinders. Instead it blasted a crater and then oozed up through the hole like dough from a cookie press, creating four adjacent lava domes. As the domes cooled the outer rock shattered into boulders, surrounding the central plug with a conical skirt of rockslides. About the same time, a similar lava dome erupted 7 miles away, much higher on Shasta's slopes. That dome is now Shastina.

To find the trailhead from Interstate 5, take Central Mount Shasta exit 738 — the *second* exit for this city in either direction. Drive east on Lake Street through downtown for 1 mile and curve left onto the Everitt Memorial Highway for 2.2 miles. Just beyond milepost 2, opposite a brown "Spring Hill Plantation" sign, turn left onto a large, unmarked gravel road. Follow this main gravel road (ignoring small dirt spurs) for 2.7 miles to a 5-way junction where the road ahead is blocked by a gate. Veer left on the best gravel road from the junction for 0.6 mile to road's end at a parking turnaround that is too small for trailers or RVs.

The trail starts at a brown post and sets off through a sparse forest. The firs

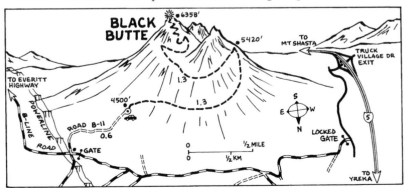

and pines here are struggling to grow amidst a jumble of gray and red andesite boulders. Black Butte's lava is rich in hornblende. If you look closely you'll see this black mineral has formed crystals resembling fossilized fir needles in the rock. At times, yellow and black lichens seem to be the only life to have gained a foothold on this relatively fresh lava. Elsewhere the trail passes surprisingly lush patches of gooseberry bushes, orange paintbrush, red fireweed, lavender pennyroyal, and yellow rabbitbrush. Viewpoints are everywhere.

At the 1.3-mile mark the path makes its first switchback, high above the double ribbon of Interstate 5. Then nine increasingly short switchbacks climb the final 1.3 miles to the cliff-edged summit and the mortared stone foundation of a long-gone fire lookout. The original cupola-style building blew off in a 1962 windstorm. Its replacement was removed by helicopter in 1975 because fire surveillance was being handled increasingly by aircraft.

From the summit, massive 14,162-foot Mt. Shasta rises above a patchwork of timber plantations—and the sharp triangular shadow of Black Butte itself. As you turn to the right, look for snowy Mt. Lassen, the flat Sacramento Valley, the jumbled Castle Crags, snow patches on Mt. Eddy to the west, the dimpled plain of Shasta Valley to the north (with Lake Shastina's reservoir below Pilot Rock's landmark knob), and Mt. McLoughlin's dark cone, 70 miles away in Oregon.

100 Mount Shasta Meadows

Easy (to Panther Spring)
1 mile round trip
280 feet elevation gain
Open mid-July through October

Moderate (to South Gate Meadows)
5.4-mile loop
1000 feet elevation gain

Left: Mt. Shasta from South Gate Meadows.

"Lonely as God, and white as a winter moon, Mount Shasta starts up sudden and solitary from the heart of the great black forests of Northern California." So wrote 19th-century poet Joaquin Miller, the first of many white visitors to leave his heart on this 14,162-foot peak. Naturalist John Muir later spread the mountain's fame with reports of his many climbs, including one harrowing trip when he was trapped overnight on the summit in a blizzard without a sleeping bag. Muir survived only by rolling all night in a sulphurous hot springs puddle.

Shasta has long inspired religious awe. The local Wintu tribe, to whom the peak was taboo above timberline, believed it to be the great white wigwam of a spirit who began creating the world from this point, and whose cooking fire sometimes wafts smoke from the summit. Those who smile at the old Indian myth should consider that a Rosicrucian author in 1931 claimed the mountain is inhabited by Lemurians, beings from the lost continent of Mu who hollowed out Mt. Shasta with supersonic bells. Later a Chicago paperhanger named Guy W. Ballard launched the I AM Foundation, based on his revelations at Mt. Shasta

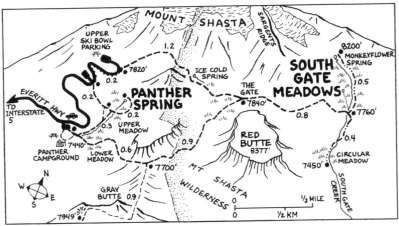

from Saint Germain, a spiritual presence from the court of King Louis XIV.

To hike through this mountain's strangely inspirational meadows for yourself, drive Interstate 5 south of Yreka 38 miles (or north of Redding 62 miles) and take the Central Mount Shasta exit—the *second* exit for this city in either direction. Drive east on Lake Street through downtown for 1 mile, curve left onto the Everitt Memorial Highway for 12.7 paved miles, and pull into the Panther Meadows parking lot on the right. From here, several little trails loop past ten free walk-in campsites with picnic tables but no water. This is the only campground on the mountain, and no reservations are taken, so come early if you want a site. Dogs must be on leash.

In the Mt. Shasta Wilderness itself, camping is banned within 100 feet of water or trails, maximum group size is ten, fires are banned, and dogs are not allowed.

To start the hike, take the leftmost trail from the parking area and keep left for 0.3 mile, following a gurgling mountain brook through Lower Panther Meadow's pink heather, orange paintbrush, yellow monkeyflower, and blue aster. Stay on the trail to protect these fragile plants! When you reach a T-shaped junction in the Upper Meadow, turn right for 0.2 mile to trail's end at Panther Spring, a gusher where devotees sometimes fill large water jugs. If you're just out for a short, 1-mile walk, simply return the way you came.

If you'd prefer a more substantial hike, head for South Gate Meadows (formerly "Squaw Meadows"). From Panther Spring, turn around, keep straight at junctions for 0.4 mile to Everitt Highway, and walk up the road 0.2 mile to the South Gate Meadows trailhead. You could drive here, of course, but by walking here from Panther Campground you'll be able to return on a lovely loop.

The trail to South Gate Meadows climbs above timberline to a pass with views not only of massive Mt. Shasta, but also of the distant Castle Crags, snowy Mt. Eddy, and the jagged Trinity Alps on the horizon. Beyond the pass the trail descends past an ice-cold spring to a sandy bowl slung between Mt. Shasta and Red Butte's ruddy cliffs. Turn left on a path that climbs through a notch ("The Gate") and contours 0.8 mile to South Gate Meadows, where creeks join at the base of an alpine valley full of heather and paintbrush. This glen is every bit as fragile as Panther Meadow, so *do not walk, sit, or camp on the delicate plants*.

To return on the loop, walk 0.8 mile back to the junction just beyond The Gate and veer left on a 1.5-mile path back to your car.

Barrier-Free Trails in Southern Oregon

People with limited physical abilities need not miss the fun of exploring new trails. Here are 19 paths within a 2-hour drive of the Rogue Valley accessible to everyone. Nearly all are surfaced with asphalt or packed gravel. Unless otherwise noted, the paths are open year round. For more information, contact the trail's managing agency, listed at the end of each entry.

UPPER UMPQUA RIVER (map on page 14)

A. Deadline Falls. The first 0.2 mi of the North Umpqua River Trail has been widened and graveled for easy access from Tioga Trailhead to an overlook of fish jumping at this river chute. See Hike #2. (Roseburg BLM, 541-440-4930)

B. Susan Creek Falls. The gravel 0.7-mi path to this waterfall (see Hike #2) is all-accessible, as are two 0.3-mi trails along the N Umpqua River from nearby Susan Creek Crampground. (Roseburg BLM, 541-440-4930)

DIAMOND AND CRATER LAKES (map on page 57)

C. Diamond Lake. The entire 11.5-mi paved lakeshore loop is accessible, as are 28 campsites at Broken Arrow Campground, 8 sites at Diamond Lake Campground, the Diamond Lake Information Center, and a fishing jetty at the resort's marina. Open June-Oct. See Hike #19. (Diamond Lake Ranger District, 541-498-2531)

D. Godfrey Glen. This 1-mi loop at Crater Lake National Park has a canyon viewpoint with ash pinnacles (Hike #28). In 2011 the park also plans to open a 1-mile path to an Anderson Bluffs waterfall. From park HQ, take E Rim Drive 8.7 miles and turn right on Pinnacles Rd 1 mi. (Crater Lake NP, 541-594-3000)

UPPER ROGUE RIVER (map on page 86)

E. Stewart State Park. A paved bike path traces Lost Creek Lake's shore 3.6 mi through woods, passing a campground, picnic area, boat ramp, and marina. For a loop, return on paved 2.4-mi path through grassy fields near Highway 62. See the map for Hike #32. (Oregon Parks, 800-551-6949)

F. Natural Bridge. A paved 0.2-mi path crosses the Rogue River to a fenced viewpoint of a lava tube where the river vanishes underground. Open Apr-Nov. See Hike #34. (High Cascades Ranger District, 541-560-3400)

G. Rogue Gorge. A paved 0.2-mi loop follows the rim of a chasm where the Rogue River churns through a 100-ft-deep slot. From Medford, drive Hwy 62 to Union Creek at milepost 56, continue east 0.2 mi, and turn left at a "Rogue Gorge" sign. Open Apr-Nov. See Hike #35 map. (High Cascades Ranger Dist, 541-560-3400)

SOUTHERN CASCADES (map on page 113)

H. Whiskey Springs. 1-mi graveled loop through meadows and lodgepole pine woods circles a beaver pond and passes a gushing spring. From Medford, drive Hwy 62 east 14.5 mi, turn right on Butte Falls Hwy 15 mi to Butte Falls, continue straight 8.3 mi, turn left on Parker Mdws Rd 0.3 mi, turn left into Whiskey Springs

Campground entrance, and keep right to the picnic area. Open Apr-Nov. (High Cascades Ranger Dist, 541-560-3400)

I. High Lakes Trail. Wide graveled 9.3-mi bike path links Fish Lake with Lake of the Woods (see Hike #51). For an easy trip, try the trail's nearly level eastern half from the Great Meadow trailhead past Lake of the Woods to the start of the Brown Mtn lava flow. Steepish grades make the western segment to Fish Lk suitable only for wheelchair athletes. Open June-Oct. (Klamath Ranger Dist, 541-885-6714)

EASTERN SISKIYOUS (map on page 137)

J. Lithia Park. The first 1 mile of the path through Ashland's Lithia Park (Hike #57) is all-accessible. (Ashland Parks, 541-488-5340)

K. Bear Creek Greenway. Entire 16-mile paved path from Ashland to Central Point is open to all (see Hike #148). (Oregon Parks, 800-551-6949)

Eight Dollar Mtn. Boardwalk.

WESTERN SISKIYOUS (map on page 173)

L. Grayback Campground. Graveled path follows Grayback Creek 200 yards from barrier-free campsite near Oregon Caves National Monument. In Cave Junction, turn west toward Oregon Caves 11.6 miles. (Wild Rivers Ranger Dist, 541-471-6500)

M. Eight Dollar Mountain. A boardwalk extends 0.2 mi to a wildflower bog, as described in Hike #80. (Medford BLM, 541-618-2200)

N. Big Pine Trail. Choice of 3/4-mi Challenge Loop, 1/2-mi Sunshine Loop, 1/3-mi Big Pine Loop, or 1/6-mi Creek Loop. See Hike #84. (Wild Rivers Ranger District, 541-471-6500)

O. London Peak. Packed gravel 0.6-mile path to clifftop viewpoint. From the Wolf Creek Inn (exit 76 of I-5), drive 0.5 mi south, but just before the freeway on-ramp turn R on Bridge Lane for 2.1 mi, turn R on gravel Rd 33-6-26 for 0.8 mi, turn R on Rd 33-6-27.2 for 1.7 mi uphill. (Medford BLM, 541-618-2200)

NORTHERN CALIFORNIA (map on page 215)

P. Klamath River. Riverside packed gravel 0.3-mi nature path from Tree of Heaven Campground (see Hike #177) includes displays describing migratory birds. (Happy Camp/Oak Knoll Ranger Dist, 530-493-2243)

Q. Lower McCloud Falls. Paved 0.2-mi trail along the McCloud River connects Fowler Campground and waterfall with a swimmable plunge pool. From I-5 south of Mt Shasta, take McCloud exit, drive E on Hwy 89 for 17 mi, and turn R at Fowlers Camp sign. (McCloud Ranger Dist, 530-964-2184)

R. Kangaroo Lake. Easy 0.2-mi path from CG to scenic mtn lake with fishing dock. Open July-Oct. See Hike #94. (Salmon/Scott Ranger Dist, 916-468-5351)

S. Juanita Lake. Start at a campground with all-accessible fishing docks to circle this lake on a 1.7-mi loop trail. Drive Hwy 97 north of Weed 38 mi (or south of Klamath Falls 36 mi) to Goosenest Ranger Station, turn west on Ball Mtn Rd, and follow signs 7 mi to Juanita Lake. (Goosenest Ranger District, 530-398-4391)

100 More Hikes in
Southern Oregon

Adventurous hikers can discover plenty of additional trails within a 2-hour drive of the Rogue Valley. The list below covers the most interesting—from park bike paths to rugged wilderness trails. Directions are brief, so be extra careful to bring appropriate maps. Estimated mileages are one-way. Most paths are open only in summer and fall, but symbols note which hikes are open all year and which are suitable for kids, horses, bicycles, or backpacking. For more information, check with the trail's administrative agency.

The appropriate ranger district or other offices are abbreviated: (AS)-Ashland, (B)-Butte Falls, (C)-Crater Lake National Park, (D)-Diamond Lake, (G)-Grants Pass, (J)-Cave Jct., (K)-Klamath, (M)-Mt. Shasta, (MB)-Medford BLM, (N)-North Umpqua, (O)-Happy Camp/Oak Knoll, (P)-Prospect, (SA)-Salmon/Scott, (ST)-Star, (T)-Tiller, (W)-Weaverville. Agency phone numbers are on page 13.

Easy / Moderate / Difficult

UPPER UMPQUA RIVER (map on page 14)

101. Wolf Creek Nature Trail. Cross the Little River on a dramatic suspension footbridge to a 0.6-mi loop through oak/ash woods with wildflowers in April and May. Start at the picnic area of the Wolf Cr Campground (see Hike #4 map). (N)

102. Little River Overhang. Basalt cliff is 0.3 mile up river path through old-growth woods. From Hwy 138 at Glide, take Little River Rd 27 for 16.2 mi, turn R on Rd 2792 for 0.2 mi to White Creek CG. (N)

103. Shadow Falls. Rock grotto with 90-foot triple cascade is the goal of an 0.8-mi downhill path. From Hwy 138 at Glide, take Little River Rd 6.5 mi S, turn right on Cavitt Cr Rd 11.5 mi to a pullout. (N)

104. Cougar Shelter. Visit a rustic 3-sided shelter by walking 0.6 mi on closed Road 630 or by climbing 2700 ft on steep 4-mile path from N Umpqua River Trail (see Hike #3 map). For upper access route, turn across Wright Cr Bridge between mileposts 33 and 34 of Hwy 138, follow Rd 4711 for 8 mi, and turn L on Rd 600 for 3 mi. (N)

105. Bullpup Lake. Easy 0.4-mi trail climbs to shallow lake with leaky shelter. Loop 0.6 mi around lake or continue 1.6 mi on Bulldog Rock Tr to

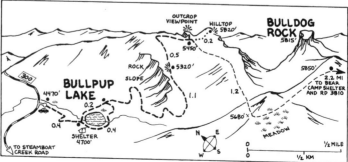

a viewpoint across the Calapooya Range to Diamond Pk. From Roseburg, drive Hwy 138 east 38.4 mi, turn L on Steamboat Cr Rd 10.4 mi, fork R on Rd 3817, follow "Bullpup Lk" signs 11.9 mi. (N)

106. Fuller Lake Shelter. Easy 0.7-mi trail drops 200 ft to a shelter by secluded, 600-ft lake. Drive as to Bullpup Lk (Hike #105), but follow Rd 3850 an extra 3.5 mi to Rd 3810 and keep L for 1 mi. (N)

107. Dog Creek Caves. Rare *Kalmiopsis* plants and endangered wildlife make this cave area so sensitive that access roads are closed Dec-July 4.4 miles before the steep, downhill 1.7-mi trail. Drive Hwy 138 east of Steamboat Cr 1.5 mi, turn L on Rd 4713 for 4.5 mi, turn R on Rd 100 for 3 mi, turn R on Rd 120 for 3.2 mi. Then walk R 1 mi on Rd 130. (N)

Bullpup Lake (Hike #105).

108. Medicine Creek Rock Art. A 0.2-mile path leads to a rock overhang with scores of red ochre paintings, including spirit masks and a horse-and-rider. Drive Hwy 138 E of Roseburg 54.7 mi. Between mileposts 55 and 56, turn L on paved Medicine Cr Rd 4775 for 1.3 mi. (D)

109. Clearwater River. Popular with mtn bikers, a nearly level 1.7-mi riverside path from Toketee Lk passes small cascades (see Hike #11 map). For loop, return on parallel path through woods. (D)

110. Cow Creek. Well-graded 6.5-mi trail starts with awkward wade of 40-ft Cow Cr, gains 1700 ft through woodsy canyon to a gravel road and the site of a former shelter at Railroad Gap. From Azalea exit 88 of I-5, take Upper Cow Cr Rd for 19 mi and turn R on gravel Rd 3232 for 1 mi to lower trailhead, or continue 6.9 mi on Rd 3232 and turn R on Railroad Gap Rd 3.5 mi to upper trailhead. (T)

111. Acker Rock Lookout. Climb 0.5 mi to a stunning, clifftop viewpoint at a staffed lookout tower. Drive as to Fish Lk (Hike #9), but drive past Tiller only 18.7 mi. Then turn R on paved Rd 29 for 5.8 mi, turn L on gravel Rd 2838 for 1.6 mi, and turn L at "Acker Rock" sign for 1.2 mi. (T)

112. Donegan Prairie. Faint but level 3.7-mi path ambles through scattered subalpine wildflower mdws (with cows July-Oct) on the Rogue-Umpqua Divide. Path starts and ends on Rd 800. From the Abbott Butte trailhead (Hike #36), drive 100 yds north and fork left for 0.2 mi to first trailhd, or continue 2.3 mi to second trailhd. (T)

Acker Rock Lookout.

113. Cougar Butte. Scattered wildflower meadows with big incense cedars (and cows July-Oct) highlight this faint 5.1-mi ridgetop spur of Rogue-Umpqua Divide Trail (see Hike #36 map). Drive as to Hike #36, but then go N toward Tiller 8 mi on Rd 68. (T)

114. Anderson Mountain. The Sandstone Trail climbs through viewless

Wilderness forest 4 mi (and up 1950 ft) to the Rogue-Umpqua Trail. Bushwhack up another 0.3 mi through a wildflower mdw to views and burned lookout remnants atop broad Anderson Mtn. Take Canyonville exit 98 of I-5, drive 23.3 mi to Tiller, fork L on Rd 46 for 5.3 mi, turn R on Rd 29 for 17.5 mi, and go R on Rd 300 for 3.2 mi. (T)

115. Castle Creek. Quiet path crosses Rogue-Umpqua Divide Wilderness, following this S Umpqua fork. Gains 800 ft in 4.5 mi, then climbs 1700 ft in 3.1 mi to Fish Cr Valley Rd 870 (see Hike #40). To start, drive as to Hike #9, but stick to Rd 2823 a total of 6.5 mi. (T)

116. Wolf Lake & Whitehorse Meadow. A 2009 fire scorched trees here but left flowers, lake, and meadow intact. Hike 0.9 mile to Wolf Lake, or continue 2.5 mi to mdws. Drive Hwy 138 to milepost 51, turn S on Rd 28 for 13.5 mi, and turn L on Rd 950 for 2.6 mi. (D)

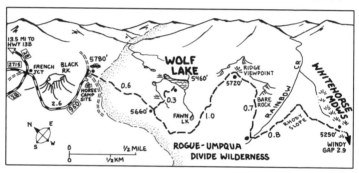

117. Calamut Lake. Easy 1.5-mi hike gains 350 ft to kid-friendly mountain lake with sandy beaches, flat campsites. From Hwy 138 between mileposts 73 and 74, turn N on Windigo Pass Rd 60 for 7 mi, turn L on Rd 700 for 2.4 mi, and turn R on Rd 740 for 0.3 mi. (D)

118. North Umpqua Headwaters. An 8-mi segment of the N Umpqua River Trail climbs valley into the Mt. Thielsen Wilderness to the river's source at Maidu Lk, gaining 1800 ft (see Hike #15 map). Between mileposts 73 and 74 of Hwy 138, turn N on Windigo Pass Rd 60 for 4.5 mi, and then keep R for 1.2 mi to the Kelsay Valley Trailhead. (D)

DIAMOND AND CRATER LAKES (map on page 57)

119. Rodley Butte. Bicycles rule this trail from Diamond Lk's outlet (see Hike #19 map). Path climbs through dry woods 3.3 mi (and 1600 ft up) to within a 0.2-mi scramble of a viewpoint atop this cone. Main path continues 3.7 mi down to Rd 4786, but becomes faint. (D)

120. North Crater Trail. Viewless 8.7-mi horse trail through woods by Diamond Lake provides a return route for equestrians making longer loops through Mt. Thielsen Wilderness. Trail starts at Howlock Mtn Trailhead (see Hike #17 map), parallels Hwy 138 to N Crater Trailhead at the Cascade summit and a Pacific Crest Trail junction. (D)

121. Red Cone. Cinder cone near Crater Lake's rim has views to Mt. Thielsen, 3 Sisters. Trailless 1.3-mi route to top gains 800 ft. Park at a turnout on the Nat'l Park's N entrance rd, 1 mi N of the Rim Drive jct. Walk X-ctry through pumice mdw toward obvious cone to NW. (C)

122. Sphagnum Bog. Floating moss landscape in Nat'l Park hosts 4 species of carnivorous plants. Park on Crater Lake's N entrance rd, 2.5 mi N of the Rim Drive jct. Hike Pacific Crest Tr W 4.8 mi (passing Red Cone Spr), turn R on Crater Spr Tr 3.6 mi to springs above bog area. Camping banned within 0.5 mi. Mosquitoes common. (C)

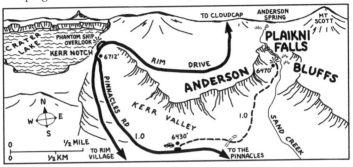

123. Plaikni Falls. The newest trail at Crater Lake is a barrier-free one-mile stroll to a waterfall glen packed with wildflowers. Fron Rim VIl-lage, drive 2.8 miles south. Just beyond park HQ, fork left on East Rim Drive 8.5 miles and turn right on Pinnacles Road for a mile.

Plaikni Falls.

123. Stuart Falls via Pumice Flat. Gentler, longer route to Stuart Falls than Hike #42 crosses a pumice plain in Crater Lk Nat'l Park. Drive Hwy 62 east of the south entrance road junction for 2.8 miles to a pullout. Hike 2.9 mi (up 400 ft) to Pacific Cr Tr, continue straight 2.5 mi (down 900 ft) to falls. (C)

UPPER ROGUE RIVER (map on page 86)

124. Denman Nature Trail. In a wildlife area beside the Rogue River, this 1-mi interpretive nature loop passes frog ponds, oaks, and grasslands. From Medford, drive Crater Lk Hwy 62 for 6.3 mi to White City, turn L on Antelope Rd 0.3 mi, turn R on Agate Rd 1 mi, and turn L on Touvelle Rd 0.7 mi to the trail on L. (Oregon Fish & Wildlife)

125. Viewpoint Mike. Path to columnar basalt overlook of Lost Cr Lake gains 1000 ft in 2.5 mi (see Hike #32 map). From Medford, drive Hwy 62 east for 30 mi. Just after Rogue River bridge, turn R on Crowfoot Rd for 0.3 mi to a pullout marked "no overnight parking." Tr starts on L above rd. (US Army Corps of Engineers)

126. Sugarpine Creek. Faint trail follows gravelly creek 3.6 mi, with shady woods, creek fords, and cows, to Road 600, gaining 700 ft. From Medford, drive Hwy 62 east for 26 mi, turn L on Elk Cr Rd 11.1 mi, turn L on Sugarpine Rd 2 mi, fork R on Rd 6610 for 1 mi. Park by Rd

243

050, walk down this rough rd 0.2 mi, and wade creek to trail. (P)

127. Bitterlick Creek. Unmaintained path descends from Grub Box Gap through lodgepole/sugarpine woods, losing 700 ft in 0.5 mi, then follows creek (with many bridgeless crossings) down 1300 ft in 3.9 mi to private land, cows. From Medford, drive Crater Lk Hwy 62 east for 26 mi, turn L on Elk Cr Rd for 13.8 mi, turn L on Rd 66 for 3.8 mi to end of pavement, turn L on Rd 6640 for 4.3 mi to signed trailhead. (P)

128. Mill Creek Falls. Spectacular 174-foot fall spills into Rogue River canyon of columnar basalt cliffs. Wide 0.4-mi trail loses just 200 ft. Spurs lead to narrower Barr Cr Falls and giant boulders by river. From Medford, drive Hwy 62 east almost to Prospect. After milepost 42, turn R on Mill Cr Rd 0.3 mi, then turn left 0.7 mi. (Boise Cascade)

129. Golden Stairs. Path climbs a rocky ridge 1600 ft in 4.3 mi to the Rogue-Umpqua Divide Tr. Then either turn L for 1.4 mi to Elephant-head Pond (Hike #36) or turn R for 0.9 mi to an upper trailhead at Yellowjacket Camp. From Medford, drive Hwy 62 east. Between mileposts 51 and 52 turn L on Rd 68 for 5 mi and turn R on Rd 550 for 2 mi. (P)

130. Anderson Camp. An early 1900s sheepherder trail gains 750 ft in 1.4 mi to wildflower meadows, views on broad Anderson Mtn. Tread becomes faint in mdws, but go straight 0.1 mi to Rogue-Umpqua Divide Tr and turn R for 2 mi to better views. Drive E of Medford on Hwy 62 to between mileposts 51 and 52, turn L on Rd 68 for 2.7 mi, go straight on gravel Rd 6510 for 5.8 mi, and turn L on Rd 6515 for 5 mi. (P)

131. Garwood Butte Lookout. A 0.7-mi path gains 660 ft to abandoned lookout tower on 7024-ft butte near Mt. Bailey. From Diamond Lk drive Hwy 230 toward Medford 3 mi to milepost 21. Turn R on S Umpqua Rd 3703 for 6.8 mi, and turn R for 1.4 mi on rough Rd 370. (D)

132. Minnehaha Creek. Motorcycle-marred path follows cascading stream through old-growth woods 2.9 mi to boggy Soda Springs. From Medford, drive 69 mi E toward Diamond Lake. Just after milepost 12 of Hwy 230 turn R at a Hamaker CG pointer. Follow Rd 6530 for 0.9 mi, and turn R on Rd 800 for 300 yds to the trail on the L. (P)

SOUTHERN CASCADES (map on page 113)

133. Varmint Camp. Steep 3.1-mi motorcycle trail along Crater Lake Nat'l Park border gains 1800 ft. Path crosses Varmint Cr, climbs wooded ridge, crosses wildflower mdw to campsite at dirt road. Take Hwy 62 east of Medford 45 miles, turn R into Prospect for 0.7 mi to hotel, turn L on Butte Falls Road 1 mi, turn L on Red Blanket Road 0.4 mi, and fork L on gravel Rd 6205 for 10.5 miles to trail sign on L. (P)

134. McKie Meadow. Loop through Sky Lakes Wilderness follows Tom & Jerry Tr 5.4 mi to McKie Mdw (1930s shelter, springs, rock outcrops) and returns on Mudjekeewis Tr past Kerby Hill's view of Middle Fk Rogue River canyon. Rocky at times, the 11.1-mi loop gains 2400 ft in all. Take Hwy 62 east of Medford 45 miles, turn R into Prospect for 0.7 mi to hotel, turn L on Butte Falls Road 2.8 mi, turn L on Rd 37 for 3 mi, fork L on Rd 3795 for 5.5 mi, turn L on Rd 650 for 0.8 mi to its end. The only horse trailer turnaround is 0.5 mi before trailhead. (P)

135. Middle Fork Rogue River. Snow-free by mid-May, this rarely maintained river valley path is the first Sky Lks Wilderness trail open each year. The first 3.2 mi gain a mere 400 ft along a colossal U-shaped valley carved by a vanished glacier. Drive Butte Falls Hwy 1 mi E of Butte Falls, turn L toward Prospect 9 mi, turn R on Rd 34 for 8.5 mi, keep L on Rd 37 for 5 mi, turn R on Rd 3790 for 3 mi. (B)

136. Alta Lake Trail. A rough long-cut to Alta Lk (see Hike #43) follows dry Gopher Ridge, gaining 2000 ft in 5.3 mi. Drive Butte Falls Hwy 1 mi E of Butte Falls, turn L toward Prospect 9 mi, turn R on Rd 34 for 8.5 mi, keep L on Rd 37 for 2.2 mi, turn R on Rd 3785 for 3.5 mi. (B)

137. Willow Prairie. 19 miles of horse-only trails explore forests, mdws from campground. Drive Hwy 140 E of Medford 35 mi. Just before Fish Lk, turn L on Rd 821 for 1.5 mi, turn L on Rd 3738 for 1.5 mi. A Northwest Forest parking pass is required. (B)

138. Rye Spur. A tough 3.3-mi viewpoint hike gains 1200 ft up this ridge. From the Lake of the Woods exit on Hwy 140, drive west 200 yds on Hwy 140, take the first dirt rd to the R, and keep R for 100 yds to the trail signboard. (K)

139. Sky Lakes via Cherry Creek. Alternate route to Trapper Lk (compare Hike #50) gains 1300 ft in 5.2 mi. Drive Hwy 140 to between mileposts 43 and 44, turn N on Westside Rd for 10.9 mi, turn L on Rd 3450 for 1.8 mi to its end. (K)

140. Mountain Lakes via Lake of the Woods. Slightly longer than the Varney Cr route into the Mtn Lks Wilderness (Hike #53), this 4.8-mi path gains 2000 ft to the central loop, passing small Lk Waban along the way. From Hwy 140 near Lake of the Woods, turn S on Dead Indian Memorial Rd for 200 yds and turn L on Rd 3660 for 1.5 mi. (K)

141. Mountain Lakes via Clover Creek. Shortcut into Mtn Lks Wilderness passes creekside meadows (with cows) and small Clover Lake, gaining 1380 ft in 3.4 mi to the central loop (see Hike #53 map). From Ashland, drive Dead Indian Mem Rd east past milepost 28, turn R on paved Clover Cr Rd for 5.7 mi, turn L on Rd 3852 for 3.2 mi to its end. From Klamath Falls, drive Hwy 66 west 8 mi to sharp curve, go straight on Clover Cr Rd for 15.7 mi, turn R on Rd 3852 for 3.2 mi. (K)

142. Brown Mountain Trail. Conveniently near the Boy Scouts' Camp McLoughlin at Lake of the Woods, this viewless 7.8-mi forest trail goes around (not over) Brown Mtn, passing lava and crossing the Pacific Crest Trail. Drive Hwy 140 to between mileposts 35 and 36, turn S on Rd 3601 and promptly turn R on gravel Rd 3640 for 0.6 mi to the poorly marked trailhead on the right just before a hill. (K)

143. Beaver Dam Creek. Beavers actually are active along this easy streamside loop. From Ashland, drive Dead Indian Mem Hwy east to between mileposts 21 and 22, turn L on Rd 37 for 2 mi. Park at Daley Creek CG, hike tr downstream 0.6 mi to start of 0.9-mi loop. (A)

144. Dunlop Meadow. Stroll 0.4 mi to a mdw (the old ranch of a 1920s bootlegger), then descend 700 ft in 1.1 mi to S Fk Little Butte Creek. From Ashland, drive Dead Indian Mem Hwy east 18.6 mi. Just past Lily Glen Horse Camp turn L on Shell Pk Rd for 1.6 mi, keeping R at forks. Then continue 5 mi on Rd 100 to Dunlop Tr on R. (A) 🐾 🚴 🏕

145. Soda Springs. Stroll 0.2 mi to mineral springs by Dead Indian Cr, then gain 1300 ft in 2.3 mi up steep ridge of oaks and pines to an upper road. From Ashland, drive Dead Indian Memorial Hwy east to between mileposts 13 and 14, turn L on Conde Cr Rd for 11.3 mi, turn R on Lake Cr Rd for 3.7 mi, turn R on Rd 800 for 0.6 mi. (A) 🌼

146. Little Hyatt Lake. Old-growth trees survive on level, 1.5-mi segment to Little Hyatt Reservoir. From Ashland, drive Hwy 66 east to Green Springs Inn (between mileposts 17 and 18), turn L toward Hyatt Lk 2.9 mi to a road jct. The PCT crosses here. Follow it L. (A) 🐾 🏕

EASTERN SISKIYOUS (map on page 137)

147. Roxy Ann Peak. In Medford's Prescott Park, this wooded knoll is circled by a hikable 2.9-mi loop road that's closed to cars in winter. From the loop, an 0.8-mi spur path and a gated 0.5-mi service road gain 550 ft as they climb to a summit viewpoint. From Medford exit 27 of I-5, take Barnett Rd E 1 mi, turn L on Black Oak Dr 1 mi, turn R on Hillcrest Rd 3.2 mi, and turn L on Roxy Ann Rd 0.4 mi to gate. If closed, walk up the road 2 mi to the start of the loop. (Medford Parks) 🌼

148. Bear Creek Greenway. Paved 16-mi bike path follows Bear Cr from Ashland through Talent, Phoenix, and Medford to county fairgrounds in Central Point. Path is often near I-5 freeway. For a stroll, walk 2 mi from Talent's Newbry Park (at I-5 exit 21) south past ponds to Hwy 99 at S Valley View Dr, near Ashland exit 19. (Ore State Parks) 🌼 🚴

149. Bull Gap. Old Mt Ashland Rd built by CCC in 1930s has been converted to 2.5-mi trail. Loses 980 ft. Drive as to Hike #56 but continue 1.5 mi to ski area parking. See map for Hike #57 to plan an 8-mi mtn bike loop via Bull Gap, gravel Rd 2080, and paved Rd 20. (AS) 🚴

150. Wrangle Gap. Follow the Pacific Crest Tr through high forest and meadows 3.8 mi around Red Mtn, gaining 850 ft. Easy 3-mi car shuttle between trailheads. Drive to Mt Ashland (see Hike #56) and continue straight on rough gravel Rd 20 another 8 mi to PCT crossing at milepost 17, just after Siskiyou Gap. For shuttle, drive 3 mi more. (AS) 🏕

151. Gin Lin Gold Mine. Interpretive 0.8-mi loop trail tours the overgrown tailings of a Chinese miner's 1881 claim. From Ruch, drive Upper Applegate Road 9 mi south, turn R on Palmer Cr Rd 0.8 mi. (ST) 🐕 🌼

152. Grouse Loop. Woodsy 2.8-mi loop with glimpses of Applegate Lk gains 600 ft. Begin at Hart-tish Park entrance (Hike #64 map). (ST) 🌼

153. Squaw Lakes (Snake Monster Lake). Easy 3.3-mi loop circles two lakes about to be renamed. From Ruch, drive Upper Applegate Rd 14.4 mi south, turn L across Applegate Dam, go straight 8.5 mi on Rd 1075 to parking area. Walk gated road L around the larger lake 1.5 mi to Mulligan Bay campsites, turn L on 1.1-mi trail through woods past the smaller lake, turn R for 0.7 mi on Rd 1075 to your car. (ST) 🐕 🌼 ⛺

154. Cook and Green Loop. Challenging 15.5-mi loop near Red Buttes tours creek canyons, Echo Lake, Siskiyou crest. Gains 3500 ft. Drive as to Frog Pond (Hike #68), but go only 3.7 mi on Rd 1040 before turning L at Horse Camp Tr pointer. Hike this trail 3.9 mi steeply up to Pacific Crest Tr (see Hike #67 map), turn L for 2.6 mi to pass, turn L on Cook and Green Tr for 8.2 mi, turn L on Rd 1040 for 0.8 mi to car. (ST)

155. Butte Fork Trail. In Red Buttes Wilderness, hike up canyon of old-growth 6.8 mi to Cedar Basin (gaining 2000 ft), then fork R for 0.9 mi to popular Azalea Lk or fork L for 1.4 mi to gorgeous little Lonesome Lk. For a grand 24.5-mi loop, keep L via PCT, Echo Lk, and Horse Camp Tr back to your car. Drive as to Frog Pond (Hike #68), but take Rd 1040 a total of 7.6 mi to Shoofly Trailhead on L (Hike #68 map). (ST)

156. Whisky Peak Lookout. Abandoned lookout building affords sweeping Siskiyou views. Steep 0.5-mi trail to top gains 580 ft. Drive to Middle Fork Trailhead (see Hike #68), then continue driving up Rd 1035 for 9 mi and turn L on Rd 350 for 2.4 mi to Rd 356 on R. (ST)

157. Miller Lake. A road washout has increased the hiking distance to this deep, swimmable mountain lake from 0.7 mi to 4.5 mi (except in late summer, when cars can cross the creek washout). An additional 2.5-mi loop climbs to viewpoints and an upper lakelet. From Medford or Grants Pass, drive Hwy 238 to the bridge at milepost 18 in Applegate, turn S on Thompson Cr Rd for 11.9 mi to a pass, veer R on Rd 1020 for 4.5 mi, and go straight on Rd 400. (ST)

Pond above Miller Lake.

WESTERN SISKIYOUS (map, p. 173)

158. Kerby Peak. Climb 2600 ft in 3.5 mi on a well-built trail to views atop this 5535-ft summit near Selma. From Hwy 199 at the flashing yellow light in Selma, drive E on paved Deer Cr Rd 8.7 mi, fork R across a bridge on White Cr Rd 38-6-18 for 0.5 mi, and turn L on gravel E White Cr Rd 38-7-13.4 for 2.7 mi to a fork. (MB)

159. Mt. Elijah. Climb past the Bigelow Lakes to a viewpoint above the Oregon Caves Natl Mon, on a 4.8-mi loop that gains 1050 ft (see Hike #70 map). From the Oregon Caves parking lot (Hike #72), drive

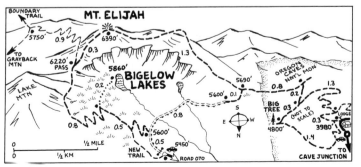

0.3 mi toward Cave Junction, turn R on gravel Rd 960 for 2.9 mi, turn R on Rd 079 for 0.6 mi, turn R on Rd 070 for 0.9 mi to barricade. Take trail up to L 1.3 mi to a pass, then keep R at junctions for 3 mi to pass Mt. Elijah's summit and complete a loop to your car. (J)   🚶🏇🐎

160. East Fork Illinois River. A rugged 9.7-mi path into the Siskiyou Wilderness fords this knee-deep river four times and passes good swimming holes en route to Youngs Valley (see Hike #77 map). Drive as to Hike #76 (Polar Bear Gap), but when pavement ends on the Bridgeview-Takilma Rd, fork R on Rd 011 for 0.8 mi. (J)   ✳🚶🐎

161. Sanger Peak Lookout. Views extend from the Pacific Ocean to Mt Shasta atop this summit, accessed by a 0.6-mi path that gains 460 ft. Rock climbing site is nearby. Drive as to Hike #77 (Raspberry Lake), but instead of turning R on Rd 4803, turn L for 1.5 mi. (J)

162. Island Lake. Rugged trail to Siskiyou Wilderness hideaway drops 700 ft in 0.9 mi to easy ford of S Fk Smith River, then gains 2100 ft in 3.2 mi to a cirque pool backed by Jedediah Mtn. Permits (available at Gasquet ranger station) are required only for campfires. Drive as to Hike #78 (Devils Punchbowl), but after 10 mi on Little Jones Cr Rd turn R on paved Rd 16N02 for 2.5 mi and turn L on rough Rd 16N28 (closed in rainy season) for 1.8 mi to its end. (SR)   🚶

163. South Kelsey Trail. This 27-mi path across the Siskiyou Wilderness is a remnant of a 200-mi Army mule train route built from Crescent City to Fort Jones in the 1850s. Drive Hwy 199 E of Crescent City 10 mi, turn R on paved S Fork Rd for 14 mi to a fork, go R on paved Rd 15 for 3.5 mi, turn L on Rd 15N39 for 2 mi to road's end. The path follows the S Fk Smith River 7 mi, climbs 4400 ft in 6 mi to Baldy Pk's views, and follows a ridge 3.1 mi to small Harrington Lk, a good goal. (SR)   🚶🐎

164. Baldface Creek. Walk a rocky roadbed 2.8 mi (and down 500 ft) to views on Biscuit Hill, then continue steeply down 1500 ft in 1.7 mi to a remote, bouldery creek. Drive Hwy 199 south of Cave Jct 7 mi to O'Brien, turn R on County Rd 5550 (which becomes FS Rd 4402) for 13 mi, and turn R on Rd 112 for 3 mi to roadbed/trail on L. (J)   🚶

165. Doe Gap. Starting point for backpack explorations of southern Kalmiopsis Wilderness trail network. Drive as to Hike #164, but continue on Rd 112 for 1.5 mi to barricade. Walk old ridgecrest road 7 mi to pass with views. Trails branch left to Chetco Pk and Vulcan Lk or right to Cold Springs Camp and Babyfoot Lk (Hike #79). (J)   🚶🐎

166. Whetstone Butte. Red rock ridgecrest route offers views of Kalmiopsis Wilderness and beyond. Path gains just 300 ft in 1.6 mi. For a longer hike, continue 1.6 mi (gaining 1000 ft) to Eagle Mtn or 3.1 mi to Chetco Pass. Drive as to Babyfoot Lk (Hike #79), but at the pass of Rd 4201 follow signs 0.8 mi R to Onion Camp. (J)   🚶🐎

167. Chetco River. Ugly mining road accessing remote center of beautiful Kalmiopsis Wilderness is drivable only in summer with a diehard 4WD vehicle. Drive as to the suspension footbridge in Hike #81, but continue across a low-water river bridge to McCaleb Ranch, take center fork through private land for 5.1 awful miles to Chetco Pass, continue 0.6 mi to gate, and park. Hike closed road 3.6 mi to knee-deep Chetco

River ford and junction with several Wilderness trails. (J)

168. Pearsoll Peak Lookout. Open for free overnight use (for reservations see page 172), this restored 1954 lookout on the Kalmiopsis Wilderness rim offers panoramic views, but lacks heat and water. Drive to Chetco Pass via awful road (see Hike #167) or hike there via nice 4.7-mi trail (Hike #166). Then walk N for 5.9-mi loop to lookout, gaining 1500 ft. (J)

169. Shan Creek. Handy 0.3-mi path to a swimming hole continues 1.8 mi up canyon slope, gaining 1100 ft to logging rd. Open to motorbikes. From Grants Pass, take Hwy 199 west 7 mi to Applegate River, turn R on Riverbanks Rd 5 mi, go L on Shan Cr Rd 1.2 mi. (G)

170. Dutchy Creek Trail. 1.8 mi of mining roads interrupt the middle of this 7.9-mi route from Sam Brown Campground (see Hike #85) over a wooded ridge to Rd 050 near Silver Falls (see Hike #172). (G)

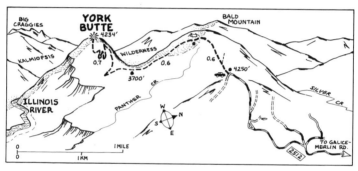

171. York Butte. The 2002 Biscuit Fire reduced the forest here to black snags, but improved views of the Illinois River's canyon. The 1.9-mi trail to the summit gains 1100 ft. Drive as to Hike #85, but continue past Sam Brown Campground on Rd 2512 for 10.4 mi. (G)

172. Silver Falls. Confusing, muddy, poorly signed, possibly gated roads make this 1-mi hike a trip for explorers only. From Galice, drive 0.3 mi toward Merlin, turn west on paved Galice Access Rd 9.5 mi to 5-way jct, turn L on Rd 35-9-1 for 4.2 mi, and fork L on rough Rd 050 for 6 mi to its end at a possibly unmarked trailhead. The path goes over rise, then loses 500 ft, to a wooded canyon with a 60-ft falls. (G)

173. Silver Peak. Through woods burned in 1987 and 2002, this wild, tough trail traces a dry ridgecrest 12.5 mi to a peak, then dives 4.5 mi down to the Illinois River Trail. From Galice, drive Galice Access Rd west 11 mi, turn L toward Hobson Horn on Rd 2411 for 4 mi to trail on R. (G)

174. Indian Mary Park. From a popular Rogue River campground, the 1.4-mi Jumpoff Joe Tr up to a viewpoint has become too overgrown with brush and poison oak for most hikers. Take I-5 Merlin exit 61, drive W through Merlin 10.6 mi. The trail begins across from the campground entrance by an old weigh station. (Josephine Co Parks, 541-474-5285)

175. Mount Bolivar. Gain 1160 ft in 2.8 mi, passing rock gardens and some burned trees, to a panoramic viewpoint in the Wild Rogue Wilderness atop

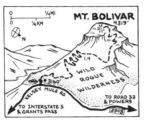

a 4319-ft peak named for the liberator of Bolivia. Drive as to Marial (see Hike #87), but at the fork 15 mi before Marial, fork *right* to stay on paved Rd 32-8-31 another 5.2 mi. At a 6-way jct in a saddle, veer slightly left to stay on paved Rd 32-8-31 yet another 3.4 mi to the trailhead. (G)

176. Wolf Creek Park. Take a break from driving I-5 to stretch your legs with a climb of London Peak, gaining 1570 ft in 1.9 mi. From the Wolf Cr exit 76 of I-5, drive to the historic Wolf Creek Inn, continue 100 ft into town, turn L on Main St 0.4 mi to a park, and keep L to a picnic area. Wade Wolf Cr to the trail, crowded in places with poison oak. (Josephine Co Parks, 541-474-5285)

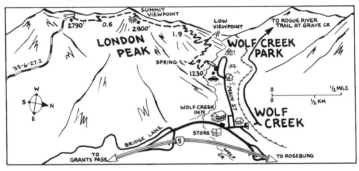

NORTHERN CALIFORNIA (map on page 215)

177. Tree of Heaven. Few trails follow the Klamath River's bank, but Tree of Heaven CG has two—a 0.5-mi bird nature tr and a 0.5-mi tr west along the shore. Drive I-5 south of Oregon border 11 mi (or N of Yreka 10 mi), turn W on Klamath R Hwy 66 for 6.7 mi.. (O)

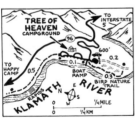

178. Devils Peaks. Challenging 4.9-mi climb on Pacific Crest Tr gains 3700 ft from Klamath River to blockbuster viewpoint atop Lower Devils Peak. Or climb another 2 mi (gaining 960 ft) to Upper Devils Pk. Drive I-5 south of Oregon 11 mi, go W on Klamath River Hwy 96 for 44 mi to Seiad Valley, continue 0.7 mi to trail sign on R. (O)

179. Grider Creek. Hike the PCT up a densely forested canyon 1.8 mi, turn R to cross a creek on a log, and return on the Old Grider Cr Tr 1.8 mi for an easy loop. Drive I-5 south of the Oregon border 11 mi, turn W on Klamath R Hwy 2.5 mi to a bridge, and turn R to stay on Hwy 96 for another 37.4 mi. Between mileposts 61 and 62, turn L on Walker Cr Rd 100 ft, turn R on Grider Rd 2.4 mi, fork R on Rd 46N66 for 2.5

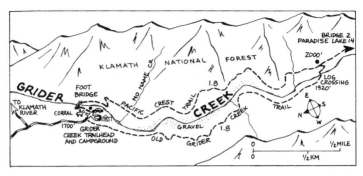

mi, and turn L for 0.5 mi to the Grider Cr Campground. (O)

180. Wright Lakes. Demanding 5.5-mi climb gains 3140 ft to spectacular wildflower mdws at Lower Wright Lk, below Boulder Pk, highest pt in the Marble Mtn Wilderness. Continue 0.6 mi (and 500 ft up) to smaller upper lk. Drive as to Hike #89 (Sky High Lks), but take Rd 44N45 for only 1.6 mi and turn L for 2 mi to the Boulder Cr Trailhd. (SA)

181. Chimney Rock. Rugged Garden Gulch Trail into Marble Mtn Wilderness gains 2300 ft in 2 mi, dips 900 ft in the next 3.3 mi to jct on shoulder of Chimney Rock. Turn R for 2.6 mi to remote Clear Lk (or for 5.8 mi to huge Hancock Lk). Drive as to Hike #91 (Paynes Lk), but continue 15 mi to Sawyers Bar, go straight on hwy another 4 mi, and turn R on a gravel road 5 mi to its end. (SA)

182. North Fork Salmon River. Trek up a long, forested valley in the Marble Mtn Wilderness 12.5 mi to this river's headwaters at English Lk, gaining 3100 ft. Then hike over a high pass 1.5 mi to huge Hancock Lk. Drive as to Hike #91 (Paynes Lk), but continue 9 mi past Etna Summit to Idlewild CG, and turn R on Rd 41N37 for 2 mi. (SA)

183. Taylor and Hogan Lakes. This broad, easy 0.3-mi path in Russian Wilderness to gorgeous Taylor Lk (Hike #91) continues faintly 3 mi to equally scenic Hogan Lk, but gains 400 ft and loses 800. (SA)

184. Duck Lakes. Large, popular Russian Wilderness lakes require 2000 ft climb. Hike 2.9 mi, partly on old roads, then fork left 0.4 mi to Big Duck Lk, or fork right 0.8 mi to Little Duck Lk. To start, drive 4.5 mi S of Etna on Hwy 3, turn R on French Cr Rd, and follow signs 8 mi. (SA)

185. Russian and Waterdog Lakes. View-packed, shadeless Deacon Lee Trail contours 3.7 mi to granite pass high in Russian Wilderness. Turn L for 0.2 mi to Waterdog Lk and 0.2-mi bushwhack route up through mdws to spectacular, swimmable Russian Lk. Drive Hwy 3 to Callahan and turn W toward Cecilville 19 mi. Past Trail Cr CG 3 mi, turn R on Rd 39 for 7 steep mi, and then turn R on a dirt road 2 mi. (SA)

186. Hidden Lake and South Fork Lakes. These cute lakes on the north edge of the Trinity Alps Wilderness are

Tangle Blue Lake (Hike #187).

251

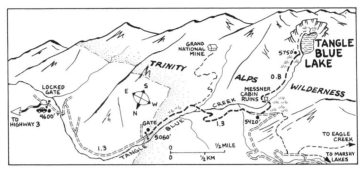

accessed from Carter Meadows Summit (see Hike #92 map). The easy
path to Hidden Lk gains 460 ft in 0.9 mi. A tougher route to South Fork
Lakes follows the PCT 1.2 mi (losing 400 ft), then climbs steeply 950 ft
in 1.2 mi. (SA)

187. Tangle Blue Lake. Massive incense cedars line the 3.4-mi trail to
this lovely lake in a granite bowl in the Trinity Alps Wilderness. The
path gains 1170 ft. From Yreka, Drive Hwy 3 through Ft Jones and Callahan a total of 49 mi. Between mileposts 80 and 81, turn R on rough,
rocky Rd 39N20 for 3.7 mi. Park and hike the gated road. (SA)

188. Big Bear Lake. A steep 4-mi trail into the Trinity Alps Wilderness gains 2800 ft to a scenic granite basin with peaks and a large lake.
Drive Hwy 3 south of Callahan 15 mi (or N of Weaverville 48 mi). Near
milepost 78 take the Bear Cr Loop 1 mi to trailhead. (W)

189. Hodges Cabin. Tour a rustic 1920s lodge in the Trinity Alps Wilderness, the goal of a 3.6 mi hike up scenic N Fk Coffee Creek, gaining
1200 ft. Drive as to Hike #96, but go up Coffee Cr Rd only 8.4 mi to the
N Fk Coffee Cr Tr, on the R just before a bridge. (W)

190. Boulder and Little Boulder Lakes. Easy hike in Trinity Alps Wilderness gains 600 ft in 1.4 mi to a fork. Go R for 0.5 mi to pretty Boulder
Lk, or go L 0.6 mi to a smaller pool ideal for a swim. Drive Hwy 3 south
of Callahan 26 mi (or N of Weaverville 36 mi). Near milepost 67, turn
W at a Boulder Lks pointer on a gravel road for 10.5 mi. (W)

191. Granite Lake. Hike into Trinity Alps Wilderness along Swift
Creek 1 mi to a footbridge, turn L on steeper 4-mi trail up Granite Cr
(with waterfall) to wildflowers of Gibson Mdw and large, lovely lake
in cliffy granite cirque. Route gains 1900 ft. To start, drive Hwy 3 north
of Trinity Center 0.2 mi, turn L at Swift Cr pointer for 6 mi. (W)

192. Stuart Fork to Sapphire Lake. Popular backpack route into the
craggy granite heart of the Trinity Alps Wilderness follows Stuart Fork
of Trinity River 13 mi to shallow green Emerald Lk and deep blue Sapphire Lk, beneath jagged Sawtooth Ridge. Gains 3200 ft. Drive 8 mi N
of Weaverville on Hwy 3 to milepost 39, turn L for 4 mi. (W)

193. Canyon Creek. Most heavily used Trinity Alps Wilderness trail
climbs wooded slope 4 mi to 20-foot waterfall with swimmable pool,
then continues 1.9 mi to jct ; either go L 1.6 mi to Boulder Lks, or go
R 1.5 mi to Canyon Cr Lks. Both are stupendous granite cirques with
flowers and views. Drive Hwy 299 W of Redding 57 mi to Junction

City, veer R on Canyon Cr Rd 13.4 mi. (Big Bar Ranger Dist)

194. Gray Rock Lakes. Cirque lakes in Castle Crags Wilderness offer views of Mt. Shasta. Take Central Mt Shasta exit of I-5, follow Siskiyou Lake signs 3.5 mi, go straight on Rd 26 for 9 mi, park at wood bridge on L. Cross bridge, turn R, hike 2.6 mi up steep, rocky road to old trailhead. Hike 0.7 mi to Gray Rock Lk, continue 0.5 mi to Timber Lk or Upper Gray Rock Lk. Entire 3.8-mi route gains 1470 ft. (M)

195. Burstarse Falls. Stroll the nearly level PCT beneath the granite spires of the Castle Crags Wilderness to a grotto with a 40-ft waterfall. Drive I-5 south of Mt Shasta 14 mi (or N of Redding 48 mi) to the Castella exit, head W on Castle Cr Rd 3.3 mi, and park at Dog Trailhead on the right. Hike 0.7 mi up to the PCT, then either go right 0.6 mi to Sulphur Cr (and Castle Crags views), or go left for 1.7 mi to Burstarse Falls. (M)

196. Goosenest. Climb 1000 ft in 2 mi to the panoramic summit of an arid 8280-ft butte 20 mi N of Mt Shasta. From I-5 at Weed, drive Hwy 97 N 20 mi. Just before Grass Lk, turn L on Rd 45N22 for 7 mi, then turn L on Rd 45N72Y for 2.5 mi. (Goosenest Ranger Dist)

197. Clear Creek Trail. Hike an ancient road to Wilderness vistas of the Watkins Glacier on Mt Shasta's rarely visited SE flank, gaining 1800 ft in 2.3 mi before the route peters out above timberline. No dogs. From the McCloud exit of I-5 just S of Mt Shasta, drive Hwy 89 E for 10 mi to McCloud, continue 3 mi farther, turn L on Rd 13 for 5 mi, turn L on Rd 41N15 for 5 mi to an X-jct, go straight on Rd 41N61 for 1.1 mi, and fork L for 2 mi. (McCloud Ranger Dist)

Mt. Bolivar's view (Hike #175).

198. North Gate. Uncrowded Wilderness path to Mt Shasta's timberline climbs 2 miles to a spring with flowers and views. Total gain: 1700 ft. No dogs. From I-5 at Weed, drive Hwy 97 north for 15 mi, turn R on Military Pass Rd 7 mi, and turn R on Rd 42N76, following signs 34mi. (M)

199. Whitney Falls. A 1997 flash flood obliterated the first mile of the 3-mi trail to a dramatic chasm with a 200-ft falls (sometimes dry) on Mt Shasta's north flank, so route finding is required. Dogs are not permitted. From Weed exit of I-5, drive Hwy 97 N 11.8 mi, turn R on rough dirt Rd 43N21 for 3.9 mi, keeping right at junctions and crossing a railroad track. (M)

200. Mount Shasta. Not a hike, the adventure of climbing this glaciated peak requires crampons, an ice axe, survival gear, good weather, the stamina to gain 7270 ft in 6 mi, and a very early morning start (at least 3:30am). No dogs. A permit for climbing above 10,000 feet costs $20. Take the Central Mt Shasta exit of I-5, drive E for 12 mi on what becomes the Everitt Memorial Hwy, and park at Bunny Flat Trailhead. From there it's 1.6 mi to the Sierra Club Hut at timberline. (M)

Index

About the Author

William L. Sullivan is the author of 17 books and numerous articles about Oregon, including a monthly "Oregon Trails" column for the Eugene *Register-Guard* and the Salem *Statesman-Journal*. A fifth-generation Oregonian, Sullivan began hiking at the age of five and has been exploring new trails ever since. After receiving an English degree from Cornell University and studying at Germany's Heidelberg University, he completed an M.A. in German at the University of Oregon.

In 1985 Sullivan set out to investigate Oregon's wilderness on a 1,361-mile solo backpacking trek from the state's westernmost shore at Cape Blanco to Oregon's easternmost point in Hells Canyon. His journal of that two-month adventure, published as *Listening for Coyote,* was chosen by the Oregon Cultural Heritage Commission as one of Oregon's "100 Books."

Information about Sullivan's speaking schedule, his books, and his favorite adventures is available online at *www.oregonhiking.com.* He and his wife Janell live in Eugene, but spend summers at the log cabin they built by hand on a remote, roadless river in Oregon's Coast Range. Sullivan's memoir, *Cabin Fever,* chronicles the adventure of building that cabin retreat.